"Walton and Walton continue their ~~~~ understood as instruction rather than law, wisdom rather than legislation. They point out how Torah is often misunderstood by Christians because they assume that it functions like modern laws or Greco-Roman laws. Instead, the authors argue, the Torah should be interpreted in its ancient Near Eastern context, where order was achieved through the wisdom of those who governed society. The collections of 'laws' contained selected illustrations, intended to teach a model for right and wrong as guidance for judges but were not comprehensive legal codes that regulated everyday life in detail. This careful and readable study will be valuable for all who are interested in Old Testament law and its relevance for Christians today."
David L. Baker, All Nations Christian College

"Walton and Walton rightly view Torah in the broader context of wisdom and as an expression of wisdom. This is exactly what passages such as Deuteronomy 4:6 and Psalm 19:7 imply."
Kevin Chen, associate professor of biblical studies, Union University

"Walton and Walton take recent scholarship on ancient Near Eastern law and apply it with great dexterity to their investigation of the biblical Torah. Ancient law codes, like the Laws of Hammurabi, very likely did not form the actual law of their respective societies, and this book is willing to face the implications of this honestly. Overall, it builds a careful and important argument for how to approach biblical law. And it is brave enough to show that most casual interpretations by modern Christians will almost inevitably go awry. One can only hope that this kind of work will begin to dampen the naive and simplistic readings that plague much of American Protestantism today."
Bruce Wells, associate professor, department of Middle Eastern studies, University of Texas at Austin

THE
LOST
WORLD
OF THE
TORAH

LAW AS COVENANT
AND WISDOM IN
ANCIENT CONTEXT

JOHN H. WALTON &
J. HARVEY WALTON

IVP Academic
An imprint of InterVarsity Press
Downers Grove, Illinois

InterVarsity Press
P.O. Box 1400, Downers Grove, IL 60515-1426
ivpress.com
email@ivpress.com

InterVarsity Press® is the book-publishing division of InterVarsity Christian Fellowship/USA®, a movement of students and faculty active on campus at hundreds of universities, colleges, and schools of nursing in the United States of America, and a member movement of the International Fellowship of Evangelical Students. For information about local and regional activities, visit intervarsity.org.

All Scripture quotations, unless otherwise indicated, are taken from The Holy Bible, New International Version®, NIV ®. Copyright © 1973, 1978, 1984, 2011 by Biblica, Inc.™ Used by permission of Zondervan. All rights reserved worldwide. www.zondervan.com. The "NIV" and "New International Version" are trademarks registered in the United States Patent and Trademark Office by Biblica, Inc.™

Cover design: David Fasset
Interior design: Beth McGill
Images: glittering silver background: © Nastco / iStock / Getty Images Plus
  starry sky: © Micael Malmberg / EyeEm / Getty Images
  Bible passages: © Ipkoe / iStock / Getty Images Plus
  black slate: © xamtiw / iStock / Getty Images Plus
  blue sky: © czekma13 / iStock / Getty Images Plus
  code of Hammurabi: © jsp / iStock / Getty Images
  Michelangelo's Moses: © powerofforever / iStock / Getty Images Plus

ISBN 978-0-8308-5241-3 (print)
ISBN 978-0-8308-7257-2 (digital)

Printed in the United States of America ∞

InterVarsity Press is committed to ecological stewardship and to the conservation of natural resources in all our operations. This book was printed using sustainably sourced paper.

Library of Congress Cataloging-in-Publication Data
A catalog record for this book is available from the Library of Congress.

P   22   21   20   19   18   17   16   15   14   13   12   11   10   9   8   7   6   5   4   3   2
Y   37   36   35   34   33   32   31   30   29   28   27   26   25   24   23   22   21   20   19

Contents

Introduction

In English we use the expression "law and order." This sort of construction is known as a *hendiadys*—two nouns joined by *and* expressing a single idea (cf. "assault and battery"). In this expression, *order* is the objective and *law* is the means of achieving it. Law is not the only way to achieve order; others would include ethics and customs of etiquette ("little ethics"). Society is regulated by mores and taboos that dictate what constitutes orderly (or disorderly) conduct. Such regulations can be formal or informal, enforced by outside agency or by social pressure, oral or written, explicit or implicit. They can be normative throughout society or subject to differences of opinion (for example, based on conflicting ideas between generations). Order is generally associated with a particular understanding of what constitutes the common good.

Law is not limited to what is perceived as moral behavior. For example, traffic laws, though essential for order, are not moral in nature. At the same time, perceptions of foundational morality are often embodied in law, but not always. In fact, some people would agree that some laws should be judged immoral and therefore should be resisted (e.g., racial segregation laws). The objective of law is order, and moral behavior is often one aspect of order. In modern Western societies, law is formal, written (codified), and enforced by agencies and institutions (police, judiciary). Such an approach to legislation is referred to as "statutory law." Given how deeply entrenched this idea of law is, it is instinctive for us to imagine that law in other societies functions in the same way. That is one of the major presuppositions that will be challenged in the following chapters.

In conjunction with assumptions about how law works, people have assumptions about how the Bible works—how it should be interpreted. In our modern world, our handling of what we call the "biblical law" teeters between heated controversy and utter neglect. Controversies arise when Old Testament laws seem either odd beyond comprehension (not eating lobster) or morally reprehensible (executing children). Neglect results when we consider the law obsolete, no longer carrying any normative power (tassels on clothing, sacrifices). Even readers who do attempt to make use of the Old Testament "law" often find it either irrelevant or so confusing that they throw up their hands in despair, frustrated at its perceived impenetrability. Despite the extremes of vitriol and dismissiveness, people—sometimes the same people who are controversial or dismissive—continue to propose moral principles from these laws and garner prooftexts to resolve the issues that arise in society by offering the "biblical view." As a result, both Christians and skeptics regularly abuse the Old Testament Law as it is misrepresented and misunderstood, and its true message too often lies either fallow or trampled underfoot.

If we seek to be faithful interpreters we need to be readers who read the text in an informed and careful manner, who are consistent in the methods that we use, who refuse to manipulate the text to our own ends, and who respect the autonomy under which divine authority operates.[1] We must interpret in light of a sound understanding of the language and literature of the text, including how the genre works. We must be committed to seeking what the original communicators intended to say—no more, no less. We dare not incorporate ideas into

---

[1]See discussion in John H. Walton and D. Brent Sandy, *The Lost World of Scripture: Ancient Literary Culture and Biblical Authority* (Downers Grove, IL: IVP Academic, 2013), 284-87, where we referred to this as competent, ethical, and virtuous reading.

the text that were not in their purview. Beyond these acts of interpretation, we must commit to being responsive to the text. Differences of opinion may well exist as to what that response ought to be, but traditionally many have agreed that in its most general sense it involves being the sort of people who represent God well in the world (whatever that entails) as we participate in his plans and purposes. As faithful interpreters of Law—more accurately, Torah—we must therefore seek understanding of how the genre works, what the paragraphs of legal sayings meant in their context, and what significance (if any) they should have for people today seeking to order their lives and society in faithful submission to God's word. The most important interpretive question is not, "what is this statement telling me to do in order to represent God properly?" The question we should ask first is, "why is this in here?"—because that will help us address the literary task.

It is the first objective of this book to provide information about the Torah that will help readers to become more aware of how this biblical literature functioned in its context—that is, why this literature was presented in this particular way, and why what it says in this form was important enough to be regarded as Scripture. We have to start in the ancient world and recognize the nature of this sort of literature in the ancient world. Then, based on that contextualization, we need to penetrate the Hebrew text to understand how the Torah was meant to function for the ancient Israelites. Only then will we be in a position to inquire what the authoritative significance of the Torah is for us.

Paul tells Timothy that "all Scripture is God-breathed and is useful for teaching, rebuking, correcting and training in righteousness, so that the servant of God may be thoroughly equipped for every good work" (2 Tim 3:16-17). Many readers think that this passage tells us what the significance of the Torah is without the need for a genre study. However, Paul is here affirming what Timothy's upbringing has already taught him—that teaching, rebuking, and so on were in fact what Jews of Timothy's day thought the Hebrew Bible (what Paul

means by the word *Scripture*) was useful for. The point in this passage—
the answer to the question "why is this in here" for 2 Timothy 3:16-17—
is to contrast that use with the innovations of deceivers (1 Tim 3:13) for
the listed functions, not with other potential uses of the Old Testament.
Scripture includes the Torah, but we should not think that Paul is offering a menu of the precise functions of Torah (or Old Testament).
Rather than asking *how* the Torah teaches, rebukes, corrects, trains in
righteousness, and equips God's people for every good work, we
should ask what it means that the Torah "is God-breathed" (inspired).

People using the Old Testament and the Torah today want to believe that they can address the significant issues of culture in "biblical"
ways and, specifically, with "biblical" answers and positions. In our
society today, as diverse and pluralistic as it is, we are faced with a
multitude of issues, including abortion, stem cell research, genetic
engineering, climate change, land exploitation, species extinction,
capital punishment, immigration policies, creation care, sustain-
ability, euthanasia, and, perhaps most pervasively, questions concerning rights and identity (gender, sexuality, ethnic, racial, etc.). We
want the Bible to give us answers, but whatever answers might be
embedded there, or whether there are any answers at all, can only be
determined by having an informed understanding of the biblical text
and by using a consistent methodology to arrive at our interpretation.
We are going to suggest that finding what we can consider "biblical"
answers to these social issues is not as straightforward as it seems
because, contrary to what many interpreters imagine, the Bible is not
a compilation of propositional revelation—a collection of facts expressing divine affirmations. Though that is a popular view, we will
contend, in contrast, that Scripture is not a body of information containing propositions that are always valid in all places and times.[2]
Instead, we will find much greater need to resist the thinking that

---

[2]Discussed and refuted in Kevin J. Vanhoozer, "Lost in Interpretation?: Truth, Scripture, and
Hermeneutics," *JETS* 48, no. 1 (2005): 89-114, esp. 94-95.

there is a divinely inspired silver bullet to resolve the complicated questions we face.

At the core of this book is the understanding that the ancient world was more interested in order than in legislation per se, and authorities were not inclined to make what we call laws (though decrees are commonplace) to regulate everyday life in society. Instead of relying on legislation (a formal body of written law enacted by an authority), order was achieved through the wisdom of those who governed society. This understanding will dramatically affect our interpretation of the text, consideration of the interrelationships of the various biblical collections, and discernment of the significance of the Torah for today. We have too often looked to the Torah to construct legislation as if the Torah were intended to be legislation. If, as we contend, it was never intended as legislation, then that is the wrong approach. If the focus of the Torah is order and wisdom, then it will provide for us an understanding of order and wisdom at least in an Israelite context.[3] We will then have to determine the relevance that has for us today.

At the start, then, we need to lay out the terminology that is used in the Old Testament and the way that it will be used in this book. First, the word *Torah* has a variety of uses. Even in the Old Testament, and throughout the history of Judaism, *Torah* has been used to describe the first five books of the Old Testament, also referred to as the Pentateuch. Some assumed such a designation in references to the "book of the Torah" in writings as early as Joshua 1:8; 8:31, 34; and 2 Kings 14:6. We will not be using the word in that general way. Second, *Torah* is a technical term in the legal literature. It describes what is given at Sinai, what regulates the purity system in Leviticus, what was delivered through Moses, and what the Israelites were expected to live by. It is

---

[3]Roy Gane indicates that the laws of the Old Testament contain "a rich source of wisdom regarding values." Roy E. Gane, *Old Testament Law for Christians: Original Context and Enduring Application* (Grand Rapids: Baker Academic, 2017), xiii. He also affirms the distinction between the Torah and legislation, pp. 28-29.

only one of the technical terms used to describe legal sayings. We will use *Torah* generally for the entire category of legal sayings, though its usage is not limited to legal contexts (for example, *Torah* is also used in connection to proverbial sayings where it refers to the "instruction" given by parents to children).

The approach of this book follows the same format as used in the previous Lost World books. Through a series of propositions, each serving as a chapter, we will build a case point by point as we address the important issues for consideration. The supporting evidence offered in each chapter will build to the final chapters, where suggestions will be made for approaching the practical issues of today using an informed understanding of the Torah and applying a consistent hermeneutic. Readers should not expect that the result of this study will be firm answers to all the controversial questions. Rather, we will conclude with a clearer understanding of how the Torah's message can be used today.

PART 1

METHODOLOGY

The Old Testament Is an Ancient Document

Any readers who have already been introduced to the Lost World series will recognize this as one of the first propositions in each of the books. The fact that the Old Testament is an ancient document means that we cannot read it as if it were a modern Western document. Its words are laden with cultural content that its audience intrinsically understood but is often opaque to a modern reader.

For instance, let's use a reverse example: imagine someone from another culture (whether contemporary with us or from ancient times) encountering an American who referred to "flying 'Old Glory.'" Even some Americans (depending on age and geographical location) may not be aware that Old Glory refers to the American flag. But let's pursue the inquiry further. In an ancient culture they would have no concept of a flag as a symbol of a country so knowledge of cultural symbolism is necessary. Second, only knowledge of semantic range would inform a reader that flying a flag is not like flying an airplane but refers to displaying it prominently. Third, they might then wonder why one would fly a flag, and our reply may have to do with patriotism, a cultural value. Patriotism would be a foreign concept in many ancient cultures since they would not have necessarily felt compelled to express loyalty to a nation-state (though they might understand the importance of loyalty to a king). Discussion about that would then open up an interesting conversation about whether national entities have value and what that value might be. Finally, we would discover that national values of today may differ considerably from national values in another culture (where their values would be cultural values rather than national values). This is simply an arbitrary example of how language is full of cultural meaning. Just as someone from an ancient culture would have difficulty understanding our ideas (even if the words were properly translated for them), we also find ourselves struggling to understand all the cultural ideas that are carried in words from ancient texts.

Translation of cultural ideas is difficult for many reasons. One of the most important is that often a target language does not have the words that would represent all the ideas and nuances present in the words of the source language. But beyond the obstacles presented by inadequate vocabulary, we encounter ideas communicated from within and with reference to an unfamiliar cultural framework. We are inclined to interpret texts from the perspective of our own cultural network without accounting for the cultural framework native to the text we are reading.

A useful metaphor for describing this phenomenon of diverse cultural settings is that of cultural rivers.[1] In our modern world, the cultural river is easily identified. Among its American (and often global) currents are various fundamentals such as rights, freedom, capitalism, democracy, individualism, social networking, globalism, market economy, consumerism, scientific naturalism, an expanding universe, empiricism, and natural laws, just to name a few. Some may well wish to float in these currents while others may struggle to swim upstream against at least some of them, but those in our modern world inevitably

---

[1]The following discussion is adapted from Tremper Longman III and John H. Walton, *The Lost World of the Flood: Mythology, Theology, and the Deluge Debate* (Downers Grove, IL: IVP Academic, 2018), 6-7.

are located in its waters. Regardless of our diverse ways of thinking, we are all in the cultural river and its currents are familiar to us.

In the ancient world, a very different cultural river flowed through all the neighboring cultures: Egyptians, Phoenicians, Assyrians—and Israelites. Despite important variations between cultures and across the centuries, certain elements remained largely static. Continual course adjustments have little effect on the most persistent currents. People from various times and cultures may indeed face some similar challenges common to humanity, but few of the currents common to the ancient cultures are found in our modern cultural river. In the ancient cultural river we would find currents such as community identity, the comprehensive and ubiquitous control of the gods, the role of kingship, divination, the centrality of the temple, the mediatory role of images, the effectual and essential role of sacrifice, and the reality of the spirit world and magic.

The Israelites sometimes floated on the currents of that cultural river without resistance, and we would be neither surprised nor critical. At other times, however, the revelation of God encouraged them to struggle out of the current into the shallows, or even to swim furiously upstream. Whatever the extent of the Israelites' interactions with the cultural river, it is important to remember that they were situated in the *ancient* cultural river, not immersed in the currents of our modern cultural river.

It is this "embeddedness" that we seek to understand so that we may be faithful interpreters of the biblical text. God communicated within the context of their cultural river. God's message, God's purposes, and God's authority were all vested in Israelite communicators for Israelite audiences, and the message took shape according to the internal logic within their language and culture. We cannot be assured of authoritative communication through any other source, and we must therefore find the message of God as communicated through those intermediaries in their ancient cultural river.

This means that if we are to interpret Scripture so as to receive the full impact of God's authoritative message, and build the foundation for sound theology, we have to begin by setting aside the presuppositions of our cultural river, with all our modern issues and perspectives, in order to engage the cultural river of the ancient communicators. The communicators that we encounter in the Old Testament are not aware of our cultural river, including all its societal aspects; they neither address our cultural river nor anticipate it.[2] We cannot therefore assume that any of the constants or currents of our cultural river are addressed specifically in Scripture. This does not mean, however, that the Old Testament becomes irrelevant to us.

How then should we proceed in order to decipher the relevance that the biblical text has for us? Our first step involves good translation of the language, but that is only the beginning. If we have any hope of understanding texts that are resident in another cultural river, we need the service of a "cultural broker."[3] Thinking back to the example used above concerning flying Old Glory, we found that understanding was not accomplished by simply translating the words. The role of cultural broker is played by someone who is sufficiently knowledgeable in both the source culture and the target culture to identify what hurdles might be encountered in trying to understand and then give explanation in terms that will make sense. As another example, consider the relatively recent practice of celebrating "pie day." At the level of translation, it sounds like an opportunity to celebrate by eating some pie, and it is, but why celebrate on March 14? For that a cultural broker is necessary. In our culture we can use a numerical notation for dates,

---

[2]Note even, for example, the line with which Walter Harrelson begins his book on the Ten Commandments: "The Bible knows little or nothing about human rights in our sense of the term." Walter J. Harrelson, *The Ten Commandments and Human Rights* (Philadelphia: Fortress, 1980), xv.

[3]For a modern example, see Anne Fadiman, *The Spirit Catches You and You Fall Down: A Hmong Child, Her American Doctors, and the Collision of Two Cultures* (New York: Farrar, Straus and Giroux, 1997).

and in America March 14 would be 3/14. A mathematical technicality is associated with these numbers when we replace the slanted line with a decimal point: 3.14, thus representing a rounded number that expresses a mathematical constant of the ratio of a circle's circumference to its diameter (a detail widely known but not universally or innately even in our culture). But still that is not enough information to make the connection. A cultural broker would next have to explain that mathematicians have agreed to represent this constant by the Greek letter pi, which happens to be a homonym to the English word *pie*, a delectable pastry. We therefore discover that the connection also makes use of wordplay.

Modern Bible readers need cultural brokers who can move beyond the translation of the ancient legal sayings of the Torah (e.g., Deut 22:11: "Do not wear clothes of wool and linen woven together") to offer an explanation of the thinking behind those sayings (why would wearing such clothes of mixed materials have been a problem in the ancient world?). A cultural broker helps build bridges between people of different cultural backgrounds in order to facilitate communication. The resulting negotiation could involve spoken words, terminology, or texts. A cultural broker must understand the values and beliefs of both cultures and be willing and able to bridge the given cultures' belief systems. This interpretive approach works on the primary assumption that various cultures do not simply have different words for the same basic ideas; they have fundamentally different ideas that they use their words to convey, and those words often have only a superficial similarity to the words another culture might use.

Torah is part of the ancient text we know as the Hebrew Bible or the Old Testament. That Bible is written for us (i.e., we are supposed to benefit from its divine message and expect that it will help us to confront the currents in our cultural river by transforming us), but it is not written to us (not in our language or in the context of our culture). The message transcends culture, but it is given in a form that is fully immersed in the ancient cultural river of Israel. This means that if we are to interpret Scripture so as to receive the full impact of God's authoritative message, we have to set our cultural river aside and try to understand the cultural river of the ancient people to whom the text was addressed. The Bible was written to the people of ancient Israel in the language of ancient Israel; therefore, its message operates according to the logic of ancient Israel.[4]

We can begin to understand the claims of the text as an ancient document first of all by paying close attention to what the text says and doesn't say. It is too easy to make assumptions that are intrusive based on our own culture, cognitive environment, traditions, or questions. It takes a degree of discipline as readers who are outsiders not to assume our modern perspectives and impose them on the text. Often we do not even know we are doing it because our own context is so intrinsic to our thinking and the ancient world is an unknown. The best path to recognizing the distinctions between ancient and modern thinking is to begin paying attention to the ancient world and at the same time imposing methodological constraints to minimize the impact of anachronistic intuition. This is accomplished by immersion in the literature of the ancient world. This would by no means supersede Scripture, but it can be a tool for understanding Scripture.[5]

We have to suppress our intuition because we are naturally inclined to read the biblical text intuitively. When we do so, we unconsciously impose our own cultural ideas on the text. We cannot help but do so—no reading is culturally neutral. Since reading instinctively inherently imposes modern cultural thinking on the text, we conclude that such reading is at least potentially unreliable. Some may object that if we read it in light of the ancient world, we are imposing that world on

---

[4]Adapted from John H. Walton and J. Harvey Walton, *The Lost World of the Israelite Conquest: Covenant, Retribution, and the Fate of the Canaanites* (Downers Grove, IL: IVP Academic, 2017), 9.

[5]Adapted from John H. Walton, *The Lost World of Adam and Eve: Genesis 2–3 and the Human Origins Debate* (Downers Grove, IL: IVP Academic, 2015), 22.

the text. We cannot impose that world on the text because the text is situated in that world. No one would ever object to using the Hebrew language to understand the biblical text by claiming that the interpreter was imposing Hebrew on the text. We cannot impose Hebrew on the biblical text—it is written in Hebrew. In the same way, we cannot impose the ancient world on the biblical text since the ancient world is its native context.

The authority of the text is found when we read it for what it is—no more, no less. For those who pride themselves on interpreting the text "literally," we can only say that a person cannot read the text more literally than to read it as the original author intended for it to be read. That is our goal, and being faithful interpreters of God's Word allows for nothing less. It takes work, and well it should. It is worth the effort.

Some would claim that such an approach takes the Bible out of the hands of the ordinary reader and might even suggest that it runs contrary to the objectives of the Reformation—that every ploughman might be able to read the Bible and understand it. We need to realize, however, that the ploughman's gain is to be able to read the Bible in his own language. The Reformers never expected that every ploughman would achieve autonomous expertise as exegete or theologian. When the Reformers insisted on the clarity of Scripture for any reader, they were contrasting the surface reading of Scripture (well informed linguistically, literally, theologically), in which anyone could engage, with a mystical or esoteric interpretation of the text available only to the initiated. Perspicuity does not override the need to acquire the arcane and esoteric skill of cultural brokerage any more than it overrides the need to acquire the arcane and esoteric skill of learning to read (whether Hebrew or Greek or one's own native language). The Reformers did acknowledge a need to translate the Bible, and cultural brokerage is part of the translation process.[6] We should not imagine

---

[6]Iain Provan, *The Reformation and the Right Reading of Scripture* (Waco, TX: Baylor University Press, 2017), 302-12.

that the Reformers would have refused to use any newly discovered texts from the ancient world. The Reformers themselves were bringing something new to the interpretation of Scripture that none of their precursors for fifteen hundred years had had—the knowledge of the Hebrew language. The fact that those before them did not have access to Hebrew did not deter them from using it for new insights. We should always use whatever tools are available to us whether others had them or not.

The Reformers certainly did not believe that all of Scripture and every aspect of Scripture were accessible and could be penetrated by any layperson regardless of training. If the Reformers had believed that, they surely would not have felt compelled to write hundreds of volumes of commentary and theology. Anyone who is literate can read that someone named David took a census (2 Samuel 24), but not everyone can read about David's census and know why he would have thought of doing such a thing, or why he thought that doing it would be a good idea, or why it turned out not to be.

Scholars have a role in the body of Christ just like everyone else does. One cannot object that it is somehow elitist for scholars to think they have a contribution to make that not just anyone can make. Not everyone is an eye, an ear, or a hand. Everyone else is gifted to do what they do, and academics are no exception—and no one should begrudge that. No person alone is the whole body of Christ; we all depend on the gifts of others. If the Bible needs to be translated—an important emphasis of the Reformation still acknowledged today—then somebody needs to translate it. Cultural brokerage, like lexical semantics, is part of the translation process and is a necessary function of a competent translator.

As we recognize the biblical text as inherently related to an ancient culture, we also realize that it communicates with goals that reflect the culture of the communicators and their audience. Communication is an *act* that intends to accomplish something—command, instruct, promise, threaten, bless, exhort, and so on. Furthermore, it is not intended to be an isolated act; rather, there is an expectation of some sort of response—obedience, learning, gratitude, caution, and so on. This understanding of how communication works is referred to as "speech-act theory." Speech-acts are launched by certain words (spoken or written). Interpretation requires careful investigation of all three aspects of each speech-act—the words, the intentions, and the desired response. Such investigation would consider linguistic aspects such as grammar, syntax, and word meanings as well as literary elements such as rhetorical devices, literary structuring, and genre.

When we apply these ideas to Torah (as we will in the following chapters), we can see that people who read the sayings as intended to provide legislation (an intended act) would understand the expected response to be obedience or even the structuring of a society. We will propose a different intention of the communicative act of Torah, based on the ancient genre, that will suggest a response of comprehending and making subsequent use of that understanding in a meaningful way. But to get to that point we must first investigate how we think about law today and how that may differ from how they thought in the ancient world.

Proposition 2

The Way We Interpret
the Torah Today Is Influenced by
the Way We Think Law and
Legislation Work

How do we think about law today? How have other people in other times and cultures thought about law? How did the Israelites think about law? Was it the same as others in the ancient world? How are the documents of the Torah related to these concepts of law? We must address issues such as these if we are to read the Torah well—that is, read it the way that it was read in its cultural time and context. To approach the issue we must ask questions about what people consider the source of law, where they believe it to be found, and how it is applied to society.

For the purposes of this book, it will be enough for us to differentiate between written documents that are *descriptive* and those that are *prescriptive*. Prescriptive documents expect obedience or conformity as a response; descriptive documents expect comprehension as a response. We will use the term *legislation*[1] to refer to the idea of legal

---

[1]Referring to positivist law, whether associated with divine command, natural law, or statutory law from the sidebar.

formulations that are prescriptive and therefore create a system of law and an obligation for those under that system. LeFebvre identifies the significant distinction between a prescriptive, legislative use of legal sayings and a descriptive function that is nonlegislative.[2] We will use terms such as *legal sayings* to refer to instruction that is largely descriptive of ideas that are current in what are generally cultures where cases are judged based on traditional wisdom. In this usage, *legislation* and *instruction* are two distinct speech-acts that in turn carry differing expected responses. Now armed with these categories we can consider how we think about law and legislation today and how that may differ from the ancient world.

In relatively recent history (post-Reformation), a major change took place in how people thought about law.[3] People grew to think of law as codified legislation that is coercive in nature. The documents of this legislation were considered prescriptive in nature and imposed an obligation on people. Consequently, today we think of law as reflected in a legal code. Furthermore, we tend to be so confident in this way of thinking that we do not remember or realize that it was not always this way or even that there could be other ways of thinking.

In contrast, prior to a couple of centuries ago (and still not uncommon in non-Western cultures), law was more flexible. Society was regulated by customs and norms that had taken shape beyond memory. Judges, who were those considered wise in the traditions of the culture rather than those who were specially educated, made their rulings based on their insight and wisdom. Any documents pertaining to law in those cultures were not codified legislation; that is, they were not

---

[2]Michael LeFebvre, *Collections, Codes, and Torah: The Re-characterization of Israel's Written Law* (New York: T&T Clark, 2006), 23-24.

[3]We will not recount the history here, but it is addressed in Christine Hayes, *What's Divine About Divine Law? Early Perspectives* (Princeton, NJ: Princeton University Press, 2015); Joshua A. Berman, *Inconsistency in the Torah: Ancient Literary Convention and the Limits of Source Criticism* (Oxford: Oxford University Press, 2017); and LeFebvre, *Collections, Codes, and Torah.*

prescriptive documents establishing law. Instead they *described* rulings (whether through actual verdicts or hypothetical examples)— reporting decisions.

This distinction is critical for us to recognize because how we think about law and legislation in our own cultural river will determine our presuppositions about and perspectives on the biblical texts and those from the ancient Near Eastern (ANE) world that contain legal information. LeFebvre contends (and we agree) that the ANE is a "non-legislative society" rather than a "legislative society."[4] In such a case, the legal structure is not based on written documents. Written documents serve an entirely different function.

---

[4]LeFebvre, *Collections, Codes, and Torah*, 23-30.

TECHNICAL TERMINOLOGY

Here is a brief review of some technical terms and their definitions from the philosophy of law.[a]

Divine command theory. In this view the source of law is God. Some believe that it is found in divine decree—written documents believed to have come from God. This requires special revelation. Others believe that no special revelation is required and that God's law is known through general sources such as conscience.

Natural law. In this view law is deduced from the functioning order of the world around us, which may include our consciences. If the world order is seen to have its source in God, this is a subcategory of divine law. It is known from observation and not from revelation in text. This view is articulated by Paul in Romans 1–2. As long as the source of law derives either from God or from the inherent nature of the world, society is not free to make its own decisions; there are universal moral truths.

Positivist law. This refers to a system of understanding whereby a body of rules is en-

forced by those in authority in accordance with their will. These rules need not be logical or rational and are not subject to being contested on their merit; that is, lack of merit does not negate their authority. No essential link to morality is necessary. Positivist law is generally undergirded by means of coercive force (though shared values will lead to conformity without resorting to force). It could have its source either in the divine world or in the king (or in both when the king is seen as the channel for the divine will), or even in a religious body (such as the Pharisees, or those who are responsible for the magisterium, or sharia). This approach to law develops in the Hellenistic period and is therefore not reflected in the Old Testament or the ancient Near East.

Common law. Once decisions are made about where law comes from (God, nature, governing body) and where it is found (divine decree, conscience, codified statutes), systems arise for applying law to regulate society's behavior. Common law (sometimes called customary

When the stele of Hammurabi was discovered at the very beginning of the twentieth century, it was immediately dubbed the Code of Hammurabi based on twentieth-century assumptions about the nature of law. Researchers assumed that it contained the law of the land for Babylon and that it was prescriptive, codified legislation. As we will discuss in proposition three, that perception gradually changed (though the label has resisted revision), but it is an important indication of what had been going on for some time in biblical interpretation, and here we arrive at what is the pivotal issue in this book.

As perspectives about law shifted over the last couple of centuries, we began to interpret the Torah in light of those new perspectives.[5]

---

[5]Other prescriptive interpretations of the Torah had existed prior to this, of course, but the specific practice we commonly find today of treating the Torah as statutory law emerged in conjunction with the development of statutory law as common civic practice.

law and generally reflected in case law) does not depend on a written code. It depends on the wisdom of the judges to issue rulings that reflect the mores and customs of the society. No particular judicial decision determines precedent for future decisions. By nature it is incomplete and fluid. Berman draws the distinction that sacred texts, when they are in play, serve in common law as a resource for judges to consult, not as a source of statutory law.[b] New circumstances and differing scenarios require revisiting of earlier decisions. Common law involves a system of reasoning rather than a code and works best in a largely homogeneous social setting (rather than a cosmopolitan or diversified one).

Statutory law. This is an application of positivist law that results in a codified text that serves as the law of the land. As positivist law, it originates from an authority and is imposed coercively. It is finite; judgments are made according to that which is written in the statutes. Its roots are found in classical Greece, but it became standard consensus in the West in the late nineteenth century.

The history of law relative to the Bible can be found in books by Hayes and Berman, already referred to, as well as in one by Michael LeFebvre.[c] The importance of that discussion is twofold: it demonstrates that our current perspectives developed relatively recently and that the ancient world did not employ positivist or statutory law.

---

[a]Information for these definitions and distinctions are drawn from Christine Hayes, *What's Divine About Divine Law? Early Perspectives* (Princeton, NJ: Princeton University Press, 2015); Roy E. Gane, *Old Testament Law for Christians: Original Context and Enduring Application* (Grand Rapids: Baker Academic, 2017), 25-26; and Joshua A. Berman, *Inconsistency in the Torah: Ancient Literary Convention and the Limits of Source Criticism* (Oxford: Oxford University Press, 2017). These definitions were refined through personal conversation with Robert K. Vischer, Dean and Mengler Chair in Law, University of St. Thomas Law School, for which I am grateful, though the final responsibility remains my own.

[b]Berman, *Inconsistency*, 110.

[c]Michael LeFebvre, *Collections, Codes, and Torah: The Re-characterization of Israel's Written Law* (New York: T&T Clark, 2006).

Specifically, we began to treat the Torah as if it were prescriptive, codified legislation, though that concept did not exist in the ancient world.
As commonly happens, interpreters were inclined to read the biblical
text through the filter of their own cultural river—their own cultural
context. As a result of such reading, people began thinking that the
Torah dictated the law of the land to Israel. And since it was considered divine revelation, it was therefore construed as God's ideal
guide to society and morality. And if it is God's guide to the ideal shape
of society and morality, then all people everywhere are obligated to
apply it; one must merely determine how to deal with idiosyncrasies
and anomalies in order to apply it to today.

This chain of logic all begins with the false assumption that the
Torah represents revelation of the prescriptive, codified legislation
given by God. Because people think this way, they try to apply the
Torah as God's revelation to offer "biblical" positions on everything
from larger questions of law and morality to specific questions that
arise from the issues of our day. If, however, the Torah was never intended to be revelation of prescriptive, codified legislation, then we
have to clear the table and start from the beginning to understand
what it is and how it works. What are the alternatives? If the intended
function is not legislation (and therefore the expected response is not
obedience), what are the intended function and the expected response? What is the revelation of the Torah intended to achieve? What
sort of speech-act is it? What is its revelation? In other words: why
does it exist in Scripture? These are the topics we will now address.

PART 2

FUNCTION OF ANCIENT NEAR EASTERN LEGAL COLLECTIONS

Proposition 3

Legal Collections in the Ancient World Are Not Legislation

Abundant documentation attests to the legal principles and practices of the ancient Near East (ANE).[1] In this critical step toward an understanding of Torah, we are ready to consider just what sorts of documents we have and what they tell us. Once we come to understand the culture of the ANE in general, we can look at biblical material to assess similarities and differences and investigate what can be learned that will help us better understand the Torah. Though we expect to find at least some differences, the similarities will show us that in the realm of legal thinking the Israelites were much closer to the thinking that existed in the ancient world than they are to the way we think today. They were fully immersed in their ancient cultural river, and the currents there were far different from what we find today. We are therefore

---

[1]Significant documents number in the thousands. If we include business transactions such as receipts, they number in the tens of thousands. Information on nearly any aspect of these documents can be found in Brent Strawn, ed., *The Oxford Encyclopedia of the Bible and Law*, 2 vols. (Oxford: Oxford University Press, 2015); see also Raymond Westbrook, *A History of Ancient Near Eastern Law*, 2 vols. (Leiden: Brill, 2003). Translations with introductions are available in Martha T. Roth, *Law Collections from Mesopotamia and Asia Minor* (Atlanta: Society of Biblical Literature, 1995).

again reminded that we cannot rely on just reading the Old Testament intuitively. Our reading instincts have been deeply affected by our own culture and the history that brought us to this present time. We begin then by summarizing the legal materials that are available from the ancient world.

We will set aside administrative texts and letters that discuss legal issues, ritual instructions, legal reform decrees, records of legal transactions (personal and public), and contracts, though all of these provide nuances to our general understanding. The most important documents for our investigation are collections of legal sayings and court documents, which attest to procedures and rulings. Of these two categories of texts, the former is the most important because these texts are most like what we find in the Torah, not only in content but, more importantly, in genre.

ANCIENT NEAR EASTERN COLLECTIONS OF LEGAL SAYINGS

The earliest collection dates to the end of the third millennium BC, but the more significant collections are primarily from the second millennium BC. The most well-known, most extensive, and the first to be found, in 1901 in excavations at Susa, is the stele that preserves 282 legal sayings embedded in a royal inscription of Hammurabi (ca. 1750 BC), hundreds of years prior to Moses. Hammurabi was a Babylonian king contemporary with Israel's patriarchs. Collections from earlier times were subsequently discovered, and the total document count is now at seven (see table 3.1). In two of the collections the list of sayings is accompanied by prologue and epilogue, a feature that offers some insight into literary use, which is one of the most important aspects of analysis. The question to be resolved concerns the purpose and function of these collections.

When first discovered, the texts were referred to as "law codes," a label that reflected a presupposition derived from our cultural river

Table 3.1. Ancient Near Eastern legal collections

PERIOD (SPONSORING KING)	CENTURY BC	LANGUAGE	LOCATION	PROLOGUE/ EPILOGUE	CONTENT
Ur III (Ur-Namma or Shulgi)	21st	Sumerian	Ur	yes	31 sayings
Isin-Larsa (Lipit-Ishtar)	20th	Sumerian	Isin	yes	38 sayings
Old Babylonian (Dadusha or Ibalpiel)	18th	Akkadian	Eshnunna	no	60 sayings
Old Babylonian (Hammurabi)	18th	Akkadian	Babylon	yes	282 sayings
Old Hittite[a] (Telipinu?)	17th	Hittite	Hattusha	no	200 sayings
Middle Assyrian (Tiglath-Pileser I)	11th	Akkadian	Assur	no	100 sayings
Neo-Babylonian	7th	Akkadian	Sippar	no	15 sayings

[a]A segment of this collection explicitly institutes reform. Among the numerous legal reform documents, two of the most important derive from Uruinimgina (Lagash, 24th century BC) and Ammiṣaduqa (Babylon, 17th century BC).

and correlating assumption about the nature of law and in part from previous decisions about the nature of the biblical "law codes." This view was believed to be supported by the relief that is found at the top of the stele containing the so-called Code of Hammurabi, which contains a picture of Shamash, god of justice, seated on a throne and extending a rod and ring to Hammurabi, who stands opposite him in a deferential pose. Early interpreters thought this represented the god giving the law to Hammurabi just as Yahweh gave the law to Moses. On further analysis, it became clear that the god Shamash was not delivering the material to Hammurabi, but the other way around. As more information about Shamash was discovered, it was learned that the rod and ring were neither the laws themselves being revealed nor even the authority to make laws. Instead, they were recognized as Shamash's symbols of authority, and he was displaying them, not giving them to Hammurabi.[2] The relief depicts the investiture of Hammurabi as the just king by the authority of Shamash. Coupled with the revised interpretation of the relief, a variety of observations over time began to suggest alternative interpretations of these ANE legal collections. When scholars began to notice that there were major gaps in the content of the law (i.e., areas that were not covered that would nevertheless have been essential for a legal code; see further below), suggestions began to be made that these collections did not constitute a law "code" (i.e., formal prescriptive legislation). Rather, it was alternatively suggested, this was a collection of model verdicts. This viewpoint fit well with the literary context of the Hammurabi collection and the interpretation of the relief. The collection of legal sayings was then reinterpreted as Hammurabi's demonstration that he was executing justice in his kingdom—a role that the gods had appointed him to carry out and for which they held him accountable.

Given this interpretation, it became less fitting to interpret the document as codified, prescriptive legislation, but adjustments in thinking continued to occur. Scholars began to suspect that these collections were the result of the scholarly creativity of the scribes rather than solely the work of legislators ruling on cases brought before them. Certainly many of the cases could have represented actual verdicts in

---

[2]This is evident from the numerous depictions of Shamash holding these symbols even when no one stands in front of him. Some believe that Shamash is giving these articles to Hammurabi and that they are symbols of royal office (scepter and nose ring), enabling the king to guide the people and administer justice. See W. W. Hallo, "Sumerian History in Pictures: A New Look at the 'Stele of the Flying Angels,'" in *An Experienced Scribe Who Neglects Nothing: Ancient Near Eastern Studies in Honor of Jacob Klein*, ed. Yitzhak Sefati et al. (Bethesda, MD: CDL Press, 2005), 142-62, discussion on 150-53. Others contend that Shamash is regularly pictured with his arm extended and holding these insignia and that he is not giving them to anyone. In this view they are understood as measuring instruments. See Thorkild Jacobsen, "Pictures and Pictorial Language (the Burney Relief)," in *Figurative Language in the Ancient Near East*, ed. M. Mindlin et al. (London: School of Oriental and African Studies, 1987), 1-11; Christopher E. Woods, "The Sun-God Tablet of Nabû-apla-iddina Revisited," *JCS* 56 (2004): 23-103. For a brief discussion of the rod and ring see Jeremy Black and Anthony Green, *Gods, Demons and Symbols of Ancient Mesopotamia: An Illustrated Dictionary* (Austin: University of Texas Press, 1992), 156.

actual cases, but there are apparent cases to the contrary.[3] If the legal sayings were not preserved as model verdicts, then what were they? Why were they recorded? We will turn attention to that question in the next chapter, but before doing that, it is important to discuss the question of the coverage of the legal collections.

COVERAGE OF THE LEGAL COLLECTIONS

One of the characteristics of the kind of prescriptive codified legislation we use today is that it has to be somewhat comprehensive in the range of topics it covers. If a society is going to be governed by law, the law must address every aspect of society. The extent to which it is selective is the extent to which it loses its effectiveness. Of course, no code can exhaustively cover every possible permutation, eventuality, and scenario. Our solution to that dilemma is to make full use of precedent to classify legal situations to align with rulings of the past. In this way, virtual comprehensiveness can be achieved. Still, every category of law and every aspect of life must be addressed. It is a gargantuan task and creates a complicated bureaucracy.

In contrast, it has been clear to everyone who has studied the ANE legal collections that they do not even try to be comprehensive; many important aspects of life and society are left unaddressed. Hammurabi covers the most area and includes paragraphs concerning both civil and criminal matters (marriage/family, inheritance, property, slaves, debt, taxes/wages, murder, adultery, rape, theft, sexual deviation, false witness, assault, and liability). The others fail to cover several or even many of these categories.[4] We might notice some categories that are not represented in any collection and many more where coverage

---

[3]Jean Bottéro, "The 'Code' of Hammurabi," in *Mesopotamia: Writing, Reasoning, and the Gods* (Chicago: University of Chicago Press, 1992), 176-77, offers the example of the "wages" for a goat trampling grain on the threshing floor. Bottéro has demonstrated that the collections seek to enumerate variations in the same sort of legal context.

[4]For a comparative chart, see John H. Walton, *Ancient Israelite Literature in Its Cultural Context* (Grand Rapids: Zondervan, 1989), 76-77.

within the category is spotty (e.g., organization of justice, fiscal policy, and animal husbandry).[5] The conclusion can only be that these documents could not possibly serve as codified legislation to regulate every aspect of society. Finally, we can glean further information from considering evidence offered by the court documents.

COURT DOCUMENTS

It has been abundantly clear to scholars studying the many thousand existing court documents that the judiciary in the ancient world did not decide cases on the basis of a formal, written, normative legal code as is done today. In all the documents that we possess, no reference is made to any resource that is consulted in order to determine the judge's ruling. For all the popularity of Hammurabi's collection, it is never cited in a court document as providing the basis for the judge's decision.[6] In our world judges make decisions based on precedents of legal rulings that have withstood scrutiny and based on legislation that has been enacted by a country's legislative body. Rulings have to be documented and supported by evidence from the written records. In contrast, judges in the ancient world did not issue their verdicts by making reference to documents that had been produced for that purpose. Instead, they depended on custom and wisdom. When those were inadequate, divine oracles would be sought (note Moses' procedure in Ex 18).[7]

When we think of laws, we imagine a normative list of rules with accompanying consequences for breaking them. When a person goes to court, the lawyers, judge, and jury try to determine if the rule has

---

[5]An extensive list of both missing and underrepresented categories is provided in Bottéro, "'Code' of Hammurabi," 161.

[6]Bottéro, "'Code' of Hammurabi," 163; and Joshua A. Berman, *Inconsistency in the Torah: Ancient Literary Convention and the Limits of Source Criticism* (Oxford: Oxford University Press, 2017), 112-13.

[7]Michael LeFebvre, *Collections, Codes, and Torah: The Re-characterization of Israel's Written Law* (New York: T&T Clark, 2006), 40.

actually been broken and to what extent the consequences should be applied. This system relies heavily on logical precision (both in the writing of the rules themselves and in the presentation of evidence) and precedent. We very specifically do *not* want the judge (or the jury) to apply their intuition about what they think constitutes "wrongness" and about what they feel should happen to this specific individual, so we force them to work within a series of methodological constraints (for example, juries are commanded to consider only evidence that the court has formally admitted and are deliberately isolated from any additional influence). People in the ancient world, however, *did* want the judge to apply his intuition about wrongness to the cases he judged and to consider each on its own merits. Our modern case law describes precedent that sets limits on what kinds of rulings the lawyers and the judges are allowed to make. Ancient legal wisdom instead tried to instruct the judge on what rightness and wrongness looked like so he (and it was usually a man) would be able to produce rightness and eliminate wrongness with his verdicts. We will develop this idea in the next chapter as we discuss the idea that these texts teach wisdom. The texts do not teach what the law is; they provide a model for right and wrong so that the judges will know it when they see it.

Ancient Near Eastern Legal Collections Teach Wisdom

The most important breakthrough for understanding the ancient collections of legal sayings developed when scholars began to note the similarity between those lists and the lists that were becoming increasingly familiar in the literature from the Sumerians, Babylonians, and Assyrians. Some of the most extensive documents from the ancient Near East (ANE) comprised lists that often, like the lists of legal sayings, used an "if . . . then" formulation (known as casuistic, i.e., case-by-case). Whether following this type of formulation or not, the use of lists was commonplace in literary circles:

- Lists of medical symptoms along with their diagnoses or remedies (whether herbal or magical)

- Lists of omens: observations along with what they portended and what should be the response

- Lists of proverbial sayings

- Lists of lexical equivalents (whether bilingual or treating synonyms)

The common ground among these lists has led to what is now a broad consensus regarding how they function.

These lists are not intended to be comprehensive; rather, they are what we can call "aspective." That is, they offer a wide variety of aspects pertaining to the topic of the list. This accumulation of aspects serves to produce a sense of understanding of the field as a whole. In a word, the accumulated aspects provide *wisdom*. The medical lists combine to provide wisdom for the care providers of the day so that they will become familiar with symptoms and recommended treatment. The omen lists provide wisdom for the divination experts that would be applied to the day-to-day decisions they had to make as they advised the king. The proverbial sayings are listed to give wisdom for preserving order in society. The lexical lists provide wisdom for the scribes who have to deal with texts every day.

In the same way, the lists of legal sayings provide wisdom for judges who have to decide on cases in their towns. These lists showcase the wisdom of the king to discern what justice will look like. They are not the laws of the land, they are not legislative decrees, and they do not constitute a prescriptive code enforced in society. The king has not promulgated these as laws. He has had them compiled to convey his wisdom because, as the king designated by the gods, his responsibility is to maintain order on behalf of the gods. Wisdom is the ability to perceive order and establish it.

In raw form the lists are pedagogical. When embedded between prologue and epilogue as in Hammurabi's stele, they serve as an accountability report to the gods. Consequently, these lists of legal sayings do not tell us what laws were in force in society, much like proverbs do not tell us how everyone lived their lives in society. Both sorts of corpus are illustrations compiled to communicate the wisdom that will lead to order and justice. Scholars who were engaged on behalf of the king sought not to define law but to offer guidance for discerning wise justice so that order might be maintained in society.

Some of the illustrations may indeed have been drawn from actual verdicts, but that is unimportant. Likewise, this instruction in wisdom should be recognized as having a very different intention from legislation. Whereas legislation has the expected response of obedience, instruction in wisdom has the expected response of comprehension and application.

A couple of examples will be helpful. In any introductory art appreciation course, the question will be asked, What is art? Ensuing discussion will address a number of issues that may include media and taste. In the end, wisdom pertaining to the nature of art will be achieved as examples are given that circumscribe the broad and unwieldy concept of art. The circle of what can be called art is now populated by many dots, each representing examples of something that is art. The result is neither comprehensive nor normative in any way. It is intended to convey an idea that is of necessity abstract. In the same way, the ancient legal sayings circumscribe the abstract idea of order and justice. Despite the abstract nature of the subject, art students are nonetheless supposed to gain some ability to know art when they see it. Likewise, pupils of the legal literature are expected to gain some ability to know justice when they see it. This intuitive recognition is what we mean by wisdom.

As a second example, consider the way that students do math problems for homework. By solving the posed problems, the students should begin to understand the concepts involved. The individual problem is of little significance in the grand scheme and may be quite artificial or even unrealistic. But the problems provide ways to practice good math and to help students achieve an informed wisdom about math, thus enabling them to use math in life and to think mathematically. If the problem involves two trains leaving from different stations and going toward each other at different speeds, the student may be asked to determine when and where they will pass each other. The students need not be interested in train schedules; such details are immaterial. They are acquiring wisdom for life, not wisdom for operating a railway. At the same time, though, math problems are not comprehensive; we do not expect math problems to provide examples for every facet of life, or even every facet that entails thinking mathematically. These analogies of art and math help to illustrate the aspective approach, which provides examples to offer wisdom to circumscribe an abstract way of thinking.

Based on this consensus, we can now revisit some of the observations made in the last chapter. The relief at the top of the stele of Hammurabi depicts the king standing before the god Shamash, the deity responsible for order and justice. Hammurabi is accountable to the gods in general and Shamash in particular to be a wise king as he establishes and maintains justice in the land. This practice of wisdom is the basis for his continued investiture (remember the symbols of investiture held by Shamash, signifying his right to designate Hammurabi as king). In the prologue and epilogue, Hammurabi recounts how he has been favored by the gods and installed by them and how he has maintained justice by means of the wisdom they have granted him. The 282 legal sayings are provided as evidence of his judicial wisdom—representing at times verdicts that have actually been handed down and at other times what the verdict would be if such a case were to come before the king. All are there to give evidence of his wisdom. All people (as well as the gods) should consider the stele as proof that Hammurabi is indeed a wise king. Judges would learn wisdom from this list, and people would be convinced that the king has been working tirelessly on their behalf to provide order for them.

The list is not comprehensive because it is intended to circumscribe, not legislate. It provides illustrations of justice and order. As judges and magistrates absorb what it communicates, they will be better able to recognize wrongness and rightness and make decisions appropriately. Since the list is not intended to regulate or legislate, there is no need for it to be comprehensive. The items in the list provide descriptive instruction, not prescriptive legislation.[1] This also explains why we find no reference to sources of law in the court documents. The list of legal sayings is not the source of law; the sayings are a resource for informing the wisdom of the judges. The court documents instead demonstrate the ways that decision were made on a more ad hoc basis, based on the judges' insight and wisdom regarding the customs and traditions of their society.

The tradition of list wisdom, the evidence from the documents concerning legal sayings, and the evidence of the operation of the courts all combine to form a picture of how law was perceived and practiced in the ancient world. We find that it is far different from the understanding and practice of law today. Rather than focusing on words that define our cultural river, words like *code, legislation, prescription, coercion, obedience,* and *obligation,* we must focus on words that define their cultural river, words like *wisdom, illustration, circumscription, description, instruction, comprehension,* and *assimilation of ideas.* In the ancient world, order was perceived as more than law-abiding obedience; it was achieved through wisdom exercised at the society level as well as the personal level. Our next step is to evaluate the Torah in light of what we have learned about the ancient cultural river.

---

[1]That is, they provide an important foundation for common law rather than representing statutory law. See discussion of statutory law in "Technical Terminology" sidebar in proposition 2.

The Torah Is Similar to Ancient Near Eastern Legal Collections and Therefore Also Teaches Wisdom, Not Legislation

On the basis of the preceding discussion of the cultural river of the ancient world, it is now clear that we cannot simply assume that legal collections are legislative in nature. It would therefore have to be demonstrated that Israel's legal lists *were* legislative, and the burden of proof would lie on those who wanted to take that position. In point of fact, however, three observations will argue strongly against understanding the Torah as constituting a legislative code. Furthermore, what we have learned from the ancient Near Eastern (ANE) lists will serve us well in accounting for and understanding what we encounter in the biblical text.

TORAH AS ASPECTIVE LEGAL WISDOM

First, as is true for the ANE legal collections, the Torah, even with all collections combined, is nowhere near being comprehensive. For example, it contains little to nothing about marriage, divorce, inheritance, or adoption. If this is not transparent enough from basic observation, it is demonstrated convincingly from the history of interpretation. Those who attempted to employ it prescriptively had to do considerable extrapolation in order to produce a code that could be used as normative. We can already see this inclination in the way that Jewish interpreters in the Second Temple period began extrapolating lines from the Torah to provide regulations for particular situations that the Torah itself did not anticipate or address. This impulse is richly worked out in the Mishnah.[1]

Second, as we found with regard to the ANE, the Torah, though clearly recognized as a document ("book of Moses"), is not relied on as the legal, normative basis for judicial decisions.[2] So, for example, David reacts to Nathan's parable with, "As surely as the LORD lives, the man who did this must die! He must pay for that lamb four times over, because he did such a thing and had no pity" (2 Sam 12:5-6). Exodus 22:1 can be cited as attesting to the custom that theft of a sheep should be repaid fourfold, but there is no indication that David had researched the law in order to arrive at his decision, nor did he substantiate it based on a legal text.[3] Texts that contain legal sayings may at times have been read aloud as exhortation to the people (as in Deut 31:10-13; Ezra 8), consulted by judges, or studied by kings who sought to be wise (Deut 17:18-20).[4] The Torah was intended to give the king

---

[1]The interpreters of the Second Temple period are not legislating—establishing a statutory law—but they are, nonetheless, trying to make the Torah prescriptive for Jewish life. They are defining a (comprehensive) cultural identity, not establishing the law of the land.

[2]Affirmed by many scholars, including Roy E. Gane, *Old Testament Law for Christians: Original Context and Enduring Application* (Grand Rapids: Baker Academic, 2017), 30.

[3]Interestingly, the Septuagint translation depicts David's judgment as requiring a sevenfold repayment so the reading of the Masoretic text is not assured. In comparison, Hammurabi indicates tenfold restitution for theft of livestock from a private citizen.

[4]Michael LeFebvre, *Collections, Codes, and Torah: The Re-characterization of Israel's Written Law* (New York: T&T Clark, 2006), 47. It should be noted that we do not have examples of the ANE collections being read aloud to the people. We contend that reading aloud is more connected to the role of the Torah in the covenant because stipulations exist for treaties of the ANE to be read aloud.

wisdom for doing his job.[5] The Torah (like the legal lists in the ANE) embodies wisdom; it does not establish legislation.

Third, we must recognize that the legal collections in the Torah are embedded literarily at several levels. Most importantly, the legal sayings are presented in the context of a covenant between Yahweh and Israel, in which case they serve as stipulations to that covenant agreement (developed further in propositions 6 and 13). Covenant (or treaty) stipulations serve a very different function from laws, whether either is represented literarily or not. Stipulations are agreed upon by both parties and generally enforced by the gods, not by judiciary institutions. Furthermore, however, the legal lists in the Pentateuch are also couched literarily in narrative or in speeches (such as Moses' sermons in Deuteronomy), as well as in what eventually became canonical books, each using the Torah to accomplish its own individual literary objectives. That means that none of these are in a literary context of legislation; they have been adopted for secondary (or even tertiary) use.

These arguments all support the idea that the Torah is similar to its ANE counterparts and therefore not legislative. However, some scholars claim that the Torah is distinct from other ANE legal collections and that the distinction specifically consists of the Torah being intended for use as legislation, though other documents were not. We will discuss the similarities and differences in the next two chapters, but before we proceed, we need to examine the evidence of the Hebrew terminology.

---

[5]The ancient world, including Israel, is hearing dominant, not text dominant, so it would not be expected that written documents served as an authoritative foundation for law. In general, there were only very specific areas where written documents served a normative function—they were written so that they could be read aloud. See discussion in John H. Walton and D. Brent Sandy, *The Lost World of Scripture: Ancient Literary Culture and Biblical Authority* (Downers Grove, IL: IVP Academic, 2013).

TERMINOLOGY

The term *Torah* is universally acknowledged to refer to instruction.[6] In fact, there is no Hebrew word for "law" (= legislation), and now it can be seen that the reason for this is that the ancient societies were not legislative societies. There is nothing like codified, prescriptive legislation in their experience. Other words that are most frequently used to describe certain types of legal sayings (along with the most common English translation used in the NIV) include:

- *mišpāṭîm*—"laws/judgments"—verdicts given in legal contexts
- *ḥuqqîm*—"decrees"—dictates delivered by a formal authority (e.g., king)
- *dəbārîm*—"words"—insights, advice, exhortations, or admonitions that should guide one's thinking
- *miṣwôt*—"commandments"—charges or mandates coming from those with recognized status (e.g., parents or elders)
- *ʿēdût*—"statutes"—used of legal sayings primarily in Psalms, not in the Pentateuch
- *piqqûdîm*—"precepts"—sayings that establish order; used only in Psalms

These terms and a few others are used interchangeably in poetic literature such as the Psalms. All of them, as well as a few others, are used throughout Psalm 119. None of them refer to codified legislation. *Torah* is most frequently used as a term that encompasses all of them. In this book we will not make an attempt to differentiate them from one another (though that can be done profitably). The term *Torah* itself is used for the Pentateuch as a whole, for the legal corpus as a

---

[6]G. López and H.-J. Fabry, תּוֹרָה *tôrâ*, *TDOT*, 15:609-46; P. Enns, "Law of God," *NIDOTTE*, 4:893-900. This conclusion has support in etymology but is even more strongly supported in the broad range of usage. Whether instruction through oracles, instruction through wisdom sayings, or personal advice, the instruction aspect remains central.

whole, and as a catchall term for the various types of legal sayings. By etymology, it is constructed from the root that refers to instruction (*yrh*).[7] Throughout the Pentateuch, the Prophets, the narrative literature, and even the Psalms, it is almost always used to refer to the legal/cultic revelation delivered by Yahweh through Moses in association with the covenant at Sinai. It is never used to refer to decrees made by kings, priests, or judges.[8]

Walter Kaiser identifies the root of the problem in how the term *tôrâ* has been rendered in translation—in each case reflecting more the cultural ideas of the translators than the cultural ideas of the ancient world. As examples he cites the decision to render *tôrâ* by Greek *nomos* in the Septuagint and the New Testament, by *loi* in French, and by *Gesetz* in German. He laments that these are all based on presuppositions concerning the nature of the material found in the Torah. He concludes that "*tôrâ* is much more than mere law. Even the word itself does not indicate static requirements that govern the whole of human experience."[9] Instead he identifies it as "directional teaching or guidance for walking on the path of life."[10]

Perhaps the main piece of evidence that leads readers to think that Torah is legislation is the repeated exhortation, or even injunction, to "obey." This warrants closer attention to the Hebrew terminology used in the Old Testament. Hebrew words that are translated "obey" in major translations are verbs from the roots *šmʿ* (usually accompanied

---

[7]A note of reminder that etymology is not a reliable guide to meaning. Meaning is determined by a word's usage, not by its history. Nevertheless, usage may at times preserve an awareness of etymology. Decisions must be made on a case-by-case basis. It is common in Hebrew for a verbal root to be given a noun form by the use of a *t* preformative, as here. Furthermore, Hebrew uses feminine forms of nouns (here represented by the *-ah* ending) to designate an abstraction.

[8]This is true also because kings, priests, and judges did not make laws. Royal decrees could be broadly included in the category of Torah, but decrees are not laws.

[9]Walter C. Kaiser Jr., "The Law as God's Gracious Guidance for the Promotion of Holiness," in *Five Views on Law and Gospel*, ed. Wayne G. Strickland (Grand Rapids: Zondervan, 1996), 192.

[10]Kaiser, "Law as God's Gracious Guidance," 193.

by a preposition) and *šmr*. The combination appears notably in one of the founding statements of the covenant:

> Now if you obey me fully [listen (*šmʿ*) to my voice] and keep [*šmr*] my covenant, then out of all nations you will be my treasured possession. (Ex 19:5)

Šmʿ means to "hear" or to "listen" (cf. Deut 6:4, "Hear, O Israel"). Beginning Hebrew students are often told that the combination of the root *šmʿ* + the preposition *b-* ("listen to") means "to obey." Note, however, that this combination almost always takes the noun "voice" (*qol*) as the object of the preposition (as in Ex 19:5), and it never has *tôrâ* or any of its synonyms as the object of the preposition. Obeying the voice of the Lord is always a good idea, but it should not be equated to obeying laws. On a few occasions the root occurs with another preposition (such as *ʾel* or *ʿal*) and is translated "obey" (e.g., Deut 11:27; 12:28, with "commands" or "regulations" as the object of the preposition *ʾel* [referring to the stipulations of the covenant], or 2 Kings 22:13 with "words of this book [= the document found by Hilkiah and Josiah]" as the object of the preposition *ʿal*). In all these cases, the fact that the content of such documents is circulated by reading aloud gives sense to the idea that the people on the receiving end should *hear*, but also *heed*, what is being said. An exhortation to heed is not solely the purview of legislation that must be obeyed. In Wisdom literature, particularly the book of Proverbs, the one being instructed is repeatedly enjoined to heed the wisdom that is being conveyed.[11] This proverbial wisdom is specifically *not* legislation. The response that we often term "obedience" pertains more specifically to aligning one's will with that of Yahweh by taking the role of a servant who is loyal.[12] This

---

[11] For the same concept concerning Hammurabi, see Joshua A. Berman, *Inconsistency in the Torah: Ancient Literary Convention and the Limits of Source Criticism* (Oxford: Oxford University Press, 2017), 146.

[12] Christine Hayes, *What's Divine About Divine Law? Early Perspectives* (Princeton: Princeton University Press, 2015), 23.

sort of response has very little to do with obeying a codified, prescriptive legislation.

The second verb, *šmr*, means to "guard, keep, or observe." Again, we find that translating such a verb as "obey" is contentious and works on the assumption that legislation is involved. Proverbial literature shows the flaw in that assumption as the student is repeatedly called upon to *šmr* as a response to the Wisdom instruction being given (e.g., Prov 2:20; 4:21)—clearly not a matter of obedience. Particularly of interest on this count are the few examples in Proverbs where the direct object of the verb is *tôrâ* or *miṣwôt* ("commandments").

> Take hold of my words with all your heart;
> keep [*šmr*] my commands [*miṣwôt*], and you will live.
>   (Prov 4:4)

> Keep [*šmr*] my commands [*miṣwôt*] and you will live;
> guard my teachings as the apple of your eye. (Prov 7:2)

> Whoever keeps [*šmr*] commandments [*miṣwâ*] keeps their life,
> but whoever shows contempt for their ways will die.
>   (Prov 19:16)

> Those who forsake instruction [*tôrâ*] praise the wicked,
> but those who heed [*šmr*] it resist them. (Prov 28:4)

> Where there is no revelation, people cast off restraint;
> but blessed is the one who heeds [*šmr*] wisdom's instruction
> [*tôrâ*]. (Prov 29:18)

These especially need to be evaluated to understand whether they refer to legislation that the Israelites needed to obey. They occur in Wisdom literature, and wisdom as a genre (like Torah) is closely associated with order. A wise person perceives what brings order, pursues that sort of life, and puts it into practice. A wise person will seek to preserve order wherever it is found and will promote it in society and in life. Such wisdom recognizes that order is important in relationships and can be undermined by careless speech or bad choices. Wisdom, then, includes prudence, but is not limited to prudence. The result of failing to heed wisdom by not keeping the Torah, as indicated in the verses cited above, is death. Death is sometimes the fate of a lawbreaker (capital crimes), but here death is the fate of anyone who fails to heed wisdom. That is because fools who undermine order or fail to embrace it face the inevitable prospect of death. This is particularly the case with covenant violations. Torah presents the way of wisdom and life (Deut 30) in the ordered world of the covenant. We can therefore see that the issues that Scripture addresses have to do with wisdom and covenant fidelity, not with legislation and its rules that must be obeyed.

Wise living cannot be legislated. It is a matter of applying principles of wisdom, not of following rules. If God did not give rules, as we have suggested, there are no rules to follow. If God did not provide legislation, there are no laws to obey. Consequently, we may conclude that translating either of these words as "obey" reflects a cultural river violation—it assumes that an idea from our culture dominated Israel's perspectives and literature. Order in society was the goal, and it was achieved through wisdom, which had its foundation in the fear of the Lord. Any individual's contribution to that order was not dependent on a set of rules and did not require that rules had been provided. Wisdom literature, like Torah, gave insights into how order was perceived, pursued, promoted, preserved, procured, and practiced.

Israel's judiciary system, like that throughout the ANE, was based on the wisdom of the judges, not on legislation. It involved a dynamic integration of custom, divine revelation (including oracles), and intuition, rather than static codes.[13] The legal collections found in the Torah and other legal collections embody that wisdom by providing

---

[13]LeFebvre, *Collections, Codes, and Torah*, 47; see also Bernard S. Jackson, *Wisdom-Laws: A Study of the Mishpatim of Exodus 21:1–22:16* (Oxford: Oxford University Press, 2006).

an aspective mosaic of sayings that manifested the sponsor's wisdom, instructed the judges, and helped the people to understand order in society.[14] The people are to "heed" this wisdom and "preserve" it. In this view, the expected response to the Torah is far different from a response to legislation. Legislation carries a sense of "you ought"; instruction carries a sense of "you will know."[15]

Consequently, we will propose that *Torah* in biblical usage is an expression of wisdom, not of legislation. It refers to a collection of examples that combine to form a description of the desired established order. We will be using the term to refer to the corpus of legal sayings found throughout the Pentateuch and will seek to demonstrate that these sayings embody standards of wisdom for the ordering of society within the covenant relationship that Yahweh had with Israel.

---

[14]We could possibly understand this by comparing it to what we refer to today as "best practices"—most responsible or effective in achieving goals in a particular field. They are not rules/laws. This example was suggested by Dan Reid.

[15]Jean Louis Ska, "Biblical Law and the Origins of Democracy," in *The Ten Commandments: The Reciprocity of Faithfulness*, ed. William P. Brown (Louisville, KY: Westminster John Knox, 2004), 146-58.

The Israelite Covenant
Effectively Functions as an Ancient
Near Eastern Suzerainty Treaty

In the covenant we find three principal genres. We have already discussed legal wisdom, and we will eventually turn our attention to ritual instruction. But now we examine the second: suzerainty treaty. Properly understood, the three genres together provide an understanding of how the covenant relationship works. The suzerain-vassal relationship is well attested in the treaties from the ancient Near East (ANE). A majority of the exemplars come from the Hittite literature in the middle of the second millennium and the Neo-Assyrian literature from the middle of the first millennium. Scattered exemplars spread through the intervening millennium.[1] It has long been recognized that the covenant between Yahweh and Israel is expressed in a literary form that was used in these international treaties

---

[1]For the most thorough treatment, see the three-volume work of Kenneth A. Kitchen and Paul J. N. Lawrence, *Treaty, Law and Covenant in the Ancient Near East* (Wiesbaden: Harrassowitz, 2012). Dialogue continues over the extent to which the biblical forms more closely resemble the first millennium exemplars (mostly Neo-Assyrian) or those from the second millennium (primarily Hittite). For our purposes it does not matter so we will not engage that controversy.

in the ancient world. The behavior of the vassal determined what steps were to be taken by the sovereign to enforce order, and the way that the sovereign treated his vassals, the suzerain-vassal relationship, established the sovereign's reputation. Consequently, to understand the Torah, we must understand the nature of the suzerainty relationship and the role that Torah plays in it.

Similarly to the legal texts, ANE treaty stipulations are aspective, not comprehensive, and their intention is instruction, not legislation. Rather than instruct judges in wisdom to properly administer justice, however, the treaty stipulations are intended to instruct the regent and his administrative underlings in the wisdom to properly serve as loyal vassals. These documents serve to delineate relationships (the role of the vassal, the role of the suzerain) and preserve order in the relationship between the parties. Treaty stipulations in the ancient world highlight the behavior expected of each party with relationship to the other. As we saw in the legal wisdom texts, here also we encounter very general statements that would resist comprehensive description, such as "violence will not flourish here."[2] Such content leads to the conclusion that, as we noted with the legal sayings, these stipulations are not a comprehensive list of everything that is expected of the vassal (i.e., if it is not on this list, you are free of obligation), but a representative list. The detailed, specific expectations should be considered real, but they are not exhaustive.

These observations lead us to inquire after the overall objective of the treaty stipulations. Importantly, stipulations were not received as revelation from the suzerain; the vassals knew what the suzerain expected of them and would not have read a treaty document in order to gain this information. What was expected was loyalty and a positive reflection on the sovereign's reputation, generally achieved by maintaining a peaceful, well-ordered state as well as an overall posture of submission.

---

[2]See the treaty between Naram-Sin and Elam, in Kitchen and Lawrence, *Treaty, Law and Covenant*, 49.

The vassal kings would have had this same understanding and would also have known what was expected of them as rulers. Rebellion was not an offense that could occur by accident; the rebels would know what they were doing, and the sovereign would have invoked generalizations in the treaty documents to demonstrate that their reactions were just. In this sense we might compare the treaty stipulations with the end-user license agreement that accompanies most software purchases. Few people ever read these documents, but we know what they say (agreements not to pirate the software, releasing the company from liability, etc.). And we know more or less intuitively what the proper use of the product entails. The license can be invoked in a lawsuit against pirates—that is its purpose—but we do not have to read the document to know that we are not supposed to steal the product. Likewise, treaty documents could be invoked in a lawsuit against rebels—the ANE often considered war to be a form of legal action[3]—but the vassals did not have to read the document to know what constituted rebellion. What the suzerain wants from the vassal is faithfulness, and he (almost always male) has both general and specific ideas concerning what that entails (see further discussion in proposition 13).

Once we recognize the presence of a stock treaty format in the Old Testament, the literary role of Israel's legal sayings can be identified: they comprise the stipulations of the covenant agreement. That is, the lists of legal collections familiar in the ancient world have been reused in a second genre, covenant/treaty, where they serve as stipulations. This important observation gives us further information by which to understand how to interpret the sayings (as treaty stipulation, not legislation). Most importantly, it indicates that though Yahweh is Israel's God, the covenant features him as Israel's suzerain king.

Taking a vassal serves to enhance the reputation of the suzerain. The treaty is not primarily about the stipulations. A treaty relationship

---

[3]Sa-Moon Kang, *Divine War in the Old Testament and in the Ancient Near East* (Berlin: de Gruyter, 1989), 14-15, 196.

has not been formed so that the suzerain can bless the vassal with stipulations. Instead, the existence of a treaty serves to communicate the greatness of the suzerain. In an act of granting royal favor he has adopted the vassal into his family (politically speaking), and the existence and condition of the vassal reflect on his power and competence as king. All of the king's royal panoply and accoutrements ultimately serve this function, not only his territories and his vassals but also his administration, his monuments and building projects, his courtiers, his largesse in all of its permutations, his treasury, his palace, his wives and concubines, his weapons, the reliefs depicting his achievements, his images, and so much more. When the Queen of Sheba visited Solomon, what impressed her was the vast display of Solomon's sovereignty. Vassals serve to demonstrate the power and competence of the king; the more powerful and more prosperous the vassal, the greater the king who rules over them. The suzerain does not support the vassals for the sake of the vassals; he supports them because the condition of the vassals reflects back on him.

The kings of the ancient world desired to label the things that were theirs. Bricks were stamped with their names, their images were placed in conquered territories, and their treaties were inscribed and displayed prominently. A vassal was a showpiece of the suzerain's grandeur. This labeling was a way to place one's name on something, just as Yahweh placed his name on Israel. For a suzerain to extend his name to a vassal was construed as an act of favor. Both in international treaties and in the Torah, this was described as the suzerain's love for his vassal. It has long been established that this love was not sentimental, emotional, or psychological.[4] Instead, it showed that the suzerain had expressed gracious preference for the vassal by extending his identity to this vassal.

---

[4]William L. Moran, "The Ancient Near Eastern Background of the Love of God in Deuteronomy," in *Essential Papers on Israel and the Ancient Near East*, ed. Frederick E. Greenspahn (New York: New York University Press, 1991), 103-15.

In all of this the stipulations served a fairly minor role. They stood as the means by which to circumscribe the shape that loyalty and faithfulness would take and what would constitute rebellion. In the end, loyalty was expected in every way since that was the vassal's expression of gratitude for having been so favored by the suzerain. Rebellion was, in theory, unthinkable and would be harshly punished. The suzerain was worthy of all praise and honor and was to be recognized for the greatness of his name. Importance was not found in what the vassal did or did not do, but in the identity of the suzerain.

A vassal could be taken by coercion (as for example, when conquered in battle, or as an alternative to conquest), but some vassals patriated themselves voluntarily, usually in exchange for military support against their own enemies. Being a vassal carried benefits, but it also came at a price. For our purposes, the most significant cost of being a vassal was the need to pay tribute. In exchange for military protection (or nonaggression), the suzerain would demand a yearly payment of various resources. Importantly, the purpose of tribute was not (primarily) to secure a revenue stream; vassal states were not a financial investment (as, for example, European colonies were). Much of the tribute became what we might refer to as "fixed assets" in the treasury of the temple or palace. The amount of tribute kings received was part of the demonstration of their power and greatness and was boasted of in their inscriptions. Heavy tribute was levied primarily to depress the economy of a conquered enemy in order to limit the vassal's resources for rebellion. Paying the tribute, in turn, was one of the primary ways by which the vassal demonstrated loyalty. Withholding tribute constituted rebellion, and the suzerain would react against this, not because the ruler needed the money but because the ability to subdue a rebellious vassal (or not) contributed to the reputation of the king. Kings did not exist in a symbiotic relationship with their vassals whereby they supported each other through mutual need. Both vassal and sovereign benefited from the relationship in their own way (protection and reputation, respectively), but in terms of dependence the relationship was entirely one-sided.

All of what has been described thus far about suzerainty treaties is resident in the concept of Yahweh making a covenant with Israel. Just as the king was not listing stipulations to legislate the society of his vassals or to implement a moral system, neither was Yahweh imposing morality or social ideals on Israel through the stipulations of the Torah. We have already demonstrated in the previous chapters that the legal sayings in the ANE and the Torah are not legislation, but wisdom. Here we have moved another step as these wisdom sayings have been incorporated into a covenant as stipulations, which likewise never served the purpose of legislating the society of the vassal.

When the suzerain imposed stipulations on the vassal, he was not asserting law. He was extending his identity (as a glorious and powerful king) to, and especially through, the vassal. The kings of the ancient world did not impose law; they gave wisdom as they forged their identity.[5] Yahweh was the source of the Torah, but since neither the treaty stipulations nor the legal wisdom can be construed as law, being the source of Torah does not make Yahweh the source of law. Yahweh was the suzerain who formed a covenant relationship with Israel, and so extended his identity to them: "I will take you as my own people, and I will be your God" (Ex 6:7 and repeated often). Yahweh, like the suzerains taking vassals in the ancient world, was acting to establish his reputation, not to give something to his vassals. He was not acting out of need and was not simply taking the role of patron or benefactor. He is the Great King.

Yahweh's suzerain-vassal relationship with Israel is established in (especially) Deuteronomy but is emphasized most strongly in the response to Israel's covenant infidelity, which is persistently referred to as rebellion (e.g., Ezek 2:3) rather than as crime or moral detraction.

---

[5]Positivist law had not yet been invented; see discussion of positivist law in "Technical Terminology" sidebar in proposition 2.

Vassals serve to enhance the king's reputation. If the vassals are loyal, the king will demonstrate his power and competence by granting them prosperity and protection from enemies. If the vassals are rebellious, the king will demonstrate that same power and competence by putting down the rebellion with brutal efficiency. The response depends on the vassal, and the same is true with regard to Israel: "Just as it pleased the LORD to make you prosper and increase in number, so it will please him to ruin and destroy you" (Deut 28:63). What pleases Yahweh is not the granting of blessing to Israel per se; what pleases Yahweh is using Israel as a means to establish his reputation. If blessing the Israelites will enhance Yahweh's reputation, Yahweh will do that; if destroying them will enhance his reputation, he will do that instead. The emphasis on Yahweh's reputation (and not the well-being of Israel) is stated explicitly in the context of exile and restoration in Ezekiel 36:22-24: "It is not for your sake, people of Israel, that I am going to do these things, but for the sake of my holy name, which you have profaned among the nations where you have gone. . . . Then the nations will know that I am the LORD, declares the Sovereign LORD, when I am proved holy through you before their eyes." This is consistent with the action of a suzerain who wishes to establish a reputation for himself through the treatment of his vassals.

Both legal wisdom texts and treaties serve to establish or enhance the reputation of the king who produced them. In the case of the legal wisdom, the text establishes wisdom and justice and thereby serves to demonstrate that the king is wise and just. In the case of treaties, the document establishes the parameters of a relationship that will demonstrate the power and competence of the sovereign based on the treatment of his vassals. The use of both genres together indicates strongly that the overall purpose of Israel's covenant is for Yahweh to establish a reputation; this is what we mean when we say that Yahweh uses the covenant to *reveal himself*. The purpose is not to give anything *to* Israel (i.e., law, moral or social enlightenment, blessings), nor is it to receive anything *from* Israel (i.e., worship, service, moral performance). The Israelites accept vassal status of their own volition (Ex 24:1-8), but once they do so, they become a medium through which Yahweh will establish his reputation one way or another, regardless of what Israel does or does not do. Whether or not Israel benefits or suffers from the arrangement is up to them: "I have set before you life and death, blessings and curses. Now choose life, so that you and your children may live" (Deut 30:19). This in turn indicates that when we turn to apply the message of Israel's covenant documents to ourselves, we should think in terms of trying to understand the reputation that Yahweh intended to establish for himself. We should not think in terms of something that Yahweh wants to give to us (law) or something that he expects to receive from us (moral performance). This idea will be explored further in chapters that follow.

However, Yahweh is not only Israel's suzerain; he is also patron deity for the people. Deities in the ancient world did not impose laws any more than kings did,[6] and they did not necessarily have reputations per se, but each did have an identity that was projected in a particular way. Yahweh's self-revelation through Israel's covenant includes establishing how he is perceived as a deity, in addition to establishing how he is perceived as a king. This is done by means of a third genre within the covenant documents, namely, ritual literature, as well as by the holy status that is conferred to Israel. This we will examine over the next chapters.

---

[6]The concept of divine law had not yet been invented. To construe the Torah as either positivist law or divine law is anachronistic (see definitions in "Technical Terminology" sidebar in proposition 2).

Proposition 7

Holiness Is a Status, Not an Objective

Basing their understanding primarily on Leviticus 19–21, many readers assume that by keeping the law Israel would thereby become holy. Many people today additionally think that *holiness* is another word for *piety* or for *morality* (generally both) and that therefore the law was intended to tell the Israelites what they ought to do in order to be pious or moral. Many today likewise think that we are to pursue holiness (the same piety and morality) by obeying the same rules in order to achieve holiness. This is mistaken and misses the point.[1] Holiness, as we will see, is connected to the objective of the Torah, but the Torah (as we have established) does not consist of rules to be obeyed. Therefore, its objective is not achieved by obeying rules. We have already laid the foundation for this concept, so we can now flesh out the idea and follow it to its logical conclusions.

It is common for people to believe that holiness is something that godly people should aspire to achieve as they attempt to imitate God. This concept is routinely drawn from Leviticus 19:2, "Be holy because

---

[1]For fuller discussion see John H. Walton and J. Harvey Walton, *The Lost World of the Israelite Conquest: Covenant, Retribution, and the Fate of the Canaanites* (Downers Grove, IL: IVP Academic, 2017), 103-17.

I, the LORD your God, am holy."[2] Careful attention to grammar, however, will show that God's people are not called to "be holy"—the verbal form is indicative, not imperative ("you will be holy").[3] God declares his people holy by election decree. It is a status that he gives, and it cannot be gained or lost by the Israelites' own efforts or failures.

Holiness is the word that identifies elements of what we can call the constellation that collectively defines divine identity.[4] Ancient Near Eastern (ANE) divine personalities were circumscribed by lists of attributes or attendant objects or minions that collectively served to establish their identities. These distinguished between different aspects of the same deity (e.g., Ishtar of Arbela vs. Ishtar of Nineveh) and between different members of the pantheon, which in turn designated their realm of patronage and function within the cosmic bureaucracy and indicated the ways in which their worshipers ought to relate to them. *Constellation* refers to all the elements that compose this list:

> Most major gods are identified with an anthropomorphically conceived divine person, a statue, a number, a semi-precious stone, a mineral, an animal, an emblem, a star, constellation or other celestial entity and various characteristic qualities. Ištar in particular is simultaneously identified as a divine person who dwells in heaven, yet is localized in various terrestrial temples (most prominently Arbela and Nineveh), the planet Venus, the number 15, the semi-precious stone lapis-lazuli, and the mineral

---

[2] Also Matthew 5:48 and 1 Peter 1:15-16. See more complete discussion in Walton and Walton, *Lost World of the Israelite Conquest*, 104-8.

[3] The Septuagint likewise uses an indicative form of the verb (*esesthe*), rather than an imperative; 1 Peter 1:15 uses a different word (*ginesthe*). The word in Matthew 5:48 translated "perfect" (*telios*) is never used by the LXX as a translation of Hebrew *qdš* ("holy").

[4] For a thorough discussion of this idea see Walton and Walton, *Lost World of the Israelite Conquest*, and the associated technical discussion found in the online appendixes, www.ivpress.com/Media/Default/Downloads/Misc/5184-appendix.pdf. See independent confirmation of the grammatical construction and association with the divine identity in Thomas W. Mann, *The Book of the Torah* (Atlanta: John Knox, 1988), 117, though he puts more emphasis on *separation* than we would.

lead, and understood as the embodiment of such qualities as love and war.

Each of these interconnected divine networks composed of many distinct elements may be viewed as a divine constellation, in which the various elements are connected to a more or less unified entity and share in its identity. In other words, each major god consists of a constellation of aspects, which may act and be treated (semi-)independently. Most divine constellations consist of several connected deified aspects, with an anthropomorphic core that is always deified and other occasionally deified elements like heavenly bodies, abstract qualities, and metals.[5]

The elements of the constellation were sometimes considered to be divine in their own right and sometimes not, depending on context and the intimacy of their association with the deity.[6] In Hebrew, one of the uses of the term *qdš* ("holy") is to designate the referent as part of Yahweh's constellation.

- As a term used in reference to Yahweh to describe the full constellation of all that is associated with him, *holiness* includes objects (the ark), places (Mount Sinai, the temple), time (the Sabbath), land (a field or city devoted to God), and communities (the nation of Israel).

- Labeling something "holy" identifies it as one of the spheres of patronage that collectively define the god's identity:[7] "I will take you as my own people, and I will be your God" (Ex 6:7).

---

[5]Michael B. Hundley, "Here a God, There a God: An Examination of the Divine in Ancient Mesopotamia," *AoF* 40 (2013): 68-107, quote on 80-81.

[6]Barbara Porter, ed., *What Is a God? Anthropomorphic and Non-anthropomorphic Aspects of Deity in Ancient Mesopotamia* (Winona Lake, IN: Eisenbrauns, 2009), 163-64.

[7]*Qādôš* is the semantic equivalent of the Akkadian determinative DINGIR, which is applied to a similar range of objects and abstractions. See Walton and Walton, *Lost World of the Israelite Conquest*, 105-16, for full discussion. For the use of DINGIR as defining divine identity, see Hundley, "Here a God, There a God."

- When a thing becomes holy, whether that thing is the abstract community of Israel or an object like the ark or the sanctuary, it means that whatever that thing is or does in some way identifies something about what God is or does.

- Holiness is a status given by Yahweh to Israel that makes the nation a part of his identity by virtue of his making a covenant with them. Israel's holy status means that Yahweh has defined himself as "the God of Israel." By making the covenant with them and giving them this status, he has brought them into his constellation.

- Holiness is a status that is conferred; it cannot be earned, acquired, or lost by behavior.

- It is the community of Israel that is holy more than each individual.[8] Only priests and perhaps prophets as individuals are holy.

- Holiness is not defined by imitating God; rather, God makes the people holy by identifying himself through his people.

- For the nation of Israel to be holy means that Yahweh will identify— that is, reveal—himself through his interaction with them.

When Yahweh makes the covenant with the Israelites and declares them to be his holy people—that is, declares himself to be their God and thereby declares that his identity will be reflected by and through them—their status changes. But what does this mean for them? What significance will this new status have for their behavior? How will this status create a different situation for them practically speaking?

Most modern interpreters assume that holiness correlates to a specific moral character. Specifically, it is assumed to refer to the moral character of God, which people, through obedience to the law, are supposed to imitate. It would be easy for us, then, to assume that reflecting Yahweh's identity entails cultivating a particular moral

---

[8]Certainly each individual has a part to play in the community identity, but like "Image of God" and "Body of Christ," the focus is on the identity of the group.

character (by means of obeying the law), which will thereby reflect Yahweh's moral character. However, this is not what the text is talking about. First, we recall that the stipulations of the Torah are not rules to be obeyed; they are descriptive. The objective of reading them is knowing, not doing or being. Second, we also recall that holiness is a status that is conferred, not earned; Israel is equally holy whether the nation keeps the covenant or not. Holy status is not an objective to strive for. A third consideration comes from the ancient context. In the ANE, people did not aspire to imitate the gods, and the gods did not expect their worshipers to imitate them. Humans were humans and gods were gods; they had different functions and different natures and were evaluated by different standards. The gods were inscrutable and unaccountable to human moral standards, and their motives and actions were mysterious and incomprehensible to humans. Israel would have conceived of Yahweh in the same way; nothing in the Israelites' literature provided them with any resource for thinking differently about their God. Because of Yahweh's role as their king, the Israelites (or at least their leaders) would have aspired to emulate God's wisdom and justice, just as a vassal regent would aspire to emulate the wisdom and justice of the king, However, such emulation is not what *holiness*, which occurs primarily in the context of ritual literature, refers to. Ruling the vassal state with wisdom and justice is the means by which to retain Yahweh's favor and blessing; it is not the means by which Israel will achieve holiness.

Holiness is always descriptive of deity, even when the referent of the adjective is something else (i.e., Israel). *Holiness* does not describe a property of Israel; it describes a property of Yahweh. In the ancient world, identifying an element as part of a divine constellation does not say anything about the element; it says something about the deity to whose constellation the element belongs. Saying that (for example) Ares is the god of war does not tell us anything about war; it tells us something about Ares.

An example might be helpful. People in our society also form a kind of identity constellation that sets us apart as unique individuals distinct from all others. The elements of these constellations include such things as our jobs, our hobbies, our political or religious views, where we live, what college we attend, which sports teams we support, and what brands of products we choose to buy and display. If you were to choose to buy Nike shoes—that is, to declare that Nike shoes are part of your personal constellation—the action says nothing about Nike. Rather, it says something about you: "I am the kind of person who would choose to wear this brand of shoe." It is your way of associating yourself with the image that Nike has projected of itself through its advertising, which in turn dictates the way that people perceive the brand and, by extension, consumers of the brand. Similarly, when Yahweh brings the nation of Israel into his constellation by declaring it holy, he declares himself to all observers to be the kind of God who would be patron to a nation like Israel.

Of course, if a company rebrands itself and alters its image to something that its consumers no longer wish to endorse, the consumers can stop buying their products. Yahweh, in contrast, has no intention of abandoning Israel; one of the qualities he wishes to project through his relationship with his people is faithfulness, expressed by the Hebrew terms ʾahab (love) and ḥesed (loyalty, kindness). At the same time, he does not want to be characterized by indulgence; rather, his character is expressed in commitment to order, wisdom, and justice. If Israel characterizes itself by order, wisdom, and justice, God will be pleased with the way the nation reflects on him and will give them blessing and prosperity so that everyone can see that he is pleased. On the other hand, if Israel characterizes itself by disorder and injustice (as they often did), Yahweh will demonstrate his own commitment to wisdom, order, and justice by inflicting judgment on them so that everyone can see that he is angry.

As a consequence of God's judgment, Israel can be perceived as a nation whose God is unable to protect it from the enemy armies who conquer his people and destroy his temple. This is demonstrated in the words of Sennacherib, king of Assyria, in 2 Kings 18:32-35:

> Do not listen to Hezekiah, for he is misleading you when he says, "The LORD will deliver us." Has the god of any nation ever delivered his land from the hand of the king of Assyria? Where are the gods of Hamath and Arpad? Where are the gods of Sepharvaim, Hena and Ivvah? Have they rescued Samaria from my hand? Who of all the gods of these countries has been able to save his land from me? How then can the LORD deliver Jerusalem from my hand?

Yahweh responds to this taunt by demonstrating his power: "That night the angel of the LORD went out and put to death a hundred and eighty-five thousand in the Assyrian camp" (2 Kings 19:35). After the Babylonian exile, a similar accusation is leveled against Yahweh in Ezekiel 36:18-23, to which he responds with the promise to restore his people to the land:

> I poured out my wrath on them because they had shed blood in the land and because they had defiled it with their idols. I dispersed them among the nations, and they were scattered through the countries; I judged them according to their conduct and their actions. And wherever they went among the nations they profaned my holy name, for it was said of them, "These are the LORD's people, and yet they had to leave his land." I had concern for my holy name, which the people of Israel profaned among the nations where they had gone.
>
> Therefore say to the Israelites, "This is what the Sovereign LORD says: It is not for your sake, people of Israel, that I am going to do these things, but for the sake of my holy name. . . . Then the nations will know that I am the LORD."

Note that Yahweh's concern is for his holy name (that is, his reputation), not for Israel's moral or social condition. Note also that the restoration is specifically for the sake of Yahweh's reputation and is not prompted by a desire to give anything to Israel. Because Yahweh is Israel's God, Israel's condition reflects on him, and Yahweh does not wish to be seen as a defeated God of a ruined and dispossessed people. All of Yahweh's interactions with Israel serve to establish his reputation, one way or another. This is once again what we mean when we say that Yahweh uses Israel to reveal himself.

Yahweh establishes and projects his identity and reputation before both Israel and the surrounding nations. All these observers belong to the cultural river of the ANE. Consequently, Yahweh establishes himself according to the principles of faithfulness, wisdom, order, and justice, as the ancient world understood those ideas, because those happen to be the highest values of the ancient world. The ancient understanding of order, justice, and faithfulness is circumscribed in the legal wisdom and treaty documents of the Torah. However, we should not assume that Yahweh wishes to stamp an endorsement on these conceptions for all time, as if all people in all places and all times who serve Yahweh would be expected to reproduce the cultural values of the ANE. Likewise, we should not assume that we can substitute our own definitions for those words and claim that *this* is what Yahweh supports instead. It further does not mean that we can assume that Yahweh endorses whatever the highest values of any given society happen to be. In our case, this would be such things as freedom, equality, self-expression, and general human flourishing. Instead, we should understand Yahweh's self-revelation not in terms of absolutes or universals but rather in terms of contrast. Faithfulness, order, and justice were not qualities that were normally associated with ANE gods (though they desired that sort of behavior from their worshipers). Yahweh has effectively told the Israelites that he is a different kind of God than their culture would lead them to expect of a deity.

Because the purpose of Yahweh's self-revelation was not to enable the creation of theology textbooks, the details of Yahweh's character remain elusive. Israel was supposed to learn, and we can learn as well, that Israel's God cares about the human world, takes responsibility for his creatures, is concerned for their well-being, and is not merely interested in exploiting them to gain some benefit for himself. Israel was a means to an end for revelation, but the people also gained benefits in the form of God's blessing, favor, and (especially) presence, which were highly desired in the ancient world. Unlike their neighbors, the Israelites knew what they had to do to retain their God's favor; they had no reason to fear retribution for random or unknown offenses. For Christians, this understanding helps us make sense of the incarnation, knowing that it is this God that is incarnate in Jesus of Nazareth and not an ANE god, a Roman god, or an abstract philosophical god. In contrast, most people most of the time do not have these assurances about their gods, especially not in the ANE, where the gods did not reveal their expectations and saw humanity only as a means to an end for serving themselves. We will examine ancient divine-human relations in the next chapter.

PART 3

RITUAL AND TORAH

Proposition 8

Ancient Near Eastern Ritual Served to Meet the Needs of the Gods

As we have seen, one of the highest priorities in the ancient world was to maintain order in the cosmos and in society. The legal collections addressed this by conveying wisdom to serve as the basis for justice, a prime necessity for maintaining order. Another important component for maintaining a stable society and equilibrium in the cosmos was ritual. Ritual is not addressed in the legal collections such as Hammurabi's stele, but many other documents provide ample insight into ritual life in the ancient Near East (ANE).

Ritual is defined in a variety of ways. Most experts agree on certain characterizations; that is, it involves ceremonial, customary routines of performance reflecting religious belief[1] about what is effective for the intended result and metaphysical notions about the nature of the object of the practices. Rituals are laden with symbolism (sometimes arcane, esoteric, opaque, and even forgotten) and provide a means whereby participants can play a role in maintaining order in the cosmos and stability in their community. As an example of wording,

---

[1]Anthropologists would be quick to point out that rituals can be sacred or profane.

Gorman indicates that ritual "refers to a complex performance of symbolic acts, characterized by its formality, order, and sequences, which tends to take place in specific situations, and has as one of its central goals the regulation of the social order."[2]

Evidence is ample and there is a wide consensus among scholars that in the ANE the cultic ritual system was designed to meet the needs of the gods.[3] The premise was that initially the gods had created the cosmos for themselves and to fulfill their desires. They were quite content without people and had no plans to include such creatures. Nevertheless, the gods had needs for food, housing, and clothing just as humans do. Eventually the gods tired of all the labor required to ensure their survival and provide the accustomed amenities that would make their existence pleasurable. Various stories circulated about how the problem finally came to a tipping point, but the upshot was that the gods decided to create people as servants to supply their needs.

For this system to work, however, it could not be just a one-way street. If people were going to meet the gods' needs successfully, effectively, and continually, the gods would have to ensure that the people had enough rain to grow food, that the crops would grow and the animals were fertile, and that the people were protected from invasion or other sorts of disaster. Dead or destitute people could not provide for the gods. The status quo, then, was a codependence built

---

[2]Frank H. Gorman Jr., *The Ideology of Ritual: Space, Time and Status in the Priestly Theology* (Sheffield: JSOT, 1990), 19. Other scholars object or take a different stance on one point or another, but much remains common; cf. Ithamar Gruenwald, *Rituals and Ritual Theory in Ancient Israel* (Atlanta: Society of Biblical Literature, 2003); and Roy E. Gane, *Ritual Dynamic Structure* (Piscataway, NJ: Gorgias, 2004). Mary Douglas is considered one of the most important scholars in this area of study. Her work goes back to her seminal study *Purity and Danger* (New York: Routledge & Kegan Paul, 1966), but her views have been modified over time. One of her more recent works is *Leviticus as Literature*, rev. ed. (Oxford: Oxford University Press, 2001).

[3]For detailed discussion see Michael B. Hundley, *Gods in Dwellings: Temples and Divine Presence in the Ancient Near East* (Atlanta: Society of Biblical Literature, 2013), as well as his *Keeping Heaven on Earth: Safeguarding the Divine Presence in the Priestly Tabernacle*, FAT 50 (Tübingen: Mohr Siebeck, 2011).

from mutual need. The gods required food, housing, and clothing, and in order to provide those amenities reliably, people needed protection and provision.

We refer to this as the Great Symbiosis because it represents the symbiotic relationship that framed the life, religious thinking, rituals, and theology of the ancient world. The gods had needs, and they wanted to be pampered in every way by the people who worshiped them. The main focus of this symbiotic relationship was the temple, the palace of a particular god, in which the god resided and from which he or she ruled, represented by his or her image, which occupied the sacred center, mediating worship, presence, and revelation. Such temples were considered the control center of the cosmos, and from there the god maintained order, sustained by the rituals of the people.

The ritual practices were overseen by the priests, who were considered the ritual specialists. They instructed the people in the standards and principles by which the needs of the gods were met. The temple complex was considered sacred space because the god dwelled there. Requirements for purity were exacting because the people did not want the gods to feel offended in any way though, unfortunately, it was not always clear how the gods' favor could be sustained or what might offend them.

The priests communicated the meticulous requirements of the gods, but there were no guarantees. The knowledge of the priests derived from training in traditional ways of thinking, not from revelation (although the gods could convey their desires through oracles or omens). They operated on the presumption that the gods were like people, only more demanding. Logically, serving a god would begin with what one would provide for the highest-ranking human and then increase exponentially. The cost for failure would be the anger of the god, resulting in all sorts of potential disaster. An angry god required appeasement to avert disorder or abandonment to the influence of demons and enemies.

In the Great Symbiosis, then, rituals provided the means by which order could be maintained. This equation was the basis of the religious system. We might well inquire, then, what role did justice, law, or morality play? The gods had no concern for the common good of humanity—only for their own good. Justice, legal governance, and what we might label moral behavior are important for order to be maintained in human society, but order was important to the gods only because it ensured the receipt of their prerogatives. In this system, humans did not have a religious obligation to be moral or just; they had a religious obligation to care for the gods, who would go to great lengths to secure their stream of revenue. Kings were established by the gods to preserve order in the human world so that humans could safely and productively carry out the duties of pampering the gods. As should now be evident, legal texts and ritual texts occupied overlapping conceptual territory. Both were strategies to ensure order and the favor of the gods. Just as the legal texts provided examples of what the wisdom of the ages would recognize as successful strategies for human justice, so the instructions for ritual performance presented all the wisdom that the priests could muster for strategies that would keep the gods satisfied. If the legal wisdom was not followed, society collapsed under the weight of injustice, resulting in anarchy and neglect of the gods. If the ritual wisdom was not followed, angry gods would turn away from the people, causing them to suffer all sorts of consequences (illness, drought, famine, invasion, etc.). Just as the judges were responsible for applying the acquired wisdom to decide cases, the priests were responsible for applying the acquired ritual wisdom for assuring that the gods were appeased.

We also find overlap in the actual practice of law and ritual. For example, in the absence of the forensic means available today, judges often had little evidence beyond hearsay or conflicting testimonies. Consequently, they relied much more on parties in a trial to swear on oath that their testimony was true. Breaking an oath sworn in the name of a god not only made a person vulnerable to reprisal if the testimony was false; it also disrupted the viability of the judicial system and therefore undermined order in society. Rituals would also come into play occasionally in the use of trial by ordeal: a person's innocence or guilt was established by subjection to a life-threatening ordeal (e.g., thrown in the river) to see if the gods would save them.

In summary, divine favor was always the objective. Both justice and ritual were time-honored means for gaining that favor, and wisdom was at the foundation of both sets of practices. As we now turn to Israelite practice, we will see that the Israelites also viewed legal wisdom and ritual wisdom as overlapping concepts associated with order—so much so that, unlike in the ANE documents, both areas were integrated into the covenant's stipulations.

Ancient Israelite Ritual Serves to Maintain Covenant Order Because Yahweh Has No Needs

Ritual in the ancient world operated in conjunction with the institutions of social order in order to please the gods by meeting their needs and thereby ensuring their favor and consequent stability and prosperity in the human world. We are now in a position to evaluate the Israelite ritual system in comparison with what we find in the rest of the ancient world. The actual shape of the rituals shows very little variation. The regular routine of sacrifices follows many of the same paths that we can trace in the rest of the ancient world. Even the designations of many of the sacrifices are the same, as we can see when we compare, for example, Israel to the society living in Ugarit in the mid-second millennium BC. To be sure, there are some notable differences. The most outstanding distinction is in the blood-manipulation rituals in Israel. The Israelite sacrifices that featured blood manipulation, primarily those commonly designated the sin offerings and guilt offerings, have no parallel in the ritual systems so far attested in the ancient world. The blood of these animals was used to accomplish *kipper* (contributing to the ritual of Yom Kippur). The term *kipper* has traditionally been translated as "atonement," but that is misleading. More recently scholars have used terms like "expiation" (Milgrom) or "clearing" (Hundley). By virtue of the death of the animal, the blood accomplished the ritual role of a detergent to expunge anything that would desecrate the sanctuary (whether unacceptable behavior or ritual uncleanness).

Although the use of blood manipulation constitutes an important distinction in the Israelite ritual system, it only serves as a minor aspect of the most significant difference between Israel and the ancient Near East (ANE): in Israel, the Great Symbiosis is gone. Yahweh has no needs—for food, clothing, or housing. He still requires rituals (and more or less the same sorts of rituals), but they have been repurposed. He still has a temple as his palatial residence, where he sits enthroned and from where he controls the cosmos, but no image of him occupies the sacred center. He is ultimately interested in maintaining order, but he is not interested in simply being pampered. Everything looks much the same from outside observance, but make no mistake—everything is different. In the Great Symbiosis of the ANE, the sacrifices and other rituals maintained the sort of relationship that was perceived to exist between humans and the gods—in that case, the relationship of mutual need. In Israel, in place of the Great Symbiosis we find that the relationship has been redefined (by the covenant) as the relationship of suzerain to vassal, in which humans display God's glory and enhance his reputation rather than providing for his needs.

In Israelite theology, Yahweh, unlike the gods of the rest of the ancient world, has no needs. The gods of the ANE created the cosmos (and eventually people) for themselves; Yahweh created for the sake of the creation, not to provide people to meet his needs. He is taking care of them, but not for the same reason that drove the Great Symbiosis. Many responses that Israel might make to Yahweh are appropriate (e.g., praise, glory, worship, order), but he does not need them, and he did not enter into the covenant relationship to get them. Likewise,

Yahweh has not initiated this relationship in order to give something
to Israel (e.g., blessing, enlightenment, happiness, prosperity, salvation,
or morality). Yahweh is proclaiming his reputation as suzerain of
Israel, his vassals. Quid pro quo is abolished.

The partnership that Yahweh set up with Israel is embodied in the
covenant, in which he is the sovereign and Israel is his vassal serving
on his behalf. These ritual exercises in Israel, though they often looked
very similar to those of their neighbors, maintained a totally different
sort of status quo. The offerings represented the tribute paid from the
vassal to the sovereign, demonstrating loyalty and submission.

> "When you offer blind animals for sacrifice, is that not wrong?
> When you sacrifice lame or diseased animals, is that not wrong?
> Try offering them to your governor! Would he be pleased with
> you? Would he accept you?" says the LORD Almighty. . . .
>
> "For I am a great king," says the LORD Almighty, "and my
> name is to be feared among the nations." (Mal 1:8, 14)

Most of the offerings are not responses to offenses. The burnt offerings
often accompanied petitions, and the sin and guilt offerings, which are
related to offenses, provided for the ongoing maintenance of purity for
the temple. These offerings did not appease the wrath of the offended
deity by bribing him with food. The sin and guilt offerings cleared
away the defilement of sins or impurities as they occurred among the
people day by day. Nevertheless, it was inevitable that some defiling
acts would go unnoticed or unaddressed. The Day of Atonement (Yom
Kippur) was designed to remove any residual defilement, serving, in
effect, as a reset button—returning sacred space to its "default settings."

The focus of the sacrificial system, therefore, was on engaging in
relationship with Yahweh as their king (e.g., thank offerings, vow offerings, free will offerings), bringing gifts when petitions were being
presented (burnt offerings), and recognizing the importance of providing the appropriate environment for a holy God. By doing so they

were maintaining an orderly and functioning cult system, which included proper respect for the purity of divine space. We might ask, however, why the ANE cult system was appropriated at all. Some of the common rituals (i.e., the practice of sacrificing outside the central sanctuary) were abolished in Israel. If the Great Symbiosis is gone, why did they bother with ritual at all?

First, as noted above, the sacrifices served the role of tribute. In order for the suzerain-vassal relationship to be properly expressed, the vassals needed to be able to demonstrate their loyalty and submission. Because Yahweh is a deity, the tribute took the established form of the means by which to present gifts to a deity, i.e., ritual sacrifice. More importantly, however, a properly functioning cultic and ritual system was a symbol of a properly ordered and functioning society. Because the purpose was revelation, Israelite society needed to be a more or less ideal embodiment of social order by the standards of the ancient world. A society that lacked a cult system would not have been seen as functioning properly. As an example, in our modern Western cultural river an important element of a properly functioning state is democracy. If a society does not appoint its leaders by means of elections, we automatically assume that that society is defective and that its government is not functioning properly, whether or not that is the case. In the ancient world, a society without a cult system would have been perceived in much the same way that we perceive a society without elections—backwards and dysfunctional. Because Yahweh does not wish to establish himself as the God of a backwards and dysfunctional nation, he establishes a cult system but repurposes it to reflect his suzerain-vassal relationship with Israel, as opposed to the mutual codependence of the Great Symbiosis.

Like all suzerain-vassal relationships, Israel gained benefits as well as obligations. One of the benefits, as discussed in proposition six, was military support against enemies, as would also be expected of a human emperor. However, because Yahweh is also a deity, the benefits of his suzerainty also included the benefits of divine favor—prosperity and fertility—but most importantly the presence of the god dwelling among them.

Israel's views on divine presence were very much like those of the ancient world. The god sat enthroned in the temple, and consequently the order established through creation was maintained, the forces threatening that order were held at bay, and the viability of the human community was maintained.[1] As the center of order and power in the cosmos and the seat of divine presence, the existence of the temple in the human community brought the hope and potential of great benefits such as fertility to the fields, prosperity, health, peace, and justice. We get a glimpse of this in the Gudea Cylinders in the speech of the god Ningirsu responding to the building of a temple for him:

> Faithful shepherd Gudea,
> When you bring your hand to bear for me
>   I will cry out to heaven for rain.
> From heaven let abundance come to you,
>   Let the people receive abundance with you,
> With the founding of my temple
>   Let abundance come!
> The great fields will lift up their hands to you,
>   The canal will stretch out its neck to you. . . .
> Sumer will pour out abundant oil because of you,
>   Will weigh out abundant wool because of you.[2]

The temple can therefore be understood as the economic center of the cosmos, which John Lundquist refers to as "the central, organizing, unifying institution in ancient Near Eastern society."[3]

---

[1]See Michael B. Hundley, *Gods in Dwellings: Temples and Divine Presence in the Ancient Near East* (Atlanta: Society of Biblical Literature, 2013); and Byron E. Shafer, ed., *Temples of Ancient Egypt*, 2nd ed. (Ithaca, NY: Cornell University Press, 1997).

[2]*COS*, 2:155, Gudea Cylinder A: xi. 5-13, 16-17 (trans. Richard Averbeck).

[3]John Lundquist, "What Is a Temple? A Preliminary Typology," in *The Quest for the Kingdom*

J. N. Postgate refers to it as "a bond holding the community together, a source of wealth and goods."[4] The same ideology and the same hope are reflected in Israel's thinking as expressed in the covenant blessings (Lev 26:3-13; Deut 28:3-14) and in Solomon's prayer dedicating the temple (1 Kings 8).

Given this understanding, it would be a mistake to think that the sacrificial system was all about sin. As already noted, most of the sacrifices are not responses to offenses. That would be indication enough, but we now turn attention to the sacrifices that are responses to offense: the so-called sin offerings and guilt offerings.[5] These sacrifices feature blood rituals prominently (whereas blood is rarely used outside of them), with the logic being that life is in the blood (Lev 17:11). Blood rituals are uncommon in the rest of the ancient world. Animals are offered to other deities, but blood manipulation is not generally involved.[6] In Israelite practice, the Torah establishes these two sacrifices as responses when some impurity encroaches on the sanctuary (sin offering) or when something that belongs to the sanctuary is appropriated for personal use (guilt offering).

The sin offering is required when violation of the Torah has taken place unintentionally. Intentional sin had no ritual response. It was understood that an unintentional offense involving ritual impurity or violation of behavioral expectations in society had a desecrating

of God: Studies in Honor of George E. Mendenhall, ed. H. B. Huffmon, F. A. Spina, and A. R. Green (Winona Lake, IN: Eisenbrauns, 1983), 213; see also Jon D. Levenson, "The Temple and the World," *JR* 64, no. 3 (1984): 298.

[4]J. N. Postgate, "The Role of the Temple in the Mesopotamian Secular Community," in *Man, Settlement, and Urbanism*, ed. Peter J. Ucko, Ruth Tringham, and G. W. Dimbleby (Cambridge, MA: Schenkman, 1972), 811-25, esp. 813-14.

[5]These labels (sin offering and guilt offering) are traditional but widely recognized by scholars as inaccurate representations. They continue to be used because English has no alternate terms that would make sense to readers. Discussions are ubiquitous in the scholarly literature; for one example see N. Kiuchi, *The Purification Offering in the Priestly Literature: Its Meaning and Function*, JSOTSup 56 (Sheffield, UK: JSOT Press, 1987).

[6]The major exception is in elimination rituals (like the Israelite Day of Atonement) where, especially among the Hittites, blood rites are evident; see Yitzhaq Feder, *Blood Expiation in Hittite and Biblical Ritual* (Atlanta: Society of Biblical Literature, 2011).

impact on the sanctuary. To give a stark physical metaphor, imagine the defilement of feces splattered on the wall of the temple. The sacrilegious defilement had to be addressed. Blood was designated as the ritual detergent to expunge the results of the offense and restore sanctity in the sanctuary and order for the community.

Given this understanding, we can see that these rituals were not designed to take away the sin of the person. They were designed to restore equilibrium to the place of God's presence. The "clearing" antiseptic role of the blood accomplishes *kipper*. *Kipper* rarely has a person or sin as its object. The verb's direct object is typically the part of the sanctuary (e.g., the veil, the ark, the horns of the altar) being expunged from desecration. A form of this verb is used in the familiar Day of Atonement (*yom kippur*), at which time any offenses that have built up over the year (not having been dealt with by sacrifice) can be eliminated (driven into the wilderness) so that equilibrium can be reestablished (reset to default settings). The result of *kipper* being accomplished by the sin and guilt offerings is that the person can be forgiven—that is, he or she will not have to be cut off from the community. If a person is not forgiven or not cut off from the community, the person's continuing presence in the community will continue to contaminate the sanctuary, resulting eventually in the withdrawal of the divine presence and favor. But the contamination remains on the *sanctuary*, not on the person, so there is no suggestion of *kipper* cleansing an individual of sin.

On the basis of this information, we can see that the translation "atonement" is quite unfortunate and misleading if we associate it with what Christ accomplished on the cross regarding our sin.[7] Instead *kipper* refers to what was accomplished on behalf of the sanctuary by

---

[7]While the letter to the Hebrews does use this imagery as part of an elaborate extended metaphor to describe the work of Christ, the metaphor works in the context of how the cult system was understood in the Second Temple period, not as it was understood in ancient Israel and the original context of Leviticus. See proposition 15.

the Israelites' ritual use of blood. If the sacrifices of Israel do not take away sin, and in fact never seek to do so, they have nothing to do with salvation (from sins; see further discussion in proposition fifteen). Furthermore, they are not simply an anticipation of what Christ would do—they do not do anything like what Christ would do.[8] Sacrifices are not just a placeholder until Jesus comes to do his work. They have a significance all their own in the theology of the Old Testament and in the role of the Torah, an important role.[9]

Since the rituals are integral to Torah, we should not artificially distinguish them from the so-called moral aspects of Torah. Rituals serve as a response to cultic contaminants. This can include moral offenses since sin is a cultic contaminant, but moral offenses in particular are not emphasized. Nonmoral contaminants, such as menstruation and other bodily discharges, required the same offerings (sin offerings) as offenses we would call sins (see Lev 15:15, 30). The rituals, like other aspects of the Torah, provide for order to preserve the favor of Yahweh as he dwells among them. We therefore review the now common litany of this book: the purpose of the Torah (including the rituals) is not legislation, not moral instruction, not to form an ideal society (see proposition sixteen), not universally applicable, not incumbent on those outside the covenant, and not connected to salvation.

The priests were charged with responsibility for maintaining the sanctity of Yahweh's sanctuary, and that involved helping the community to maintain ritual purity. This meant that they had to be ritual experts and instruct the people in all the aspects of Torah so that the community could remain in good standing in the covenant and honor

[8]The only real similarity would be based on the metaphor that the church is comparable to a temple. God dwelled in the temple, and he also dwells in his people (in quite a different way). Following the metaphor, if blood was used in the temple to expunge the effects of offense so that God's dwelling place remained pure, we could talk about the blood of Christ expunging the effects of offense to purify his people so that he could indwell them.
[9]For more extensive discussion of the relationship between Christ and the sacrificial system, see John H. Walton, *Old Testament Theology for Christians: From Ancient Context to Enduring Belief* (Downers Grove, IL: InterVarsity Press, 2017), 261-63.

the God who had made them holy. We often think of priests as those who performed sacrifices—and that was certainly among their responsibilities—but to posit that as the main description of their identity is reductionistic. They offered the sacrifices because they knew what the rituals required in terms of quality of the offering, ritual status of those bringing the offering, proper procedures for the offering, and maintaining their own ritual purity to make sure that their mediation would be guarded. They were guardians of sacred space. Instruction in all aspects of Torah observance and performance of rituals were both important aspects of their position but should not be considered the whole of their responsibility.

As an illustration, we might consider those who protect the life of the ruler of a country (for the United States, consider the Secret Service agents who guard the president). It would be a mistake to say that their main role is to make sure that the leader does not get assassinated. Certainly that is one of their tasks, it but represents only a small part. They have the job of making sure that nothing interferes with the leader carrying out his or her role. Security for the leader results in stability for the people and order for the community's covenant relationship.

In conclusion, the rituals associated with the Torah maintained an appropriate relationship between Israel and her sovereign—the one who has made a covenant with them. The rituals (mediated by the priests) allowed them to express their worship to Yahweh and to remediate any threat to the sanctity of Yahweh's presence, of which they were hosts. It would be easy to think of the sacrificial rites as constituting commands that must be obeyed (and thereby sounding like legislation), and it is true that the priests were required to adhere precisely to the sacrificial instructions, but these instructions were not commands per se—they described a procedure that had to be executed properly if the people wanted to receive a desired result (like the procedures essential to the successful use of an ATM). Nevertheless, these stood as Yahweh's communication of what was acceptable to him, how they could prevent angering (or disgusting) him, and how they could safely come into his presence. Impurity had its consequences, just like touching a hot stove does; there are properties that cannot be safely ignored. These were not commands that told them what they ought to do as replacement for what they naturally would want to do (coercive law); they represented, instead, Yahweh's active communication with them of what was essential to their relationship. This can be contrasted to the ancient world at large where gods did not inform people of what was considered essential, yet held them accountable anyway.

In our modern way of thinking, which values individualism and freedom, we might be inclined to consider divine expectations and accountability negatively; we label it legalism and consider it oppressive. We might prefer being free from divine expectations. This is what appeals to us about the New Testament indicating that we are free from the law, though we apply "freedom from the law" well beyond its original intention. In Israel such freedom could result only in anarchy, as was evident in the Judges period when "all the people did what was right in their own eyes" (Judg 21:25 NRSV); that was not good and it did not bring order. The Israelites welcomed the guidance and instruction that Yahweh gave them and counted it a blessing and an act of grace.

PART 4

CONTEXT OF
THE TORAH

The Torah Is Similar
to Ancient Near Eastern
Legal Collections Because
It Is Embedded in the Same
Cultural Context, Not Because
It Is Dependent on Them

In proposition one, we introduced the metaphor of the cultural river as a way of understanding that our own world is very different from the ancient world. Rather than reading the Old Testament as if it is embedded in our contemporary world, we need to read it as embedded in the ancient world, in which the humans communicating God's revelation did not anticipate our culture or any other throughout the history of cultures. This cultural embeddedness gives the Torah inevitable similarities with what we find in the rest of the ancient Near East (ANE), but now we are ready to address the question of whether the Old Testament's embeddedness in the ancient world makes it indebted to particular pieces of literature from the ancient world. Furthermore, does either its embeddedness or any discovered indebtedness undermine its identity as God's revelation?

When we engage in comparative studies between Israel and the ANE, we should not assume that any similarities that we might find between their texts suggest literary indebtedness—that is, that Israelite scribes were copying or translating existing documents from say, Babylon, by making minor, cosmetic modifications. We need not deny that such adaptation may have occasionally taken place,[1] but often the evidence simply does not substantiate so close a relationship. For borrowing to be determined, one must demonstrate near identical words, phrases, and ideas at multiple places, and also propose how the Israelites would have had access to the other piece of literature (which requires discussion of geographical and chronological proximity). The burden of proof for indebtedness (i.e., literary dependence) is very stringent and cannot be established simply by observing that two texts describe similar ideas in similar ways. For example, today it would not be uncommon to hear someone voice the philosophy "eat, drink, and be merry, for tomorrow we die." Most people who might say that have not read those words in the work of Epicurus and don't know that they came from him. Instead, the saying has diffused into our cultural river, but we get it by being embedded in the river, not by borrowing it from the literature.

In a similar fashion, comparison of the Old Testament literature in general and the Torah in particular with ANE documents often produces similarities that can be explained by the fact that Israel was simply embedded in the ancient world. Therefore, Israelite writers were inclined to think like the people around them and have a rough familiarity with the traditions of the surrounding culture (perhaps more by oral diffusion than by literary access).[2] The traditions of any

---

[1]Inspiration could feasibly operate in the context of a biblical author choosing to adapt a well-known work from the ancient world to a new purpose. Solomon is said to be well acquainted with the wisdom of the East and could easily have made use of some world-renowned proverbs as guided by God.

[2]This is not the place to explore it, but various categories of embeddedness have been identified by scholars working in this area, including literary strategies that are called "counter-texts" or "polemics." These studies recognize the role of diffusion and allusion (echoes) that are common within a broader cultural milieu. See Eckart Frahm, *Babylonian and Assyrian Text Commentaries: Origins of Interpretation* (Münster: Ugarit-Verlag, 2011), 364-68; and

culture (oral or literary) flow into the broader cultural river and from there can be drawn on in subtle and untraceable ways by others who are immersed in that same cultural river.

More important, however, is the question of how people react to the currents (ideas) that flow in their cultural river. They may float comfortably along on those currents, or they may fiercely resist them. We can observe ways in which Israel's Torah contains features that we can also recognize in the ancient cultural river. The question is not, What have they borrowed?, but rather, How does Israel's Torah represent the revelation of God? The Torah may adopt some aspects of the cultural river (e.g., the idea that divine presence is something to be desired) and may resist others (e.g., the idea that humans are supposed to provide for the needs of the gods), but our interest is in how the Torah uses these aspects. It is in the interaction with the ideas that we will find the revelation of God that makes Torah Scripture. In other words, the potential source of the information (e.g., from this or that piece of ANE) matters much less than the use the author has chosen to make of it.

In the table 10.1, Comparison of Similar Legal Sayings in the Bible and the Ancient Near East, we examine some of the similarities between the legal sayings of the Torah and those from the ANE. We provide this so that the readers will see the nature of the similarities.[3] These will bolster our contention that the legal sayings of the Torah share genre characteristics with the legal sayings of the ANE.

John H. Walton, "Biblical Texts Studied in Comparison with Other Ancient Near Eastern Documents," in *Behind the Scenes of the Old Testament: Cultural, Social, and Historical Contexts*, ed. Jonathan S. Greer, John W. Hilber, and John H. Walton (Grand Rapids: Baker Academic, 2018), 573-85.

[3]Discussion of similarities between biblical and ANE legal collections can be found in a number of sources. A whole volume devoted to the subject is David P. Wright, *Inventing God's Law: How the Covenant Code of the Bible Used and Revised the Laws of Hammurabi* (Oxford: Oxford University Press, 2009). Pamela Barmash, "Ancient Near Eastern Law," in *The Oxford Encyclopedia of the Bible and Law*, ed. Brent Strawn (Oxford: Oxford University Press, 2015), 1:17, contains an extensive list of similarities between the ancient Near Eastern legal collections. For more comprehensive book-length treatment see Samuel Jackson, *A Comparison of Ancient Near Eastern Law Collections Prior to the First Millennium BC* (Piscataway, NJ: Gorgias, 2008).

Table 10.1. Comparison of similar legal sayings in the Bible and ancient Near East[a]

SEXUAL RELATIONS IN CITY OR COUNTRYSIDE	
Torah (NIV)	Deuteronomy 22:23-27 If a man happens to meet in a town a virgin pledged to be married and he sleeps with her, you shall take both of them to the gate of that town and stone them to death—the young woman because she was in a town and did not scream for help, and the man because he violated another man's wife. You must purge the evil from among you. But if out in the country a man happens to meet a young woman pledged to be married and rapes her, only the man who has done this shall die. Do nothing to the woman; she has committed no sin deserving death. This case is like that of someone who attacks and murders a neighbor, for the man found the young woman out in the country, and though the betrothed woman screamed, there was no one to rescue her.
ANE[a]	Hittite 197 If a man seizes a woman in the mountains (and rapes her), it is the man's offense, but if he seizes her in her house, it is the woman's offense: the woman shall die. If the woman's husband discovers them in the act, he may kill them without committing a crime.

GORING OX	
Torah (NIV)	Exodus 21:28-29: If a bull gores a man or woman to death, the bull is to be stoned to death, and its meat must not be eaten. But the owner of the bull will not be held responsible. If, however, the bull has had the habit of goring and the owner has been warned but has not kept it penned up and it kills a man or woman, the bull is to be stoned and its owner also is to be put to death.
ANE[a]	If an ox is a gorer and the ward authorities so notify its owner, but he fails to keep his ox in check and it gores a man and thus causes his death, the owner of the ox shall weigh and deliver 40 shekels of silver. Hammurabi 251: If a man's ox is a known gorer and the authorities of his city quarter notify him that it is a known gorer, but he does not blunt its horns or control his ox, and that ox gores to death a member of the *awilu*-class, he (the owner) shall give 30 shekels of silver.

WOMAN INTERVENING IN FIGHT BETWEEN MEN	
Torah (NIV)	Deuteronomy 25:11-12: If two men are fighting and the wife of one of them comes to rescue her husband from his assailant, and she reaches out and seizes him by his private parts, you shall cut off her hand. Show her no pity.
ANE[a]	Assyrian A-8: If a woman should crush a man's testicle during a quarrel, they shall cut off one of her fingers.

FIRST WIFE RIGHTS WHEN MAN TAKES SECOND WIFE	
Torah (NIV)	Exodus 21:10-11: If he marries another woman, he must not deprive the first one of her food, clothing and marital rights. If he does not provide her with these three things, she is to go free, without any payment of money.
ANE[a]	Hammurabi 148-149: If a man marries a woman and later *la'bum*-disease seizes her and he decides to marry another woman, he will not divorce the wife whom *la'bum*-disease seized; she shall reside in quarters he constructs and he shall continue to support her as long as she lives. If that woman should not agree to reside in her husband's house, he shall restore to her her dowry that she brought from her father's house, and she shall depart.

LOST ANIMAL	
Torah (NIV)	Deuteronomy 22:1-3: If you see your fellow Israelite's ox or sheep straying, do not ignore it but be sure to take it back to its owner. If they do not live near you or if you do not know who owns it, take it home with you and keep it until they come looking for it. Then give it back. Do the same if you find their donkey or cloak or anything else they have lost. Do not ignore it.
ANE[a]	Hittite 71: If anyone finds an ox, a horse, or a mule, he shall drive it to the king's gate. If he finds it in the country, they shall present it to the elders. The finder shall harness it (i.e., use it while it is in his custody). When its owner finds it, he shall take it according to the law, but he shall not have the finder arrested as a thief. But if the finder does not present it to the elders, he shall be considered a thief.

BESTIALITY	
Torah (NIV)	Leviticus 18:23: Do not have sexual relations with an animal and defile yourself with it. A woman must not present herself to an animal to have sexual relations with it; that is a perversion.
ANE[a]	Hittite 187-188: If a man has sexual relations with a cow, it is unpermitted sexual pairing: he will be put to death. They shall conduct him to the king's court. Whether the king orders him killed or spares his life, he shall not appear before the king (lest he defile the royal person). [188 gives similar instruction if the object is a sheep.]

SORCERY/WITCHCRAFT	
Torah (NIV)	Exodus 22:18: Do not allow a sorceress to live.
ANE[a]	Assyrian A-47: If either a man or a woman should be discovered practicing witchcraft, and should they prove the charges against them and find them guilty, they shall kill the practitioner of witchcraft.

WANDERING LIVESTOCK	
Torah (NIV)	Exodus 22:5: If anyone grazes their livestock in a field or vineyard and lets them stray and they graze in someone else's field, the offender must make restitution from the best of their own field or vineyard.
ANE[a]	Hammurabi 57: If a shepherd does not make an agreement with the owner of a field to graze sheep and goats, and without the permission of the owner of the field grazes sheep and goats on the field, the owner of the field shall harvest his field and the shepherd who grazed sheep and goats on the field without the permission of the owner of the field shall give in addition 6,000 silas of grain per 18 ikus (of field) to the owner of the field.

MOVING BOUNDARY MARKERS	
Torah (NIV)	Deuteronomy 19:14: Do not move your neighbor's boundary stone set up by your predecessors in the inheritance you receive in the land the LORD your God is giving you to possess. Deuteronomy 27:17: Cursed is anyone who moves their neighbor's boundary stone.
ANE[a]	Assyrian B-8: If a man shall incorporate a large border area of his comrade's (property into his own) and they prove the charges against him and find him guilty, he shall give a field "triple" that which he had incorporated; they shall cut off one of his fingers; they shall strike him 100 blows with rods; he shall perform the king's service one full month.

Source: List derived from William J. Doorly, *The Laws of Yahweh: A Handbook of Biblical Law* (Mahwah, NJ: Paulist Press, 2002), 119-22. For more treatment, look up any legal saying in any biblical passage in John H. Walton, ed., *Zondervan Illustrated Bible Backgrounds Commentary* (Grand Rapids: Zondervan, 2009), vol. 1.

[a]Translations from Martha T. Roth, *Law Collections from Mesopotamia and Asia Minor* (Atlanta: Society of Biblical Literature, 1995).

It should be no surprise that legal wisdom would find common ground across cultures and that God's people would reflect some of the same sort of understanding about order in society that has been common to human beings throughout time and history. It is not the content of the legal wisdom that stands as God's unique revelation—everyone in all cultures knew, for example, that murder was disruptive to order in society. Some might suggest that Yahweh upgraded Israel's perspectives about murder, and we could not rule out such enlightened innovations, but at the same time, we need not feel obliged to find such upgrades to validate Torah's revelatory status. In fact, as the examples in table 10.1 demonstrate, it would be difficult to do so consistently. The content of Torah's legal wisdom is embedded in the culture and contains ideas that more or less reflect what everyone already knew. This does not jeopardize the Torah's status as revelation once we recognize that the revelation in the Torah is not found in the contents of the law. If the Torah is not revealing law, it does not have to offer a distinctive viewpoint of the nuts and bolts of law. We need to explore why the Israelites believed that they had experienced something unique at Sinai.

The Differences Between the Torah and the Ancient Near Eastern Legal Collections Are Found Not in Legislation but in the Order Founded in the Covenant

The Israelites were like the other people in the ancient Near East (ANE) in many ways. For our purposes, we should note that they largely agreed about what brought order in society, and both groups had literary legal collections that gathered illustrations of wisdom for executing justice in society. Those superficial (though pervasive) similarities pale in comparison to the perspectives that distinguished the Israelites' thinking from those around them. They attributed these differentiating perspectives to the revelation of Yahweh, their God.

DIFFERENCES BETWEEN TORAH AND
ANE LEGAL COLLECTIONS

Source. We recall that in the stele of Hammurabi the king is reporting to the god Shamash, not receiving from him. It should not be denied that the king was believed to receive wisdom from the gods, but the application of that wisdom to the task of ruling justly was the responsibility of the king. The king's perception of order and the wisdom that established it were therefore reflected in the collections of legal sayings. In contrast, Israel did not view a human authority (i.e., Moses) as the source for the Torah.[1]

Scope. The theology of the Old Testament considers Yahweh to be the center and source of order and wisdom for both the cosmos and the human world. When Adam and Eve ate from the tree of the knowledge of good and evil, they had understood it as a wisdom tree (Gen 3:5), and by taking its fruit they were "becoming like God" in that they attempted to make themselves the center of order and wisdom. They were subsequently sent out to establish order for themselves (see proposition fourteen). In the ANE, it likewise fell to humans to establish order in the human world because the gods were only concerned with themselves. Outside of Israel, human efforts in this regard—specifically the establishment of cities and civilization—were considered to be more or less successful. The Old Testament is more pessimistic about the ability of humans to order their own world and instead portrays a divinely administered order (through the covenant) as essential.

The Torah, which has its source in Yahweh, is concerned with the establishment of order in human society. This is different from the rest of the ANE. Yahweh, as ruling king, issues decrees from Sinai that serve as the basis for order in the human realm of Israel.[2] This is an

---

[1]Comparisons between the "books of Moses" and the stele of Hammurabi typically cast Moses as the lawgiver (Hammurabi) and Yahweh as the transcendent divine sponsor (Shamash). However, in the epilogue of Hammurabi's Code, the following appears: "These are the just decisions which Hammurabi, the able king, has established and thereby has directed the land along the course of truth and the correct way of life" (translation by Martha T. Roth, *Law Collections from Mesopotamia and Asia Minor* (Atlanta: Society of Biblical Literature, 1995), 133. In the biblical text, no such statement is ever attributed to Moses; the law is established by Yahweh, the decrees are Yahweh's, and the refrain throughout is "I am Yahweh." Yahweh is the lawgiver; Moses is merely the scribe.

[2]Note that even what we call the Ten Commandments are referred to in the Hebrew text as the "ten words" (using the same Hebrew word as Ps 33:6).

important difference, but we should also realize that Yahweh has acted as Israel's king in offering the Torah so, as in the ANE, these decrees come from the king, albeit the divine one. The source is significant, but the main factors differentiating Israel from the rest of the ANE are the aspects of holiness and covenant.

Holiness and covenant. We introduced our core understanding of holiness in proposition seven. We are now ready to pick up that thread in analysis of the difference between the legal sayings in Israel and in the ANE. Yahweh entered into a covenant relationship with Israel. It began with Abram when God established a relationship with him (Gen 12) and then ratified a covenant with his family (Gen 15). That covenant got extended to Israel, the family of Abraham, in Exodus 6:6-7 (see further Ex 19:5-6), and also to the descendants of Abraham and Isaac in Deuteronomy 2:2-23. This sort of act between a god and a people group is not attested in the ANE, where gods generally restrict themselves to making sponsorship agreements with kings.[3] Land grants are also normally made by kings, not gods, although in Judges 11:24 Jephthah claims that the god Chemosh has given the Amorites their land (just as Yahweh gave land to Israel), which indicates that this is something that ANE gods could do. However, when God made the covenant with Israel at Sinai, he co-identified himself with them and

---

[3]One Phoenician (some say Aramaic) amulet from Arslan Tash dated to the seventh century BC is translated as referring to an "eternal covenant" between the god Ashur and "us." It further elaborates that it was done "with a covenant of the Heavens and Eternal Earth." For the text see "An Amulet from Arslan Tash" (trans. P. K. McCarter), *COS*, 2.86, pp. 222-23. For full discussion, see Ziony Zevit, "A Phoenician Inscription and Biblical Covenant Theology," *IEJ* 27 (1977): 110-18; S. David Sperling, *Ve-Eileh Divrei David: Essays in Semitics, Hebrew Bible and History of Biblical Scholarship* (Leiden: Brill, 2017 [from a conference presentation in 1981]), 60-69. The problem is that the word translated "covenant" in this text is a word that typically refers to an "imprecation" associated sometimes with oaths and covenants. See the lengthy discussion of the term in Herbert Chanan Brichto, *The Problem of "Curse" in the Hebrew Bible* (Philadelphia: Society of Biblical Literature, 1963), 22-71. For the god Ashur to attach an imprecation to himself is not necessarily equivalent to entering a covenant. This issue needs more scholarly attention before it can be considered a parallel, especially since a few lines further in the text is a reference to this imprecation in connection to an oath (presumably for protection since this is an amulet).

them with him: "I will take you as my own people, and I will be your God" (Ex 6:7). Yahweh becomes the "God of Israel" (Ex 5:1). This co-identification expands the identity of Yahweh (since it is new) just as it expands the identity of Israel.[4] As a result of this co-identification, Israel is made holy because Yahweh is holy. The holy status was not conferred on any of the other nations who participate in the Abrahamic blessings of land and nation. As we have indicated, this statement does not refer to holiness as something that Israel should strive to achieve; it is the status that Yahweh has given them. He, by definition, is holy (*holy* essentially means "divine"), and since he is identifying them with him, they are holy (part of his divine constellation). This status cannot be gained or lost by anything that they do, though they may or may not reflect that status appropriately.[5]

The Torah, then, far from being legislation, has as its objective *to define the nature of the order that defines the people who in turn give some definition to the identity of Yahweh.* The wisdom of the Torah instructs its primary audience—the kings and priests and their subordinate administrators—on the nature of the order they should be upholding if they want to reflect Yahweh's identity properly and thereby retain his favor in the form of the covenant blessings. Nothing in the ANE equates to this conception of holiness—that is, ANE gods are not concerned with the integrity of their identity as reflected through the objects of their patronage. The identity of the god of war is defined by the phenomenon of war (just as the identity of Yahweh is defined by the character of the nation of Israel), but the god of war does not

---

[4]This expansion of God's identity can be compared to the incarnation. Yahweh "becomes" the God of Israel here just as he "becomes" human later.

[5]For more discussion see Walton and Walton, *Lost World of the Israelite Conquest* (Downers Grove, IL: InterVarsity Press, 2017), 103-17 (proposition 10) as well as the online appendix providing a full technical profile of the root *qdš* ("holy") in classical Hebrew usage (www.ivpress.com/Media/Default/Downloads/Misc/5184-appendix.pdf). Recent scholarly analysis can be found in Michael B. Hundley, "Here a God, There a God: An Examination of the Divine in Ancient Mesopotamia," *AoF* 40 (2013): 68-107; and idem, *Keeping Heaven on Earth: Safeguarding the Divine Presence in the Priestly Tabernacle*, FAT 50 (Tübingen: Mohr Siebeck, 2011), esp. 71-72.

instruct the people in war so that the conduct of war will reflect his identity. Further, the patron gods of nations, cities, or other human demographics do not identify themselves with their people as intimately as Yahweh identifies with Israel.[6] The revelation element that distinguishes Sinai as unique is connected not to legal content or to genre but to the covenant context and the way that the covenant granted the Israelites a status (i.e., as being holy) whereby their community served to define Yahweh's identity. He is their suzerain and king, and he defines what order should look like just as the kings of the ANE did. The Torah therefore is not focused simply on maintaining order in the cosmos and society by executing justice; it is designed to define the covenant order so that it will reflect the identity that Yahweh wishes to establish for himself. Given this understanding, it is no surprise that the wisdom contained in the Torah not only instructs judges in wisdom for executing justice; it instructs all of Israel in wisdom for maintaining order in all spheres of life.[7]

Given this understanding, we can reiterate that we should not think of the Torah as giving Israel an upgraded sense of law or an improved legislation. That is not the lens by which we should understand its revelation or its distinction from the ancient world. This is true, first of all, because we have seen that neither Torah nor the ANE collections are legislation or have direct connection to the practice of law, which itself operated very differently in the ancient world than it does today.

---

[6]In the ANE when they wanted to designate something or someone as part of the divine constellation, they marked it with the determinative DINGIR (= ^{d} placed before the noun). Gods are so designated as well as the objects belonging to the gods. Kings are very occasionally so designated, but never a group of people. For extensive discussion see Walton and Walton, *Lost World of the Israelite Conquest*, 108-16.

[7]Note that Exodus 18:20-23 indicates the importance of teaching and exhorting the people. See discussion in Michael LeFebvre, *Collections, Codes, and Torah: The Re-characterization of Israel's Written Law* (New York: T&T Clark, 2006), 46-47. In a vague way the people of Babylonia were expected also to be instructed since in the epilogue Hammurabi enjoins those who have been wronged to come and hear the stele read aloud so that they might hear the pronouncements and have wisdom regarding their cases.

Second, Torah is not trying to improve on ancient law, and the Israelites are not arguing against the premise or practice of law in the ANE. While we may identify places in which the Torah seems more sensible to us than what we find in, say, Hammurabi, in other places we may find it less "enlightened." That is not the point. The Torah is not polemical; it is foundational to the Israelite order located in the covenant. No one else is supposed to define order by the covenant; no one else has one (more about this in proposition thirteen). The revelation of the Torah is not a revised law; it is covenant order.

This leads us to inquire preliminarily, what would keeping the Torah look like? As we have been saying, the Torah is not intended to be a normative set of rules to be obeyed; it is a list of illustrations that collectively circumscribe the nature of the covenant order, which can guide the Israelites as they seek to be the people of Yahweh, in vassal relationship with him by virtue of the covenant. The Israelites will (ideally, in theory) live according to the covenant order as their community serves to define the identity of Yahweh because they are his holy people. If they do not live according to the covenant order, Yahweh will define his identity by withdrawing his presence and favor and by punishing them, just as a responsible suzerain would punish rebellious vassals. Whichever treatment Israel prefers, Yahweh's identity and reputation will be established either way.

EXCURSUS: OBSERVATIONS ABOUT COMPOSITION

In this book we will not be investigating the composition of the Pentateuch or discussing the various source-theory schemes.[8] In this brief excursus, however, it is important to unpack the significance that our assessment of Torah as wisdom has for understanding what we have in the Pentateuch.

---

[8]For important analysis of the limitations of source theory, see Joshua A. Berman, *Inconsistency in the Torah: Ancient Literary Convention and the Limits of Source Criticism* (Oxford: Oxford University Press, 2017).

When previously the Torah was considered normative legislation, it was worrisome to those who took the Bible seriously to find that there were legal sayings scattered through the Torah that appeared to stand in contradiction to one another.[9] This was even more the case for those who are inclined to characterize the Bible as "inerrant" or "infallible." How could it be inerrant if two different books had differences of opinions on the same legal case? Some interpreters who were not as concerned about the Bible being monolithic used such cases to propose either that different sources from different times indeed stood in contradiction to one another or that the Torah represented an artificial compilation from different sociological periods of Israel's national life.[10] We may not find reason to deny sources or stages, but our reconstructions in either case depend heavily on speculation, and we need not resort to such hypotheses.

Once we adopt the view that Torah is wisdom rather than legislation, we are no longer compelled to reconcile apparent contradictions. Wisdom provides much greater latitude for such variations. Consider the following from Proverbs 26:4-5:

Do not answer a fool according to his folly,
    or you yourself will be just like him.
Answer a fool according to his folly,
    or he will be wise in his own eyes.

Which couplet is right? Both of them. Which one is wisdom? Both of them. Which one should a person do? If they are wise, they will have the discernment to know. Both embody valid principles. It doesn't matter that they offer conflicting advice.

---

[9]Christine Hayes, *What's Divine About Divine Law? Early Perspectives* (Princeton, NJ: Princeton University Press, 2015), 19-21, gives examples of contradiction among laws in the Bible; see particularly the comparison between Exodus 21:2-11 and Deuteronomy 15:12-18. Lefebvre, *Collections, Codes, and Torah*, provides a chart on pp. 69-70 that highlights differences between the Book of the Covenant (Ex 20:23–23:19) and the Deuteronomic Laws (Deut 12–26), both of which include legal sayings regarding building of altars, slavery, marriage/adultery, carcass disposal, seven-year release, gleaning, and festivals.

[10]Cf. William S. Morrow, *An Introduction to Biblical Law* (Grand Rapids: Eerdmans, 2017).

This example can serve as a paradigm for thinking about Torah. We need not worry that different responses to a fool might have been considered wise in different contexts, and the same is true of Torah.[11]

> Such cases attest to the fact that in ancient Israel, the law's divinity was not perceived as entailing its fixity or absolute nature. Terms of the divine law were modified, revised, updated, and interpreted in the course of their transmission. . . . The postbiblical claim that Yahweh's revealed divine law is fixed and immutable is not consistent with the Pentateuchal evidence. For the biblical writers and redactors, the flexibility, evolution, and even self-contradiction of divine law do not appear to have impinged upon its authoritative or divine status.[12]

Such examples in the Torah need not be taken as the evidence of pluralistic voices or contradicting opinions and should not become the most important tools for determining the composition of the Pentateuch. We have to remember that the primary transmission of traditions (whether narrative, legal, or wisdom) was oral. Documents served very restricted functions.[13] The admixture of oral and textual traditions greatly complicates our ability to unravel the process of composition. Nothing existed in the ancient world comparable to the books and authors of today. It was a world of scribes and documents whenever written records were made—which was not done regularly and was not essential. The authority of a document was not in its author but in the authority that stood behind it.[14] In this way, Moses could theoretically be the authority behind the Torah without having actually written any of it with his own hand. At the same time, there is no good reason to deny him a role in the written tradition.

---

[11]Berman, *Inconsistency in the Torah*, develops this at length.

[12]Hayes, *What's Divine About Divine Law?*, 21.

[13]See discussion in John H. Walton and D. Brent Sandy, *The Lost World of Scripture: Ancient Literary Culture and Biblical Authority* (Downers Grove, IL: IVP Academic, 2013), especially 17-29.

[14]Walton and Sandy, *Lost World of Scripture*, 24-26, 216-23.

What we do know is that the tradition is tightly connected to Yahweh whenever it was finally written down in the form that we have. That could have been a lengthy process that combined oral and textual phases. In a hearing-dominant culture in which oral tradition often carried more authority than written tradition, it would not be expected that text would precede speech. In other words, in the history of compilation and composition, a "book" would be more likely to be the last step rather than the first step. For that book eventually to be attributed to Moses would mean only that he had long been identified as the authority figure at the fountainhead of the tradition. That would be sufficient to justify its being attributed to him. Furthermore, the Torah's authority as Scripture is not based on whether any or all of the written documents can be attributed to Moses at any level.

CONCLUSION

In summary, we have discussed the nature of the legal sayings in the Pentateuch and have found them similar to those found throughout the ANE. Our comparative study has revealed significant overlap in genre and in content. In the course of the study, we have proposed, in keeping with the consensus that exists among scholars of the ANE, that the collections of legal sayings are not legislative but focus on wisdom for preserving justice and order in society. This results in a considerably different perspective from what a modern reader's intuition would be about such texts.

At the same time, we have identified the most significant differences in the connection to holiness and covenant. In the Old Testament the similar genre and content known from the ancient world have been repurposed—used in a new way with a new function. Yahweh is not just communicating to Israel standards for justice but is delivering standards by which his people can reflect their holy status. The wisdom embedded in the Torah will enable them to maintain covenant order.

As a final note, we might ask, if it is not legislation, then what is the significance of not adding to it or subtracting from it (Deut 4:2; 12:32)? Statements such as this do not refer to an eternally static situation in which legal perfection has been achieved. Such admonitions are found in the legal literature of the ANE (epilogue of Hammurabi) as well but also in other sorts of literature (such as the Erra Epic or treaties). Significantly, however, in the Old Testament they are also found in relation to prophetic oracles (Jer 26:2) and even Wisdom literature (Prov 30:5-6).[15] It is therefore evident that such warnings are not specific to legal documents and do not refer to a complete and unchangeable legislation. Instead, the warnings are addressed to scribes as a way to secure the integrity of the text—whatever sort of text it is.[16] It has to do with textual tampering, not with legislative innovation.[17]

Even as the Torah differs from the ANE literature, however, it is still fully embedded in the cultural river of the ancient world. Thus even the innovations it introduces still have to be understood within the context of the ancient world. We will examine the cultural "situatedness" of the Torah in the next few chapters.

---

[15]LeFebvre, *Collections, Codes, and Torah*, 67.
[16]LeFebvre, *Collections, Codes, and Torah*, 68.
[17]Berman, *Inconsistency in the Torah*, 191.

Torah Is Situated in the Context of the Ancient World

Over the next chapters, we will address and define the "situatedness" of the Torah as it is embedded in a number of important contexts. By situatedness we mean that the Torah cannot be read as though it fell out of the sky. The Torah is written to a people of the ancient Near Eastern (ANE) world within the language and logic of the cognitive environment. Thus we say that it is situated in its ANE cultural context. But the Torah was also given to Israel as part of Israel's covenant with Yahweh; thus it is situated within the terms of the Israelite covenant. Finally, that covenant operates within a very specific conception of the nature of divinity and the relationship between God, people, and land. Thus the covenant is situated within the Israelite theology concerning sacred space—Yahweh living among them. These three defining features will be addressed in this and the next three chapters. The main goal is for us as modern readers to recognize that the Torah has a context and to understand the various ways in which that context influences what the words and phrases of the Torah mean—because the meaning of language is determined by context.

The statement that the Torah is situated in the ancient world could easily be perceived as a truism—a simple factoid. But when we make such a statement, we are referring to more than just the chronological place of the literature. To say that the Torah is situated in the ancient world is another way of recognizing that its communication and conversations are embedded in the ancient world. Consequently, every aspect of it must be interpreted within that ancient context; extrapolation outside of that context is hazardous. That does not mean that we cannot extrapolate, only that it has to be done very carefully with full knowledge of what we are dealing with (genre) and how extrapolation can take place effectively (methodology and hermeneutics). One cannot seek to extrapolate it on the assumption that it is legislation or a moral system. It is neither a question, then, about the unchanging law of an unchanging God nor a presumption that morality is relative. If the Torah is neither a law code nor a moral system (more discussion in proposition twenty-one), then its lessons cannot be learned from following those pathways.

When people try to sort out which parts of the Old Testament "law" are still relevant and which parts are not, they are really trying to determine which sayings are culturally relative and which are not. When we read statements like "don't murder," we naturally assume that they are not culturally relative but universal. Such a thinking process reflects a basic assumption that the sayings are law—a concept that we have already suggested is misguided. We therefore have to start our evaluation process from the beginning.

If the Torah gives illustrations of ways that order can be maintained in the society of ancient Israel—covenant order defined by preserving the sanctity of sacred space as God's holy people—it is *all* culturally relative. How could it be otherwise? Only the Israelites were in a covenant relationship with Yahweh; only the Israelites experienced Yahweh's presence dwelling among them in his tabernacle or temple. We must therefore conclude that the Torah, as an instrument to give definition to this covenant relationship, is fully situated in ancient culture, fully situated in the covenant relationship, and fully situated in temple ideology.

Modern Bible readers are inclined to regard the Torah as universal because they have assumed that it is God's law, that it is to be equated with a moral system, that it reflects God's (unchanging) ideal, and that it is in the Bible—God's revelation to all his people. What compels us to conclude that it is fully situated and relative? We can address this by turning the question around: What compels us to believe that it is *not* culturally situated?

To begin with, then, we note that, in the Christian world, virtually no one treats the entire Torah as universally applicable so we cannot say that it is universal just because it is in the Bible. Christians are not typically concerned with whether one wears cloth mixed of linen and wool or how to avoid cooking a kid in its mother's milk. If it is acknowledged that parts of the Torah are not universally applicable, we learn that universality is not the nature of Torah. If universality is not the nature of Torah, then any sense we might have that some of it is universal results from the fact that our understanding of order is similar to theirs in certain cases. Consequently, we are not treating the Torah as something that carries authority over us; we are simply using our own good sense and logic to identify those aspects that we already are inclined to agree with.

In contrast, upon investigation, we will find that the internal logic of the Torah is ancient and the conditions it advocates are ancient, rather than ideal. Some passages address economic concerns like loans and debts (Ex 22:25-27; Deut 23:19-20). The economy that they reflect is an agropastoral economy, not a service economy operating within a capitalistic market system. The Torah is based on ideas of class and status that differ from ours and was devised to provide for economic recovery for farmers when drought or crop failure threatened survival (see further discussion in proposition sixteen).

These ancient cultures were characterized by community identity, and that affected every aspect of order within society. People found their identity in the role and status that they had in the community and in whether they brought honor or shame to their community.[1] This conception of identity is reflected in practices such as arranged marriages where marriage was not based on feelings of love but reflected the commitment of two families to one another for the benefit of the community (see further discussion in proposition sixteen). Likewise, when identity is located in the community (especially within the family/clan), the values of independence, autonomy, and democracy are absent and undesirable. All members of the community place a higher value on the community than on themselves and seek to submit to the authorities in the community rather than demanding their rights or seeking an equal voice.[2] One could object that the characteristics we have described are not patently ancient; they are just not what we experience in our modern Western (American and European) culture. It could be argued that one might find such features in many Asian or African cultures today. True enough—but that still indicates that these features are culturally relative.

In such cultures, the highest order is not individual human happiness. Instead, the highest value is order in society. Consequently, the focus of the legal sayings is order, not happiness. So, for example, lay members of the Israelite community do not wear clothes of mixed wool and linen (Deut 22:11); priests wear garments that contain that mix. Order is maintained in the community when the status and the status markers are recognized and respected. In a similar way we consider it unlawful for someone who is not a policeman to wear the uniform of a policeman.

---

[1] For insightful examples see the comparison of Western to Mediterranean cultures in John J. Pilch, *Introducing the Cultural Context of the Old Testament* (Mahwah, NJ: Paulist, 1991), 96-98; ample additional examples can be culled from Victor H. Matthews, *The Cultural World of the Bible: An Illustrated Guide to Manners and Customs*, 4th ed. (Grand Rapids: Baker Academic, 2015).

[2] Or at least they were supposed to. Those who did not would have been seen as dangerous threats to the social order, much as we today consider psychopaths to be a dangerous threat to social order.

The final issue, and for this chapter the most important, concerns the question of how Torah functions as God's revelation. It *is* appropriate to consider it God's revelation. But the most significant question is, revelation of what? It is certainly correct that anything God reveals is of enduring value and should be considered to have universal relevance. Nevertheless, before we get there we have to consider what it is that God is revealing. In the previous chapters we have already presented the case that the Torah contains illustrations of wisdom delivered in the context of ancient Israel's situation, which in turn describes the nature of God's covenant with Israel through which God reveals *himself* (as opposed to revealing an ideal society or revealing his moral expectations for humanity). The revelation of what the covenant is and what it tells us about how God chooses to work in the world provides a context for us today in understanding the New Covenant found in the New Testament. We will develop this further in subsequent chapters.

In conclusion, we return to the metaphor of the cultural river. God communicated in the Hebrew language to the Israelite culture, not in every language or in a common language into a culturally neutral environment (neither of which exists or has ever existed). Meaning derives from context—that is, language and culture. Just as Hebrew words are not universally meaningful, the cultural and logical context of the Bible is not universally relevant. Since the Old Testament message communicates in a language and a culture, it is necessarily situated in that language and culture. The belief that it is God's revelation does not change that. As we have said before, it is written for us, but not to us. Like the rest of the Old Testament, then, Torah is situated in the ancient world—in the language and culture of the ancient Israelites. We have to take that into account when we seek to translate its meaning to discern the enduring value that it has by virtue of being God's revelation.

Proposition 13

Torah Is Situated in the
Context of the Covenant

Stipulations in ancient treaties establish obligation on those who are the participants in the agreement (see proposition six), but it is important to develop a nuanced understanding of the nature of this obligation. It goes without saying that those who are not participants are not under obligation. Furthermore, we note that the obligation established by stipulations is of a different sort from that established by legislation. First and foremost, a general distinction can be made in that stipulations are a matter of mutual agreement whereas legislation is imposed by virtue of one's membership in a community.[1] As George Mendenhall, one of the early pioneers of the comparison, pointed out, covenants and treaties create a relationship and an identified community whereas law presupposes a social order and seeks to maintain it.[2] To clarify this

---

[1]Both of these characterizations would require qualification when subjected to close scrutiny. It may be that two nations agree to the terms of a treaty, but military or political pressure may be responsible for coercion. Legislation, while imposed, can also be considered to be subject (at least indirectly) to the desires of the people in the ideal forms of democracy (election of legislators, referenda, etc.).

[2]George E. Mendenhall, "The Conflict Between Value Systems and Social Control," in *Unity and Diversity: Essays in History, Literature and the Religion of the Ancient Near East*, ed. Hans Goedicke and J. J. M. Roberts (Baltimore: Johns Hopkins University Press, 1975), 169-80 (chart on 174-76).

distinction, we could think about the US Constitution, which is essentially a treaty between the people and the government. It describes how the people will be governed but does not contain legislation.

When we read the stipulations in treaties from the ancient Near East (ANE), we find outlined a sort of obligation that differs from the obligation imposed by law. As we saw in proposition six, the topics discussed in stipulations pertain to the corporate body (city or country, and their representation by the king), as would be expected, and offer details concerning expected behavior by the vassal toward the suzerain.[3] Some of the categories and obligations that can be found among the stipulations include both general expectations and specific details of what the vassal's duties are:

General

- Acknowledgment of suzerain as only master[4]
- Loving the suzerain as you love yourselves[5]
- Faithfulness to suzerain by not making alliances against him, joining revolts against him, or cursing him
- Recognition that unfaithfulness will result in forfeiture of land[6]
- Acknowledgment of allegiance or submission
- Suzerain's promised protection to vassal
- Not coveting land or inhabitants of other allied vassals[7]

---

[3] Almost all the treaties are vassal treaties, though even the few parity treaties feature similar types of stipulations.

[4] In treaty between Suppiluliuma I of Hatti and Huqqanas and the Hayasa people. Kenneth A. Kitchen and Paul J. N. Lawrence, *Treaty, Law and Covenant in the Ancient Near East* (Wiesbaden: Harrassowitz, 2012), 1:441.

[5] Esarhaddon of Assyria and the Medes. Kitchen and Lawrence, *Treaty, Law and Covenant*, 1:979.

[6] In the treaty between Abba-AN of Aleppo and Yarim-Lim of Alalakh. Kitchen and Lawrence, *Treaty, Law and Covenant*, 1:233.

[7] Treaty between Mursil II of Hatti and Manapa-Tarhunta of Seha River-land. Kitchen and Lawrence, *Treaty, Law and Covenant*, 1:531.

- Not speaking evilly against the suzerain and punishing those who do[8]
- Respectful treatment and display of the image (or stele) of the suzerain (in Naram-Sin's treaty with Elam, "Everyone shall fear this deposit by Naram-Sin")[9]

Provision of specific details

- Water management and rights
- Establishment of boundaries
- Provision of troops for battle: supplies and garrisons
- Duty to report sedition and any who are in violation
- Extradition of rebels or fugitives
- Punitive treatment of offenders
- Payment of tribute
- Trade and tariff restrictions or requirements
- Behavior of citizens in relation to the other party
- Debts and lawsuits between the citizens of the two parties
- Restitution for theft
- Division of spoils in joint military operations
- Treatment of envoys

Some observations can help us apply information learned from these stipulations to the interpretation of the Torah. First, we can see that many of the specific stipulations do not find easy parallels in the biblical material since they pertain to political relationships between communities. At the same time, the stipulations in the

---

[8]Treaty between Muwatallis II of Hatti and Alaksandus of Wilusa. Kitchen and Lawrence, *Treaty, Law and Covenant*, 1:557
[9]Kitchen and Lawrence, *Treaty, Law and Covenant*, 1:51.

general category are transparently similar to the concerns that are expressed in the Torah.[10]

Second, we can note that at times the stipulations of treaties take on the same sorts of form and content that we find in the legal collections. As an example, consider this interesting case from the twenty-fourth-century treaty between Ebla and Abarsal, stipulations 37-41:[11]

> [37]Who steals in the sheepfold, who steals in the city gate area, who steals in the walled settlements, shall die.
>
> [38]In the house of an Abarsalite an Eblaite may stay over: and the house owner will get up for him.
>
> [39]If he robs the house, he shall replace stolen goods; if the Eblaite kills an Abarsalite 50 rams as penalty he shall pay.
>
> [40]Whoever lies with a [married?] woman, he shall pay a fine of a bundle of multicolored garments and 3 oxen.
>
> [41]If it was an unmarried girl, a girl he respects, then he shall confirm his proposal. And this guest will marry her.

We can see then that the legal collections and the treaty stipulations share some stock phrasing and have overlapping content. We might even surmise that formulations from the legal collections could be reused in treaty stipulations, though that would be difficult to substantiate.

On the basis of the observations of the last chapter, we are now prepared to reconsider the nature of the Torah. Like the treaty stipulations, covenant stipulations address how Israel should relate to Yahweh. Just as the treaty stipulations provided examples of faithfulness to the suzerain, the covenant stipulations address faithfulness to Yahweh. Like the treaty stipulations, the covenant stipulations give definition to order in the relationship between Yahweh and his people, that is, how Israel is to be faithful to Yahweh and respect the suzerainty of Yahweh.

---

[10]For examples of stipulations in Torah similar to those in the general list above, see Exodus 22:28; Leviticus 24:16; Numbers 15:30; and Deuteronomy 4:25-26, 39; 6:5; 8:19; 11:16; 12:10.

[11]Translations simplified from Kitchen and Lawrence, *Treaty, Law and Covenant*, 1:27, 29.

These stipulations provide examples of loyalty and faithfulness. In that way they overlap not only with the legal collections but with the Wisdom literature. Note that in Israel, the "fear of the Lord" that is the beginning of wisdom refers to loyal submission to the will of the suzerain. Though the stipulations include detailed particulars, in the end they are aspective, just like legal collections, but with different focus:

- Legal collections of the ANE give examples of what justice in society looks like.

- Treaties of the ANE give examples of what faithfulness to a suzerain looks like.

- Ritual instructions (e.g., Hittite instructions to priests[12]) give examples of what purity in sacred space looks like.

---

[12]Jared L. Miller, *Royal Hittite Instructions and Related Administrative Texts* (Atlanta: Society of Biblical Literature, 2013), 244-65.

APODICTIC AND CASUISTIC FORMULATION

On the formal side, it is interesting to note that many of the stipulations in the treaties are apodictic in nature ("you shall/shall not"). When the legal collections from the ancient Near East (ANE) were first analyzed, it was observed that most of them use a casuistic form (case law, "if someone does X, then Y will be the response"). In the Torah, examples of casuistic formulations are found in some of the sections, but many others use a variety of other forms,[a] and the Decalogue, the most well-known collection, uses apodictic formulations. We can now see that this combination of apodictic and casuistic in the biblical Torah is accounted for when we recognize that it reflects both genres: legal collection and treaty stipulation. It has been observed that even though the legal collections use casuistic formulations instead of apodictic ones as found in the Decalogue, the subject matter of commandments 5-9 of the Decalogue is addressed in the legal collections.[b] When we turn to the treaty stipulations, however, we can easily find comparable issues addressed (except the Sabbath), often in apodictic formulations.

The following are examples from treaty stipulations chosen to illustrate parallels with the Decalogue:

- Don't have any other suzerain.[c]
- Respect the image of the suzerain.[d]
- Do not speak evilly of the suzerain, and do not hold guiltless those who do.[e]
- [nothing comparable]
- Give honor to the suzerain that your days may be long in your land.[f]
- Do not commit murder against any of the people of the suzerain.[g]
- Do not engage in sexual behavior with any of the suzerain's family.[h]

We can now see that the Torah, situated in the covenant, includes all three of these focus elements (justice, purity, and faithfulness), but more than all of them as it gives examples of the order that will define Yahweh's identity (= holiness). The attribute of holiness (the status conferred on Israel) is the underlying reason why justice, faithfulness, and purity are necessary. Upon the ratification of the covenant, Israel receives its holy status. Holiness is therefore not the stipulation of the covenant and not simply an amalgam of conditions such as justice, purity, or faithfulness.

All these genres pertain to maintaining order in various respects and are aspective. In the treaty stipulations, general statements show that there are more obligations than the examples specify; for example:

- totally devote your heart to the suzerain

- commit no wrongdoing

- Do not steal what belongs to the suzerain.[i]
- Do not swear falsely (violate the oath made to the suzerain).
- Do not covet what belongs to the suzerain.[j]

None of this is offered to suggest that the Torah is borrowed from ANE documents. As we discussed in proposition ten, the issue is not literary indebtedness. Rather, cultural embeddedness influences an inclination to use similar genres, though they may be reshaped in the Torah. The Torah may also use stock phrases present in the documents created by scribal schools throughout the ANE (in treaties or in legal collections).[k] These comparisons give an improved understanding of what the Torah is (literarily) in light of the cultural river in which it is immersed, a unique part of the cultural river but not a replica.

ed. John H. Hayes (San Antonio: Trinity University Press, 1974), 106.

[b]Karel van der Toorn, *Sin and Sanction in Israel and Mesopotamia: A Comparative Study* (Assen, Netherlands: Van Gorcum, 1985), has a chapter on each commandment, employing information gleaned from the ANE legal collections.

[c]Suppiluliuma I and Huqqana, Gary M. Beckman, *Hittite Diplomatic Texts*, ed. Harry A. Hoffner Jr., 2nd ed., WAW 7 (Atlanta: Society of Biblical Literature, 1999), par. 2, p. 23.

[d]Naram-Sin and Elam, Kitchen and Lawrence, *Treaty, Law and Covenant*, 1:51.

[e]Muwattalli II and Alaksandu, Beckman, *Hittite Diplomatic Texts*, par. 13, p. 85.

[f]Suppiluliuma I and Huqqana, Beckman, *Hittite Diplomatic Texts*, par. 22, p. 27.

[g]Ebla and Abarsal, Kitchen and Lawrence, *Treaty, Law and Covenant*, 1:27.

[h]Ebla and Abarsal, Kitchen and Lawrence, *Treaty, Law and Covenant*, 1:29.

[i]Ebla and Abarsal, Kitchen and Lawrence, *Treaty, Law and Covenant*, 1:27.

[j]Murshili II and Manapa-Tarhunta, Beckman, *Hittite Diplomatic Texts*, par. 7, p. 79.

[a]See a convenient compilation of the Hebrew syntactical forms in M. Clark, "Law," in *Old Testament Form Criticism*,

[k]Not unlike boilerplate legal documents today, e.g., house closings or even book contracts.

- do not commit offense or violence
- do nothing against the suzerain
- do nothing bad
- do not sin in any way
- do not neglect to support the suzerain
- do not set in your mind an unfavorable thought
- do not do anything that is not good

These are open-ended and cannot be defined in any exhaustive way, but they still address what is expected.

In conclusion then, we had previously noted that the Torah's legal collections offered wisdom, using an aspective approach, to circumscribe and thereby to understand the nature of the order that was expected to pervade in Israel, particularly in relationship to justice. Since the characteristics of Israel give public definition to the characteristics of God (they have been identified as holy as he is holy when chosen as his people), Israel must manifest justice according to the values of the ancient world in order to reflect God properly and thereby retain his favor. Treaty stipulations do not offer wisdom per se, though the wise person will give heed, but they are also aspective treatments of faithfulness. That is, because the characteristics of Israel give public definition to the characteristics of God (holiness), the Israelites must manifest loyal service to their sovereign (God) according to the values of the ancient world in order to reflect God/sovereign properly and thereby retain his favor. Although the stipulations are not wisdom lists, wisdom lists can play a role in stipulations, and we believe that is true of Torah.

The Torah therefore reflects a combination of both of these well-known genres from the ancient world, and from that we conclude that the Torah is aspective, not comprehensive, and that it calls for Israel to be characterized by faithfulness and justice. But, as we have noted, this obligation, as defined in the Torah, falls to Israel and Israel alone, as Yahweh's covenant partner. The Torah is situated in the covenant relationship and cannot be extrapolated as binding on anyone else— no one else was designated as holy. The Torah stands as Yahweh's revelation of the role that he has for Israel, his covenant people, in his plans and purposes for the world and for history. The Torah communicates to Israel, by means of familiar literary genres, how to play that major role. That role is not offered to everyone, but it represents the great enterprise that Yahweh has undertaken, which we will learn more about in the next chapter.

Torah Is Situated in the Context of Israelite Theology Regarding Yahweh's Presence Residing Among Them

Just as Torah is situated in the ancient world (not the modern one) and in the covenant with Israel (not universal), it also must be understood in its contingent relationship to the presence of Yahweh dwelling in the midst of Israel. To understand this concept, we must begin with a discussion of the temple ideology of divine presence in the ancient Near East (ANE).

The temples in the ANE were the palatial residences of the deities. There the gods rested, and from there they ruled. The temple provided housing for the god just as sacrifices provided food—all serving what we have called the Great Symbiosis. In the temple the god was pampered, but the temple was also viewed as the hub of cosmic control. The people desired to have the temple with its resident god in their midst because they could then serve him and thereby gain his favor. Having the favor of a god could bring safety and prosperity. To maintain the presence and favor of the deity, his needs would have to be met consistently and even lavishly.[1]

Since, as we have discussed, Israel gave no credence to the Great Symbiosis and Yahweh had no needs, the temple ideology in Israel, despite considerable overlap, differed from that in the ANE in a number of important ways. The ideological aspects of presence, rule, and favor remained, though the ways to retain them differed. In the Old Testament, God's residence among people is a common recurring theme that is addressed in various texts in a variety of ways.

Bible readers first encounter this theme in Genesis 1:1–2:4, though we often fail to recognize it because we are no longer aware of what is involved in divine rest, or we are distracted by questions of science. In our interpretation, the seven days of creation are primarily concerned with God ordering the cosmos to serve as the domain over which he will rule when he takes up his residence and rest in Eden (which is effectively a cosmic temple). In the ANE, the world outside of the divine realm was divided broadly into two areas: the human realm, where order was established and maintained, and the liminal realm, where it was not. The liminal realm existed on the periphery of creation and was home to dangerous animals; harsh and inedible plants; hostile terrain such as deserts, mountains, or the sea; and unworldly entities such as demons, wandering spirits, or monstrous demihuman barbarians. The ordered world was protected and sustained by the gods as they took their rest in their temples; *rest* here refers to active residence and rule, not passive relaxation. The gods do not rest in a bed or on a couch; they rest on the throne. In Genesis, the seven days of creation describe the establishment of the ordered world. The process is completed on the seventh day when Yahweh enters into his

---

[1]For more information see John H. Walton, "Temples," in *Behind the Scenes of the Old Testament: Cultural, Social, and Historical Contexts*, ed. Jonathan S. Greer, John W. Hilber, and John H. Walton (Grand Rapids: Baker Academic, 2018), 586-96.

rest.[2] When Adam and Eve choose to take wisdom (the "knowledge of good and evil," Gen 2:17) for themselves, they simultaneously become like God (Gen 3:22) and thereby inherit the responsibility to establish and sustain order. Consequently, they are sent out into the liminal world and charged with setting it in order themselves, which they attempt to do by establishing cities and civilization, the structures that were thought to establish order in the human world throughout the ANE. Genesis 4–11 records that these attempts were unsuccessful; cities and civilization do not, in fact, lead to an ordered condition. The remainder of Genesis provides the setup for Israel's proposed alternative, which is an order established by God through the instrument of the covenant. The covenant is not a return to Eden (which is neither anticipated nor desired in the Old Testament), but it does represent a kind of order that is sustained by the gods (Yahweh) rather than by humans through human efforts. This divine-centered order is finally established in Exodus with the ratification of the covenant and the construction of the tabernacle, where God takes up his rest among the people (Ex 40:34).

To develop this concept in connection with Torah, we must begin with an understanding of the centrality of God's presence in the book of Exodus, where it stands as the theme around which the rhetorical strategy of the book is shaped. Yahweh appears to have been long absent as the book opens and then gradually manifests his presence (burning bush, plagues, pillar of cloud/fire, tent of meeting, Mount Sinai). At the climax, God descends to take up residence in the newly constructed tabernacle. This establishment of God's presence among his people is a recurring theme in the Old Testament, and indeed throughout the entire Bible (e.g., "I will put my dwelling place among

---

[2]Details of the interpretation and support for it can be found in John H. Walton, *Lost World of Genesis One: Ancient Cosmology and the Origins Debate* (Downers Grove, IL: IVP Academic, 2009); and idem, *Lost World of Adam and Eve: Genesis 2–3 and the Human Origins Debate* (Downers Grove, IL: IVP Academic, 2015).

you," Lev 26:11). Divine presence in the ANE, and also in Israel, is a sign that order is being maintained and the world is functioning properly.

The covenant defines a formal relationship that will serve as a mechanism for establishing a divinely centered order where Yahweh will be king and provider to his people. This covenant eventually (by the end of Exodus) leads to the establishment of his terrestrial presence—his rest/residence among them. He lives in the midst of his people and, as their suzerain, establishes order for them through his presence and his rule. The tabernacle provides an initial place for God's presence to dwell and is eventually replaced by the temple. These sanctuaries, from which Yahweh rules, serve as the palace of the Great King but also as the place where his presence dwells among his people to bring order. The Torah is given so that Israel might learn from the wisdom of the king (Yahweh) how to retain his favor and presence, enhancing his reputation through the order they establish proclaiming his rule and honoring his name. If they fail to do so, they may jeopardize their lives, they may be driven from the land (once they take residence there), or he might abandon them.

Yahweh furthermore has a land for his people. It is his land, but he grants them tenancy. Leviticus 25:23 makes this fact clear: "The land is mine and you reside in my land as foreigners and strangers." Thomas Mann expresses it succinctly: "As an alien, Israel does not possess the land as an inalienable right."[3] Yahweh indicates his possession by the frequent claim that he has "put his Name there" (e.g., Deut 12:5, 11, 21). When a king places his name in a land (literally, by engraving it on a victory stele), it indicates his lordship over a vassal state to which he has laid claim.[4] Because the land belongs to Yahweh, Israel's residence in Yahweh's land is conditional on their fidelity to their vassal treaty, as was normal for vassal relationships throughout the ancient world.

---

[3] Thomas W. Mann, *The Book of the Torah* (Atlanta: John Knox, 1988), 123.
[4] Sandra L. Richter, *The Deuteronomistic History and the Name Theology:* lᵉšakkēn šᵉmô šām *in the Bible and the Ancient Near East*, BZAW 318 (New York: de Gruyter, 2002), 217.

By faithfulness to the sovereign, Israel will retain God's presence and the associated benefits of divinely established order, in contrast to the symbiosis of the rest of the ancient world.

The theme of divine presence continues to appear as the prophets speak both of the future dwelling of God among the Israelites (Is 2; Mic 4) and of pending abandonment and punishment at the hands of the Babylonians (Ezek 10). The hope oracles of the prophets, on the other hand, look forward to a time when God will restore his people and dwell among them again (Ezek 40–48).

The Torah has no role apart from the sanctuary—the place of Yahweh's presence from which he rules over his people as he dwells among them in a covenant relationship. The Torah is therefore contingent on the tabernacle/temple—the establishment of God's presence among the Israelites. The Torah is given so that God's covenant people Israel can order their lives and society in a way that will retain Yahweh's favor and his presence residing among them. It is designed to provide examples of covenant order and to help Israel understand how they can

IMPORTANCE OF THE TABERNACLE

In accordance with this interpretation, we might propose the possibility that Yahweh's ultimate reason for coming down to the top of Mount Sinai is not to deliver the Torah; rather, he descends to the mountain to inaugurate the construction of the tabernacle as a place of his presence. If this is so (and it cannot be proven), the primary objective was not Torah; the tabernacle was not constructed to support Torah. The ultimate objective was for God to give instructions for the construction of the tabernacle so that Yahweh could come to reside on earth among his people. The covenant is preparatory for the tabernacle/temple, and the Torah gives wisdom for living in and retaining the presence of God. This finds support in the layout of the book of Exodus, in which the reference to the tablets frames the tabernacle instructions. From this we might consider the possibility that the tablets may have included the instructions for the tabernacle and perhaps even a diagram of its design. In the ancient Near East, the gods frequently gave instructions for the building of temples and also provided diagrams (such as the one pictured on the lap of Gudea in a well-known statue from about 2000 BC). In fact, the biblical text refers to God's provision of such a diagram (*tabnît*; Ex 25:9, 40; 26:30; 27:8; Num 8:4).[a] We also learn from the Gudea Temple dedication cylinder that temple-building instructions and diagrams could represent sworn agreements. On this cylinder, Gudea refers to a "firm promise" of the gods, which is represented by the decision to build a temple for a dwelling place.[b]

bring honor, rather than shame, to the name (that is, the reputation) of Yahweh because they have been identified with him by being designated as holy.[5] As they are faithful to the covenant by heeding the wisdom of the Torah, they will preserve God's presence among them. Failure to establish covenant order will result in Yahweh's departure, to their great loss. Furthermore, this failure will expose them to harm, not only from enemies that Yahweh would send to discipline them but from Yahweh himself, who fulfills the responsibilities of a suzerain against rebellious vassals.

This contingency of the Torah on the presence of God provides significant perspective on how we think about Torah. Just as Torah cannot be mechanically extrapolated beyond its ancient context, and cannot be adopted outside of its covenant context, Torah cannot be removed from its context of the manifest presence of God in his terrestrial residence (tabernacle/temple). The Torah is precisely about

---

[5]Note the point repeatedly made in Deuteronomy that Yahweh would choose a place for his name to dwell (e.g., Deut 12).

Furthermore, the connection between written instructions and the construction of sacred space is found in Esarhaddon's description of his work at the temple of Ešarra: "I made [it] beautiful as the heavenly writing."[c] The sworn agreement between Yahweh and Israel might then refer to Yahweh's promise to come to dwell among his people when they prepare an appropriate place for him. All this evidence then suggests that in Exodus the tablets were provided, first and foremost, for the building of the tabernacle while the Torah serves contingently as instructions for living in proximity to sacred space.[d] This distinction does not mean that none of the Torah instructions were included on the tablets,[e] but it does suggest that we would be remiss to exclude the instructions for the tabernacle from among its contents.

[a]Victor Hurowitz, *I Have Built You an Exalted House: Temple Building in the Bible in the Light of Mesopotamian and Northwest Semitic Writings* (Sheffield, UK: JSOT Press, 1992), 168-70.

[b]Otto Edzard Dietz, *Gudea and His Dynasty*, RIME 3/1 (Toronto: University of Toronto Press, 1997), Cyl B: 24.11-14, p. 101.

[c]Hurowitz, *I Have Built You an Exalted House*, 245.

[d]See William Schniedewind, "Scripturalization in Ancient Judah," in *Contextualizing Israel's Sacred Writings: Ancient Literacy, Orality, and Literary Production*, ed. Brian B. Schmidt (Atlanta: SBL Press, 2015), 313.

[e]Exodus 34:1, 4, 27-29, when read together, seem to suggest that at least the "ten words" were included on the tablets and that they represent the covenant (*bərît*).

establishing order in accordance with ancient ways of thinking, within the covenant relationship, for a people living in proximity to the manifest presence of Yahweh. Whatever its relevance for today (and it *is* relevant as revelation), that relevance must be derived in careful recognition of its situatedness. We will discuss this relevance further in proposition nineteen.

PART 5

ONGOING
SIGNIFICANCE OF
THE TORAH

Discussions of Law in the New Testament Do Not Tell Us Anything About Old Testament Torah in Context

The history of interpretation of the Torah has consistently recognized an important and transparent reality: we cannot adopt all of Torah as regulations for Christian living. With no temple, no sacrificial system, and no society the shape of ancient Israel (which included, for example, polygamous solutions to certain problems), direct application is simply not possible. Yet, if all Scripture is inspired and useful for instruction, what are we to do with this "problem child" that even New Testament authors at times seemed to dismiss?

The problem is that most Christians throughout history who have written about the Torah are really writing about law in the New Testament. They do so under the assumption that there must be continuity between the Old Testament and the New Testament in how to think about law. In fact, however, we would contend that there is not. By suggesting this, we are not proposing that the testaments stand in contradiction to one another, only that they have different perspectives and are addressing different issues. They are both operating from their own cultural rivers, and the Greco-Roman cultural river is notably different from that of the ancient Near East (even though they are more similar to each other than either is to ours). To study Torah in the Old Testament cultural river, we cannot use the New Testament as a source of information.

LAW AND GOSPEL

It is not our intention to investigate the New Testament use of law (*nomos*) and what Paul thought about the moral law of God or what Jesus taught about his connection to the Law/Torah.[1] All those discussions take place against the backdrop of what the Law had become during the Hellenistic period leading up to the New Testament.

Having said that, the discussions about the New Testament understanding of Torah can highlight some of the important issues to be considered. The conversation often takes place under the rubric of "law and gospel," though that putative dichotomy may itself be misleading because it assumes that law and gospel are somehow doing the same or similar things. Paul occasionally addresses what the law does or does not do in contrast with the gospel, but that is strictly a New Testament issue. A prior dichotomy should be considered between Old Testament ideas of law and New Testament ideas, independent of questions concerning the gospel and salvation. Even the New Testament authors make this clear as, for example, the author of Hebrews indicates that the blood of bulls and goats cannot take away sin (Heb 10:4). The sacrifices that included blood rituals in the Old Testament maintained purity of the temple compound and allowed the offenders to remain in good standing in the covenant community (see proposition eight); it did not take away their sin (more about this in proposition seventeen).

---

[1]For a listing of Paul's positive and negative views of law, see Greg L. Bahnsen, "The Theonomic Reformed Approach to Law and Gospel," in *Five Views on Law and Gospel*, ed. Wayne G. Strickland (Grand Rapids: Zondervan, 1996), 93-94.

New Testament authors have their own significant issues to deal with, which are derived from their cognitive environment and the theological controversies of their day. They are making no attempt to reconstruct the theological and cultural issues of an Old Testament context though they obviously draw information for their discourse from the Old Testament as they understood it in their time. Most discussions of the Torah today, filtered through the New Testament, want to examine either the issue of salvation or the issue of moral absolutes for the church or for humanity in general—New Testament questions. This is no surprise, but it does not give us a contextual reading of the Torah. The Old Testament Torah is not trying to define the nature of righteousness or justification. Righteousness (by ancient Near Eastern standards) would be one result of Israel's adherence to Torah—but this is not the absolute righteousness (implicitly, by divine standards) provided by Christ, and not a righteousness concerned with salvation. Furthermore, it is certainly not a righteousness that conforms to our modern cultural river's definitions of values (modern standards). To understand the Torah in the context of the Old Testament we have to stop thinking in New Testament theological categories.[2]

As we have previously discussed in proposition five, we cannot speak of keeping the whole Torah any more than we can speak of keeping the whole book of Proverbs. Both offer wisdom insights. New Testament authors and scholars talk about the hypothetical but unrealistic idea of keeping the law in its entirety to achieve righteousness or salvation, and generally note that it simply cannot be done. This is not to say that the Second Temple community did not try to keep the law in its entirety—the exposition of the Mishnah indicates that they did—but in doing so they were forced to embellish the material substantially. Even then, the righteousness and salvation that they hoped

---

[2]See discussion by Walter C. Kaiser Jr., "The Law as God's Gracious Guidance for the Promotion of Holiness," in Strickland, *Five Views on Law and Gospel*, 192-93.

to achieve were forgiveness for the infidelity of their ancestors and restoration of God's favor to Israel, not moral or social perfection or an impeccable status before God. But this approach to the question already misunderstands Old Testament Torah. While the New Testament insists (on theological grounds) that even perfect Torah observance would not restore God's favor, there are also practical reasons why "keeping the law in its entirety" cannot be done. In previous chapters we have proposed that the Torah, like the comparable ancient Near Eastern (ANE) documents, is aspective. If that is the case, it does not represent an entirety—there is no entirety. It was never more than selected illustrations for the larger calling to reflect order. Even if one successfully adhered to all the stipulations of the Torah, one could not claim to have fulfilled the expectations of Torah because even though they are stipulations, they are not intended to be comprehensive. It is not a checklist to be marked off—the law is "kept" by order being reflected in every aspect of life. The goal of the Torah is order, not legislation or salvation. Sometimes order is even sustained by violating the stipulations, as Jesus frequently demonstrates concerning the Sabbath. Likewise, even "obeying" the commandments of the Torah did not result in the rich young ruler in Luke 18:18-23 embodying the covenant order. The Torah is a guide to what order looks like, not a checklist that can be followed to attain it.

CHANGES IN THE HELLENISTIC PERIOD

It was only when Torah was adopted as legislation in the Hellenistic period that a community discussed the idea of keeping all the law as if it were legislative and comprehensive. As we have seen in our previous discussion, in both Mesopotamia and Israel, the only form of divine law is found in the decrees issued by the gods that maintain order in the cosmos. In contrast, the Greek concept was that law emanated from the gods in the sense that the divine realm was the source of rationality and reason, which in turn served as the foundation for an understanding of natural law. In their view, this law is universal and unchanging, and resulted from general revelation.[3] The model seen in the ANE fits the Torah data better. If that is the case, Torah can be considered neither divine legislation nor a manifestation of the inherent functioning of the world. This is important to recognize if we are interested in reading the text in accordance with its genre and context.

Torah in its Old Testament context differs from Greek conceptions of the world order in that Torah is not based on the concept of natural law woven into the fabric of the cosmos. Torah differs from what we find in Hellenized Israel in that it is not legislation that has its source in divine, special revelation. Torah arises in the context of the culture of the ANE, and similarly is not law but instead represents an impressionistic description of the shape of the world order as desired by the gods. At the same time, Torah differs from the primary culture of the ANE in that it derives from a suzerainty relationship (covenant), not from a symbiotic relationship of mutual need. It is evident in the writings of Paul that viewpoints about the Old Testament Torah shifted dramatically over the time that passed between the testaments. That is expected because culture has changed and Paul has to deal with issues as they exist in his cultural river.

THE NEW TESTAMENT UNDERSTANDING OF TORAH

Many people who object to the idea of the Bible's cultural embeddedness argue that the practice of saying different things to different cultures undermines the idea that a single God inspired the Bible. This objection is misguided because it assumes an overly simplistic understanding of how the Bible communicates. If it were the case that the Bible communicated by presenting a series of relatively simple, universally true factual propositions about life, the universe, and

---

[3]Christine Hayes, *What's Divine About Divine Law?: Early Perspectives* (Princeton, NJ: Princeton University Press, 2015), 2-3.

everything, then it would perhaps be legitimate to claim that a single speaking voice would require all those propositions to be more or less homogeneous in meaning. Many people in fact do believe that the Bible communicates in this way although that conception itself is deeply flawed. Effective communication does not consist of broadcasting a single message over and over like a parrot; rather, it involves a dynamic interaction with the intended audience to ensure their comprehension. One of the most basic elements of successful interaction is speaking in the audience's own language; thus, the communication in the New Testament changes from Hebrew to Greek. Speakers, however, cannot assign any meanings they want to words if they expect to communicate effectively. Instead, they have to use words according to the meanings that the audience expects them to have. Communicating new ideas does not involve assigning new meanings to words; it involves combining existing ideas (using existing words) in new ways. Thus, even if speakers want to convey the *same* new idea in two different contexts/languages, they will have to use different existing ideas in order to communicate.

An example might be helpful. In optics, the colors of lights can be changed by placing colored filters in front of them. If you have a yellow light and wish to change its color to white, you have to put a blue filter in front of it. On the other hand, if you have a purple light and wish to change its color to white, you have to put a green filter in front of it. Now, some people might argue that, in order to get the same color light, you should always use the same color filter, but that misunderstands how light works. The result you get is derived from an interaction between the element you choose to use (the filter) and the elements that you had to work with originally (the colored light). In the same way, saying that you must always use words with the same meaning in order to convey the same message misunderstands how language works. The message you convey is derived from a combination of the elements you choose to use (the words and phrases) and the elements you had to work with originally (the meanings those words are given by the intended audience in their cultural context).

Of course, that assumes that every message in the Bible is intended to say more or less the same thing. If the Bible were God's revelation on life, the universe, and everything—which we could argue does not change—then perhaps that would be the case. However, we have argued that the Bible is God's revelation of *himself*. We could argue that God does not change either, but God is also complex;[4] new revelation might be intended to reveal new aspects of God, as opposed to reiterating the same aspects. The divine personality is in fact so diverse that later theologians had to break it apart into three distinct personae (Greek *prosopon*; English "person"). If God reveals something new about himself, we would not expect it to simply duplicate the information that came before. Further, we have argued specifically that the Bible reveals God's purposes, that is, what God is doing. God is not a machine doing only one thing over and over, and a single individual can do two different things without becoming two different people. To return to the metaphor of the lights, if you have a red light and want to make it yellow, you put a green filter in front of it. If you have a blue light and want to make it purple, you put a red filter in front of it. The fact that you wanted two different colors of lights—and of course used different filters to get them—does not therefore mean that there is more than one person (you) applying the filters. In this conception, God would begin by establishing and sustaining the world order; then, while still doing that, would do something new by establishing and sustaining the Israelite covenant; and then, while still doing both of those things, would do something else new by establishing and sustaining the New Covenant. The point is that the "unity of Scripture" does not mean that it says the same thing in the same way all the time. Instead, it means

---

[4]This observation is unrelated to the technical theological discussion of divine simplicity; we refer here to complexity in terms of depth of personality and diverse functions, not metaphysical composition of the divine *ousion*.

that all of Scripture describes the same God (as opposed to several different gods; see for example Marcion's thought) and that all of it describes that God accurately. That is, it is not a mix of true theological fact and flawed human speculation. That in turn means that in order to gain full understanding of who that God is and what he is doing, we have to pay attention to all of Scripture in accordance to the particular way each part conveys its message. We cannot alter and distort parts of it in order to make its statements superficially homogeneous and thereby expect to come to any real understanding about God.

When we look at the two testaments, then, we should understand that different issues may drive the respective discussions. The cultural river of the Greco-Roman period differs significantly from that of the ANE. The Old Testament, including the Torah, is embedded in the ancient cultural river. By the time we get to the New Testament, influences from the Persian cultural river and the Hellenistic one have led to the Greco-Roman period in which the New Testament is embedded. Just as we do not expect the Old Testament to anticipate the issues in our cultural river, we do not expect it to anticipate the perspectives of the Greco-Roman period. Furthermore, the New Testament writers were not trying to engage the ancient cultural river; they were dealing with their own. This is indeed what we find in the treatment of Torah (and New Testament *nomos*) as the writers address their respective cognitive environments. We can take both testaments seriously, but at the same time, we must recognize each for what it is. The New Testament does not instruct us on how we ought to interpret the Old Testament, though the New Testament authors have much to say about the significance of the Old Testament (as they understood it in their time) for the issues they address. In order to take the New Testament seriously, we need to understand what it does say in its own cultural and literary context.

In previous chapters we have already presented a view of the Torah and its role in the Old Testament and suggested that moral formation was not its literary-theological objective. A next step is to explore whether Paul presents the law (*nomos*) as it was understood in his time as having the function of providing moral formation. Although Paul at times shows a general interest in moral behavior in the churches, we would contend that he does not view the Torah as providing the foundation for that. A number of passages could be cited, but by all accounts one of the most important references is Galatians 3:24, where Paul refers to the law as *paidagōgos* (NIV: "guardian").[5] Modern scholars agree that the Greek term is not to be understood according to its traditional translation as a "tutor" that would lead people to Christ; rather, it should be understood as something more like "custodian" or "babysitter."[6] The role in Greek culture for the person so designated has been recognized as not primarily educational but one in which the appointed individual supervises mundane aspects of life like a nanny or au pair. Although in Greek culture the "pedagogues" were sometimes rather crude or harsh, their job was to protect and to guide through the daily routines of life. They did not have educational objectives, suggesting that Paul did not see the pedagogue as providing training in moral law. Instead, like the Torah, the pedagogue ensured that the subject remained safe and participated in the routines that were appropriate to the subject's status and identity. It would not matter if Paul emphasized a different function for the Torah than could be found in an Old Testament context, but this one (possibly incidentally) seems remarkably close to the role of Torah in the life of Israel. Consequently, even though Jesus and Paul were willing to engage in moral instruction, they did not identify the Old Testament Torah as having that role.

---

[5]The interested reader may find full discussion throughout Wayne G. Strickland, ed., *Five Views on Law and Gospel* (Grand Rapids: Zondervan, 1996).

[6]All the various views presented in Strickland, *Five Views of Law and Gospel*, affirm this to be the case. They direct us to articles such as J. W. MacGorman, "The Law as a *Paidagogos*: A Study in Pauline Analogy," in *New Testament Studies: Essays in Honor of Ray Summers in His Sixty-Fifth Year*, ed. Huber L. Drumwright and Curtis Vaughan (Waco, TX: Baylor University Press, 1975), 102; and Richard N. Longenecker, "The Pedagogical Nature of the Law in Galatians 3:19–4:7," *JETS* 25, no. 1 (1982): 53-61.

Furthermore, we contend that neither Paul nor even Jesus provides hermeneutical models from which we can infer a methodology that can then be applied consistently to arrive at the authoritative message of Old Testament texts that we are interpreting. The New Testament authors use the methods of their day, but their use of them does not validate them.[7] This is the same stance that we take on numerous other issues.

- The New Testament use of Hellenistic traditions and literature does not validate those literatures (e.g., Paul quoting Stoic philosophers in Acts 17:28; Peter referencing 1 Enoch in 2 Pet 2:4).

- The New Testament author's choice to quote from one version (say, the Septuagint) rather than another version (say, what would become the Masoretic tradition) does not validate a text-critical decision.

- The New Testament author's interpretation of a passage in the Old Testament does not attempt to offer an analysis of the Old Testament author's intention or the exegetical meaning of the Old Testament context (e.g., Jn 10:34 treatment of Ps 82:6; Zech 13:7 in Mt 26:31).

- The New Testament author's identification of fulfillment does not show us the original message of the prophet (e.g., Hos 11:1 in Mt 2:15).

- The New Testament author's views of Christ in the Old Testament cannot be used as license for us to find Christ wherever we want (e.g., in the wrestling angel in Gen 32; Arius found him in Prov 8 and used that as a basis for the idea that Jesus was only adopted as the Son of God).

The reason that we cannot imitate the methods of the New Testament authors in these areas is because there are insufficient controls to

---

[7]Richard N. Longenecker, *Biblical Exegesis in the Apostolic Period*, rev. ed. (Grand Rapids: Eerdmans, 1999).

assure the results. In the end, this is because the interpretations of the New Testament authors do not derive from hermeneutics. This is something that we need to unpack.

The authority of Paul's statements is derived not from his hermeneutics but from his apostolic inspiration. Today, we are obligated to use hermeneutical principles to validate our interpretations because we are not inspired. Paul's authority derived from his apostolic status, but in our case whatever authority we have derives from the integrity of our method. Sound hermeneutical principles are essential to place necessary restrictions on us as interpreters because we do not have authority. If we were all inspired, we would not need hermeneutics. What makes the New Testament authors different from us is that they *are* inspired; we are not. Consequently, we should never conclude that we could reproduce their methodology; the authority of their message is vouchsafed from their inspiration no matter how sound their methodology may or may not be. That is to say, we cannot confidently transfer their methods and be assured of guaranteed results. When we try to derive methodological principles and apply them to texts on our own, we have no means of validating whether we have made legitimate use of the method in our extension of the principle. Without controls, there can be no authority.[8] The history of interpretation is filled with examples of interpreters and methods that have ranged out of control and resulted in fanciful and destructive readings. Therefore, just because Paul or Jesus derived a principle from the Torah and extended it to a related situation, we are not therefore justified in attempting to do the same since we do not possess the authority they had. Our

---

[8]Or, said another way: if we do consider ourselves to be inspired, we do not need to derive the authority of our proclamations from the text via hermeneutics; we need only support our conclusions with "thus says the Lord." Citations of biblical material in this case would reduce to creative or aesthetic supplementation, as we see for example in biblical references by, say, Dante or Milton. Granted, Paul, Jesus, et al. are not always being simply creative (though sometimes they are), but when they are not, they are using the best hermeneutical principles as understood in their time. Therefore, in order to imitate them, we should use the best hermeneutical principles as understood in our time as well.

accountability is to the authors of Scripture since they were the instruments for conveying God's revelation. This means that we are accountable to an Old Testament author's intention in context. We are also accountable to a New Testament author's intention in context. When the New Testament authors are interpreting the Old Testament, we accept the authority of that interpretation, but we cannot repeat the way that they derived it any more than we can repeat how the Old Testament authors got their messages. We validate those messages because we have accepted their authority, not because we can legitimate their method.

The biblical text never points to a method of interpretation and then instructs us to go and do likewise. So, for example, on the road to Emmaus, Jesus "explained to them what was said in all the Scriptures concerning himself" (Lk 24:27). Luke does not say that he told them how to do the same thing or exhorted them to do so. In this sense, we could say that the text does not offer us hermeneutical principles any more than it offers us cosmic geography. Likewise, regarding ethical principles, we can observe the principles employed, but that does not mean that they are universal principles. We will discuss this further in proposition nineteen.

Proposition 16

The Torah Should Not Be
Divided into Categories to Separate
Out What Is Relevant

As indicated in the introduction to proposition fifteen, Christians have long recognized the problem that the Torah is not something that can be fully obeyed once the temple has ceased to exist. The rituals can no longer be performed. Furthermore, many of the sayings found in the Torah gradually became obscure or were recognized to apply to the context of the ancient world, which no longer existed.

This dilemma resulted in a solution that has become commonplace in Christian interpretation—to divide the Torah into categories—ritual/ceremonial, social/civil, and moral. As a result, the ritual law was considered fulfilled in Christ and therefore no longer relevant while the social law was considered applicable only to Israelite society. This left only the moral law (the weightier issues of the law) judged to be still binding on us today.[1] In this way, it was believed that the moral

---

[1]For a summary of the categories propounded by Thomas Aquinas, see Michael Dauphinais and Matthew Levering, "Law in the Theology of St. Thomas Aquinas," in *The Ten Commandments: The Reciprocity of Faithfulness*, ed. William P. Brown (Louisville, KY: Westminster John Knox, 2004), 45-50. Evidences of at least a twofold distinction go back to early writers such as Justin Martyr, Origen, and Augustine; see Harold G. Cunningham, "God's

law of God, considered to be reflected in the Torah, could be carried
over beyond the confines of Israel and the Old Testament. In some
cases the core of the moral law was located in the Ten Commandments.

Two immediate problems arise. The first is that this approach treats
the Torah as legislation. Even by the time we get to the New Testament,
cultural perceptions have changed, and both the Jewish scholars and
the New Testament authors who interact with them are thinking of
Torah in terms of legislation (see proposition fifteen). But as we have
demonstrated in the previous chapters, that is not its purpose in the
ancient Israelite context. When attempts are made to preserve the
moral law from the Torah, the decision has already been made that the
focus of the Torah is not only law (normative legislation) but morality.
These presuppositions do not square with the Old Testament context.

The second problem concerns the coherence and integrity of the
Torah as a whole. The Israelites would not have considered it legitimate to make such distinctions and thereby choose what has validity
and what does not. Nor would Jesus or the New Testament authors.[2]
The Torah, in contrast, in its entirety, pertains to order and provides
wisdom for that order to be maintained. That order integrates all three
of the categories that are identified in the Torah; its integrity and coherence resist dissection. It is only when we are thinking of legislation
that is normative as rules to be obeyed that we encounter the problem.
In the proposal that is at the core of this book, all of the Torah is culturally relative in that it is all situated; it is neither a legislative system
nor a moral system. Douglas Moo indicates that even the Jews of the
first century considered the Torah a unity and so did not make distinctions between categories.[3]

Law, 'General Equity' and the Westminster Confession of Faith," *Tyndale Bulletin* 58, no. 2
(2007): 289-312, esp. 292. Various perspectives have been presented in Wayne G. Strickland,
ed., *Five Views on Law and Gospel* (Grand Rapids: Zondervan, 1996).
[2]Affirmed by Douglas J. Moo in his response to VanGemeren, in Strickland, *Five Views*, 85.
[3]Moo's response to Greg L. Bahnsen, "The Theonomic Reformed Approach to Law and
Gospel," in Strickland, *Five Views*, 167. See Moo's longer statement in "The Law of Christ as

In contrast, Walter Kaiser raised objections to this perspective by noting that in the Old Testament itself there seemed to be some prioritizing. In support he points to passages such as Micah 6:6-8:

> With what shall I come before the LORD
>   and bow down before the exalted God?
> Shall I come before him with burnt offerings? . . .
> He has shown you, O mortal, what is good.
>   And what does the LORD require of you?
> To act justly and to love mercy
>   and to walk humbly with your God.

Similar arguments are presented in 1 Samuel 15:22-23, Isaiah 1:11-17, and Jeremiah 7:21-23, as well as in texts in the Psalter such as Psalm 51:16-17. From these he concluded that "the moral law of God took precedence over the civil and ceremonial laws in that it was based on the character of God. The civil and ceremonial laws functioned only as further illustrations of the moral law."[4]

We will discuss in later chapters (see proposition twenty-two) the degree to which we should consider the Torah to be based on the moral character of God, but for now it should be noted that the passages Kaiser cites do not necessarily convey what he suggests. Instead, these passages assert that covenant faithfulness is not achieved simply by rote ritual performance. We will recall that the primary paradigm in the ancient Near East (ANE) was the Great Symbiosis. In that system, ritual performance met the needs of the gods and constituted the full religious obligation of the people. The Great Symbiosis was a strong current in the cultural river of the ANE, and Israelites found it a natural way of thinking and an easy routine to adopt. The behavior

---

the Fulfillment of the Law of Moses: A Modified Lutheran View," in Strickland, *Five Views*, 336-37.

[4]Walter J. Kaiser Jr., "The Law as God's Gracious Guidance for the Promotion of Holiness," in Strickland, *Five Views*, 189-90.

that the prophets are criticizing comes from an assumption, based on symbiotic thinking, that the gods did not care about order in the human world as long as they were properly fed. While this was true in the ANE, in Israel Yahweh was a suzerain as well as a deity, and so he cared about social order in his realm because order in his realm (or lack thereof) reflected on his competence as king. All these passages are insisting that ritual performance (feeding the gods) is insufficient for covenant faithfulness (which entails loyalty to a suzerain). That does not mean that the ritual performance was a lesser priority, only that it could not stand on its own. Covenant order requires much more than ritual to work, but it does require ritual for order to be maintained because in Israel the rituals represented tribute offered as an expression of loyalty and faithfulness. A vassal who withheld tribute stood in violation of a treaty just as much as a vassal who failed to preserve order in the king's realm.

In summary, dividing the Law into categories is not the means by which we can come to appreciate the value that it has for us today.

THE TORAH AND IDEAL SOCIETY

Since the Torah cannot be divided into categories of ritual, moral, and social, if we read any of it as divine legislation, we must read all of it as divine legislation, with social ideals standing equally beside moral ideals. Some interpreters, of course, are inclined to read the social stipulations of the Torah as divine ideals anyway. On this point, it is common for skeptics who level criticism at Christians to ridicule the Torah. If this is this great law of God that was transforming the paganism of the ancient world and providing a system whereby all people could flourish in love and harmony, why is it characterized by primitive flawed institutions such as slavery, by condoning rape (in town, Deut 22:23-24), and by an institutionalized patriarchal misogyny, all neglecting basic social sensibilities of freedom and equality? As they push their case point by point, Christians are often left with mouths agape stuttering through some objection that Yahweh's law treated people better than was characteristic of the rest of the world at that time. Whether or not that is the case, it is little consolation and does not salvage the reputation of God or Scripture in anyone's minds—believer or skeptic.

Many interpreters, as far back as Justin Martyr, tried to mitigate the problem based on an understanding of Ezekiel 20:25-26, where the prophet reports that in response to Israel's rebellion and unfaith-fulness, Yahweh "gave them other statutes that were not good and laws through which they could not live; I defiled them through their gifts— the sacrifice of every firstborn—that I might fill them with horror so they would know that I am the Lord." One common approach uses these verses to suggest that Yahweh gave the Israelites the Torah as punishment (according to some views, for their general lack of faith; by other views, as punishment specifically for the golden calf incident[5]). Irenaeus suggested that the Torah was given to bring the Israelites into slavery.[6] Others divide the law into two—one that brings life and a second that brings death. It is then the first that is carried forward by the work of Christ and the latter from which he set us free. Still others suggest that what were good laws became bad laws through the disobedience of the Israelites.[7] In these ways, the Torah became dispensable even as it remained in some way the foundation for morality and society.

In Ezekiel 20, as in Genesis 1, the designation of something as "good" indicates that it is ordered.[8] For something to be "not good," means that it does not produce order (note Gen 2:18, which states that it is not good for man to be alone). We consider it likely that Ezekiel

[5]Cf. Justin Martyr, *Dialogue with Trypho the Jew*, chaps. 18–21.
[6]Irenaeus, *Against Heresies*, 4.15.1.
[7]This summary is indebted to the thorough treatment in Daniel I. Block, *The Book of Ezekiel, Chapters 1–24* (Grand Rapids: Eerdmans, 1997), 636-41.
[8]For discussion see John H. Walton, *Lost World of Adam and Eve: Genesis 2–3 and the Human Origins Debate* (Downers Grove, IL: IVP Academic, 2015), 53-57.

is not talking about the Torah at all; the passage does not use that word. The passage more plausibly refers to God's judicial decisions regarding Israel, which were not favorable to the unfaithful Israelites and were not done for their good. They did not produce order for Israel. He decreed war, drought, and exile rather than blessing.[9] Yet, at the same time, it is evident throughout the Old Testament that even though the Israelites struggled to conform to the Torah, they considered it to be a joy, not a burden—a gift of Yahweh in conjunction with the gifts of his covenant and his presence.

We will find that the previous chapters have laid the foundation for finding our way through these complicated issues. We start by reminding ourselves, most importantly, that the Torah is a variously situated document: a covenant agreement locked in an ancient culture and the product of a geo-theological setting in which Israel serves as host to the presence of Yahweh. The Torah, for the most part, did not promote a different order from that familiar to the ANE and therefore did not offer an ideal social structure. Indeed, since the point was to establish a reputation for Yahweh as a patron of order, this could only be done using more or less the conception of order that the observers could recognize. Instead of describing an ideal society, it addressed how the Israelite people should maintain their culture's conception of order in the relatively unique context of a vassal relationship with a deity, that is, the covenant relationship with Yahweh. Such order enhances the sovereign's reputation as a competent, wise, and just administrator of the world order. It operates within the confines of the ancient cognitive environment. We can understand how the Torah's social stipulations are situated in the cognitive context of Israel by looking at a number of examples. As we do so, we will note that there were practices characteristic of the world around them that the Israelites were supposed to resist or abandon. But those prohibited practices generally

---

[9]Supported also by Block, *Book of Ezekiel, Chapters 1–24*, 640.

pertained to what represented order in the relationship between people and the gods, not in what represented order in society.

Marriage. The Torah assumes the Israelite institution of marriage, which was virtually identical to that found in the ANE and which was very different from that of today. In the ancient world, marriage was primarily focused on establishing a relationship between families (more than between individuals) and on producing offspring (providing continuity of identity to the next generation). Of course, people "fell in love" with each other, and sometimes that could become the basis for an arranged marriage, but love and the feelings of individuals were not fundamental to the system. People of that time and place did not prioritize freedom of choice for individuals. Since offspring were essential to the success of the institution, divorce was often associated with inability to bear children, and polygamy was a strategy to ensure that children resulted. Polygamy could provide for a first, infertile wife (and the family alliance created by the marriage) to be retained while a second fertile wife could be taken. It also served to mitigate the high mortality rate among children and women in childbirth.

The Torah assumes this particular shape of the institution of marriage. It neither criticizes it nor offers it as an ideal. In this sort of system, the exchange of goods (dowry and bride price) was part of the transaction for a new relationship between families. The dowry (given by the father to the bride) provided security for the wife in the possibility that her husband would die, abandon her, or divorce her. The bride price (given by the groom to the bride's father) reimbursed the bride's family for a lost laborer. We might think that these exchanges reflected a belief that the woman was a commodity to be purchased, but that would be a misunderstanding. Both the woman and the man, along with the exchange of goods, were part of a community merger.

The Torah does not mandate a transformation of the institution by promoting monogamy, by focusing on individual feelings and relationships, or even by talking about what an ideal family ought to be regarding the roles of husbands, wives, and children. In Israel's covenant relationship with Yahweh, integrity in the marriage institution was expected, but this was no different from the rest of the ANE and was relative to the institution as it already existed in that world. Fidelity ensured the paternity of the offspring and therefore the legitimacy of heirs, which in turn was important because property and goods were owned by families, not individuals. If Israel was to be the covenant people of God serving as hosts to his presence, they were expected to maintain order in the conduct of marriage and family, according to the concept of order as it was perceived in the ancient world.

Economy. Israel, along with the rest of the ancient world, had a particular economic system that can be labeled agropastoral: a single family both grew its own food and raised its own flocks and herds. This system was nothing like the market economy, service economy, or supply-and-demand system that exists globally today. The reflection of this system in the Torah does not make it a better economic system and is not one that in general could be maintained today. In such systems, there was little that could insulate people against the vicissitudes of weather patterns. Even one season of low rainfall could result in lack of food for that year and lack of seed for the next. One of the strategies to cope with these potentially life-threatening patterns was what is referred to as debt-slavery. It was an alternative to starvation as it provided a way for those in need to recover from bad seasons.

Today many Americans, under combined taxation of 40 percent or more, in effect work for the government for free for 40 percent of the year. As many build up debt to buy commodities that they need/want, they work another percentage of their year to pay off the banks. Student loans are paid off as people work for years passing the money on to creditors. It makes little difference whether one makes money and passes that on to others (our system) or whether one just works for free for those to whom they are in debt (ancient system). We have little justification for pontificating about the ills of slavery in the ancient world. Furthermore, and in contrast, the debt slavery of the ancient world, in which slaves were more like indentured servants, bears little resemblance to the slavery resulting from ethnic domination in early American history.

Consequently, we are more judgmental of their system than we have a right to be, but at the same time we recognize that the Torah was not seeking to transform their economic system into something that was somehow more God-like. There is no ideal economic system because people will always find a way to corrupt any system and abuse others through it. Any system can be operated with integrity or alternatively be used repressively or oppressively. The Torah insisted that God's people should not abuse people through the system that was in place in their world. The Bible does not call on us to return to an agropastoral economy, and it did not call on them to abolish debt-slavery.

Political systems. One does not have to read much about the ancient world to see that the dominating political system was that of monarchy. In Israel's early years they had a tribal system of governance rather than a monarchy (though priests also had some governing roles), but God eventually instituted one. The Torah does not require a monarchy but allows for one. It does not, however, consider the merits of a democracy, which today is exalted as the best political system, despite its obvious flaws.

We today tend to locate good and evil in the details of institutional structures because we believe that humans themselves are inherently good. Thus, for us it is oxymoronic to talk about executing righteousness and justice in a system that, for example, is not a democracy because we consider a system that is not a democracy to be inherently unrighteous and inherently unjust. The reason why people are concerned that Yahweh did not establish democracy (or feel a need to pretend that he did) is because they believe (probably subconsciously) that a just society cannot exist in any capacity in any other form.

We should not be dismissive of the Torah because it did not institute democracy, nor should we abandon democracy in favor of a "biblical" political system. The Torah does not undertake the installation of a better or ideal political system. Even though God eventually works through a king, the Torah remains neutral about kingship (Deut 17:14-20). Given as little as it has to say about political systems, we recognize that its objective is not to provide an ideally structured society. A structured society requires some sort of political system, which the Torah does not contain. This is another instance of the limited coverage of the legal wisdom genre (see proposition five).

Social status and hierarchy. All societies have structure, whether based on wealth, power, education, family connections, or vocation. Regardless of (theoretical) commitments to considering all persons to be of equal worth, society has its ranks, and rank has its privileges. The Torah does not seek to establish an undifferentiated society, even if such a thing were possible. The status and hierarchy that are evident in the Torah and in Israelite society are not noticeably different from the world around them, and are not presented as ideal. A structured society was an ordered society—each person fulfilling his or her role for the good of the family, clan, community, and nation.

The ancient world was a patriarchal world, and, unsurprisingly, the Torah reflects a patriarchal paradigm. That does not mean that it endorses a patriarchal paradigm as God's will for all people of every place and time. In this, as in other aspects under discussion, the Torah is descriptive. Consequently, we should avoid the complementary though opposite reactions: we should neither criticize the Torah for condoning patriarchy, nor should we seek to enforce or imitate patriarchy today. Both extremes represent a flawed understanding of Torah.

International relations, warfare, and diplomacy. Today we speak of "just war" and have developed criteria to determine the purpose of warfare, how it should be conducted, and what role the threat of war and the objectives of war play in international relations. When people look to the Torah for guidance on these matters, they are often disappointed. For those who feel that war is never justified, they are disconcerted that the Torah even allows for it. But even those who are convinced of the necessity of war look at passages like Deuteronomy 20 and find little guidance.

Again, we find that the discussion of warfare in the Torah does not differ greatly from what one could find in the rest of the ANE. In the ancient world, war was not considered the opposite of peace; it was considered a response to encroaching disorder. Warfare brought disorder to individual lives and even whole communities, but it was justified on the basis of bringing order to the world that, in their estimation, the gods required. This is not dissimilar to a common modern conception that sees war as an evil that prevents greater evils, as long as it is waged in a particular manner according to prescribed limits and rules. The ancients had an orderly way of waging war that prevented greater disorder. Part of the way that they went about conducting war in an orderly manner was ensuring the support and approval of the gods; war was provided with divine justification.

We can see many ways that such a perspective could be abused to create propaganda for all sorts of oppression. The Torah does not provide a theory of warfare that is going to prevent abuse, or one that is going to always represent the best for all parties. No ideal theory of war exists, and the Torah should not be evaluated on that basis.

Diplomacy and international relations. In the same way, we cannot look to the Bible to give universal guidance on how to engage in international relations. In fact, the Torah says little about that (though Israelite practices are evident enough in the narrative literature). Even the observation that the Torah says little about such topics indicates that it does not offer a comprehensive social system. Such gaps show the inadequacy of the Torah to provide universally for the shape of society.

Nonetheless, in this category we do notice a difference between the normal practice in the ancient world and what Yahweh calls for in the

Torah. In the discussion of marriage above, it was noted that marriage was primarily an alliance between families. It is not surprising, then, that international and political alliances also came to be established by marriage among the parties. These marriages were purely diplomatic and did not serve any of the purposes that marriage serves in the modern Western world. Interestingly, we find that the Torah's description of kingship stipulates that the king should not take multiple wives (Deut 17:17). Royal polygamy was essential for international treaties and also demonstrated the power of the king; prohibiting the practice to Israel's king does not represent some monogamous ideal. The reason for the prohibition is given in the text ("or his heart will be led astray"). Israel is thus called to resist what was a standard behavior in the ancient world because such a practice would prove detrimental to the nation's covenant loyalty to Yahweh, who is their suzerain (Solomon and Ahab especially are made examples of in this regard). It is not unusual for suzerains to limit the kinds of political alliances that their vassals are permitted to make. While making treaties with nations outside the land is permitted, turning to other gods would violate the exclusive loyalty owed to the suzerain and constitute (political) rebellion. It is therefore motivated by covenant order, not societal order or moral order.

Respect of personhood. We have already discussed social hierarchies and indirectly noted the role of slaves and women. Many people who read the Torah get the impression that it fails to respect personhood or protect civil rights or personal freedoms—issues that rank high in American values. However, America's value system is not the same as the ancient value system. The Torah does not seek to communicate a "biblical" value system; it reflects an ancient value system exercised with integrity. Respecting persons did not carry the same requirements in the ancient world as it does today; those societies were more interested in preserving order and structure in the community, which meant keeping everyone in their place. We may think that our ways are better, and maybe they are in some regard, though the ancient world would likely not have thought so. That is not the point. The Torah is telling the Israelites some of the ways that they could reflect their culture's values in their world, in their system, and in their covenant relationship with Yahweh, and in so doing reflect favorably on Yahweh "in the sight of the nations" (Lev 26:45). This does not accord with our modern individualism, but it does relate to their ideas about corporate humanity being in the image of God and the importance of maintaining the integrity of social structure within the covenant community.

In ancient society, order and stability in the community took precedence over personal freedoms. We recognize the same principle today when we prohibit someone from exercising freedom of speech by yelling "fire!" in a crowded theater. Whereas we limit such prohibitions to extreme situations, in the ancient world personal freedoms were limited in many more ways in favor of community stability. Again, different societies will prioritize differently, and the Bible does not dictate whether one or the other is right or wrong. The Torah simply operates within the priorities that the ANE cultural river maintained.

Taxation. The economy in the ancient world was based on the exchange of goods and services as currency, not on money. Silver was used as a commodity of exchange, but coins were not minted until the Persian period. Taxation worked within the goods-and-services system. The government or the temple received its due by exacting crops from the harvest, animals from the flocks and herds, or service in the form of corvée, unpaid labor. This was the only form of taxation that was possible in the ancient agropastoral economy. The Torah does not talk about limits on taxation by the government, nor does it discuss how the government ought to use what it receives. When Torah prohibits the king from acquiring great numbers of horses (Deut 17:16), it is exhorting the king not to rely on military capabilities. Vassals were supposed to be dependent on the military support of the suzerain to ensure their continuing loyalty, and pious kings were supposed to be dependent on the support of their gods for military victory, not on the strength of their armies. In the *Cuthean Legend of Naram-Suen* the Babylonian king is chastened by his gods after trying to defeat his enemies by his own strength without their consent. Israel's king, as a (theoretically) pious ruler and loyal vassal, therefore has two reasons not to put too much emphasis on his own military strength. At the same time, the king's military might serve as an indication of the power and favor of his gods; Solomon's chariotry is recounted with pride in 1 Kings 4:26. The prohibition does not provide principles for defense spending.

Property ownership and rights. In ancient Israel as in the rest of the ancient world, the people did not have the same perspective on property ownership as we do today. Land belonged to the gods and was administered by the king, but primary rights were vested in clans and families (as opposed to ownership by individuals). It was a complex balance that is reflected in many of the stipulations of Torah (such as the prohibition of moving boundary stones) and in the narratives of the Old Testament (for example, the conflict of Naboth, Ahab, and Jezebel, 1 Kings 21). The Torah can be seen as promoting the property rights that existed in the ancient world but does not offer reflection on the proper way to understand inalienable property rights.

Crime and punishment. Many find reason to criticize the Torah's views on crimes and punishments (eye for an eye, killing the rebellious son, death penalty for a variety of sexual violations), and many others promulgate ideology based on the premise that the Torah gives God's opinion of how crime and punishment ought to be viewed (e.g., with regard to capital punishment). The Torah's positions in this area follow the pattern that has been well established in the preceding paragraphs. It is descriptive of what was considered to represent justice in the ancient world. In some cases it reflects what we might consider an improvement over what is evidenced in the ancient world (such as children not being punished for the crimes of their parents),[10] while in other cases we might find ANE punishments to be more lenient and (to our minds) more reasonable. For example, in the case of a habitually goring ox that attacks and kills a person, the collections of Eshnunna and Hammurabi call for a payment to be made to the survivors of the victim. That is the sort of thing we would consider reasonable. In the Torah, in contrast, the owner of the ox was to be put to death (Ex 21:29).

As in other categories, we will find that the Torah has little to say about some of what we consider the more important issues. For example, it says nothing about incarceration as a strategy or remedy for criminals or about how to ensure that a criminal has been rehabilitated.[11] These were simply not the issues in the ancient world. Very little is known about prisons in the ancient world though we have reference to them in the early second millennium BC.[12] People were imprisoned when awaiting trial or execution. Once they were tried, they were either released with instructions regarding a penalty, whether flogging, fines, banishment, or execution. The state did not provide care for those in prison except minimal sustenance, which is one of the reasons for emphasis in especially the New Testament to care for those in prison (see also Jeremiah in the cistern, Jer 38). Locking people away for months and years at the expense of the state as a form of post-trial punishment (our idea of prison) is unattested in the ancient world. More frequently, prisons incarcerated debtors or political rivals, not criminals. This gives a very different meaning to the word *prisoners* in the ancient world. Therefore, we cannot draw

---

[10]This reflects the practice that is evident in ANE sources that if a person brings about the death of someone's son, that person's own son's life will be taken. It does not suggest that children would not suffer along with the parents for the sins committed by the parents. Instead, it says that children should not be punished *instead* of the parents—a practice that is attested in the ancient world.

[11]Christopher D. Marshall, *Beyond Retribution: A New Testament Vision for Justice, Crime, and Punishment* (Grand Rapids: Eerdmans, 2001).

[12]Raymond Westbrook, *A History of Ancient Near Eastern Law* (Leiden: Brill, 2003), 2:967.

principles about these issues from the Torah since it did not address the conditions that we encounter in the modern world.

Consequently, we cannot use the Torah to talk about the pros and cons of capital punishment or about what should be considered a capital crime. Capital punishment was a given in the ancient world for good or ill. Indeed, the "state" took much less of a role in enforcing justice than it does today. Ancient societies had none of our alternatives (e.g., institutional prisons for long-term incarceration). For example, for them, the principle of vigilantism made sense, as we can see in the practices concerning the avenger of blood, where the family of the one wronged carried out justice. Furthermore, they did not have the forensics available today for all of its advantages or disadvantages; their judicial system was based on the use of oaths in the testimony of witnesses. Finally, the rights inherent in the modern legal system (e.g., trial by jury) were not recognized in that world. Any principles that we could draw are only valid in relation to the ways in which the ancients thought.

Some approach the issue by saying that since the Torah allows for capital punishment, we cannot say that capital punishment is abhorrent to God or contrary to the moral character of God. Obviously, something God commanded at some point cannot be inherently contrary to his character or nature, but this argument still misses the point because this assumes that the Torah is reflecting the moral character of God or is drawn from it. In proposition twenty-one, we will suggest that this paradigm cannot be maintained.

We can conclude neither that capital punishment is acceptable nor that it is unacceptable to God based on the Torah. The Torah reflects how capital punishment is integrated into society when capital punishment is viewed as a legitimate recourse (number of witnesses, cities of refuge). Order in the ancient world, and even covenant order, employed capital punishment, but that does not supply any sort of universal guidance for structuring society and the criminal system, or for understanding the nature of God. Covenant order is about enhancing the reputation of Yahweh in accordance with the perceptions of the ancient world.

Sexual ethics. Because sexual ethics has become such an important discussion in contemporary Western thinking, this aspect of the Torah has become a hotbed of controversy, both as a target of criticism and as a justification for "biblical" positions. As we encounter the various stipulations in the Torah, we must recall that it is designed to promote a particular understanding of order, not an absolute morality or an ideal way of thinking. Most of the sexual ethics of the Torah had to do with what was perceived to bring order throughout the ancient world.[13] This order prohibited incest as well as uncontrolled sexual relations, either outside of marriage or inside, because they jeopardized the paternity of resulting children, an important concern since marriage and children related to clan relationships. With polygamy being an option, it also provided a deterrent to male promiscuity; if a man had sexual relations with an unmarried woman, he would be required to take her as an additional wife, which would tax his resources. All of these stipulations preserved order as it was understood in the Israelite (and ancient) institution of arranged marriages, which were perceived as clan alliances. We may well adopt similar ideals (prohibiting sexual promiscuity and demanding fidelity within marriage), but given the radically different shape of the institution of marriage in modern Western culture, the same principles are not being applied. The same conclusions are simply being drawn. Our practices may occasionally look the same, but they exist for very different reasons.

When we turn to issues such as same-sex activity and the related issues of gender identity and gender roles, we should be warned against a naive extraction of sentences from the Torah for "biblical principles" to substantiate a particular position today as if that position is thereby

---

[13]Interestingly, we find the Patriarchs violating a few of them in Genesis, but we must also remember that the Patriarchs are not presented as perfect models of order.

built on moral absolutes or on universal dictates. We will return to this in a more focused way in proposition twenty-one. Sexual ethics in the ancient world were built on the premise of what constituted order in an ancient worldview—everyone conforming their behavior to the expectations associated with their roles. We recognize that order may be construed differently in different cultures and that roles may often be restructured. Indeed, societies may place differing values on order in general however that order might be defined.

Doing business. A high percentage of the documents that have been recovered from the ancient world pertain to business (contracts, inventories, receipts, etc.). The earliest writing was developed with business needs in mind, and writing was most often used for this purpose. Most other categories of literature were more commonly preserved in oral tradition and were written primarily as scribal exercises.[14] In the Torah, as throughout the ANE, justice was maintained through fair business practices (true weights, charging of interest, etc.). We can describe these practices in the Torah and in the ANE and compare and evaluate them, but they reflect a far different society from our modern Western one—a market economy that is increasingly service oriented. The Torah conforms much more closely to the rest of the ancient world in business practices than to our modern world.[15]

Relationships with outsiders. In the ancient world a strong sense of outsider status versus insider status is evident in all aspects of society. Warfare against outsiders, social relations with outsiders, interacting with outsiders living among them (Hebrew: *gērîm*), and

---

[14]For more information about the use of writing in a hearing-dominant culture, see John H. Walton and D. Brent Sandy, *The Lost World of Scripture: Ancient Literary Culture and Biblical Authority* (Downers Grove, IL: IVP Academic, 2013).

[15]In this, as in many of the other categories we have discussed, further information describing, comparing, and evaluating specific practices can be found in Westbrook, *History of Ancient Near Eastern Law*, and in Raymond Westbrook and Bruce Wells, *Everyday Law in Biblical Israel: An Introduction* (Louisville, KY: Westminster John Knox, 2009).

marriage to outsiders (exogamy) are all subjects of discussion and considered of utmost importance in cultures in which preserving clan or ethnic identity was given high value. It is of little significance whether we can find ways in which the Israelites were more open or more charitable to outsiders (or, conversely, less so) than was the rest of the ANE. Such differences may reflect a distinct sense of how order in society should be maintained, but more importantly we must recognize that the Torah emphasizes covenant order. Therefore, the Torah is going to address the extent to which outsiders can be incorporated into the covenant relationship with Yahweh rather than the extent to which they can achieve insider status in society. We cannot draw on the principles illustrated in the Torah because we are not in the same sort of covenant relationship as that which governed the Israelites and that Torah was given to promote. Ancient Israel was not a nation-state as we conceive of the term, that is, a geopolitical unit whose legal citizens were beholden to an established authority. Instead, Israel was a geographic territory ("from Dan to Beersheba," e.g., Judg 20:1) in which a particular standard of order was expected, both from ethnic Israelites and from anyone else residing in the territory. See, for example, Leviticus 24:22: "You are to have the same law [read: the demands of covenant order apply equally] for the foreigner and the native-born." Non-native Israelites do not have to observe the feast of tabernacles (Lev 23:42) since this commemorates God's provision for Jacob's descendants. And, with the exception of Caleb and his family, non-natives could not own property in the land since the land was given to the descendants of Abraham. Foreigners were therefore expected to observe the covenant order within the land but were not brought into full participation in the covenant made with Israel. Such stipulations reflect the nature of the covenant as well as concerns of the ancient world. They are not given as universal moral principles for all people for all time and will not help us to resolve the complicated immigration issues of today.

Relationships within the community. Many stipulations of the Torah include affirmations to care for the poor, the widows, or the orphans. In the ANE such concerns were pervasive and stood as intrinsic aspects of what it meant to establish and maintain order in society. Each person had a role and status in the community, and order in the community was enhanced and sustained as these vulnerable classes received provision and protection. It would be difficult to assess the goal of such affirmations in relationship to our modern concerns about the rights of each individual to dignity and "the pursuit of happiness." Order in the community, not personal flourishing, was the chief end of such concerns. If we were to try to contend that Israel was different from their neighbors on this count, we would have to demonstrate a concern for the individual and for personal flourishing that transcended the significance of covenant order within the community. The affirmation that humans are created in the image of God (Gen 1:27), as a statement concerning corporate identity, is not in itself a warrant to claim that the Torah has a special concern for personhood, dignity, or human flourishing. In any case, this statement is never offered within the text as a reason to care for the poor.

CONCLUSIONS

In all of this it is clear that those who criticize the Bible for promoting a social system that is primitive and barbaric in contrast to our own enlightened views; those who believe that the Torah presents an ideal social system that all should follow as "God's way"; those who argue that the society created by the Torah, if not ideal, was at least an improvement over the ANE status quo; or even those who point to isolated passages in the Torah as representing God's moral or social ideals have all misunderstood the Torah. It is also clear that Israel's own society was little altered by Torah and that it did not differ in any significant ways from the other societies in the ancient world. Torah was not the revelation of a new society. It was revelation pertaining to how

God's chosen people were expected to participate in the plans and purposes of God by reflecting well the name of Yahweh, with whom they were identified. This called for integrity as people living in the society in which they lived, as they promoted an order that would be the envy of the nations around them and give honor to Yahweh, their covenant God.

Torah Was Never Intended to Provide Salvation

Since most Christian Bible readers throughout the centuries have encountered the "law" as a topic of New Testament discussion, it is no surprise that they think of it in relationship to salvation (see proposition nine where this was introduced). The author of Hebrews insisted that the blood of bulls and goats could never take away sin (Heb 10:4), and Paul argued stringently against relying on works to produce righteousness (Rom 4:6; 11:6; Gal 3:1-14) as he stressed that we are saved by grace, through faith, not by works (Eph 2:8-9). Though all these statements deny that the law provides salvation, they all relate the law (as it was understood in Paul's time) to salvation.

New Testament scholarship today is engaged in a great debate about what the Jews of the first century AD believed about salvation and the role of Torah in that. They discuss whether Paul was caricaturing his fellow Jews incorrectly or perhaps was misrepresenting them. More often, questions are raised about whether we are reading Paul with post-Reformation eyes and perhaps misunderstanding the issues. This is a complex discussion swirling around what has been termed the New Perspective on Paul.[1] We have no intention of entering that conversation or trying to sort it out here. If the Jews of the first century had gradually developed a different way of understanding the Law (see proposition fifteen), that becomes its own conversation. The places in Pauline literature where we find negative assessments of the Torah are based on how people perceived it in the first century, not a critique of what it was in the Old Testament.

What is important for our study is that we understand that Torah, in the context of the Old Testament, was never intended to provide a way to heaven or a way to pay the penalty for sin fully and finally. It was never intended to do what Jesus accomplished through his death and resurrection. It is therefore not a failed approach; it did precisely what Yahweh intended for it to do. When we talk about Christians not being under law, but under grace, it is a reflection on what Christ has done for us, not a biblical rejection of the Torah as a means of salvation (which it never was intended to be). Non-Jews can neither accept nor reject the Torah because it was never offered to them.

Christians today have furthermore been inclined to think of the Torah in terms of salvation because they have been taught that the metanarrative of the Old Testament—the big picture—is salvation history: it is all about God bringing redemption to his fallen people. When we think of the Old Testament as having such a metanarrative, it is understandable that we may consider the Torah as inevitably propounding a flawed means to salvation. This way of thinking is problematic on a number of counts.

---

[1]For reading in this area, see the seminal works of E. P. Sanders, *Paul and Palestinian Judaism* (Minneapolis: Fortress, 1977); James D. G. Dunn, *Jesus, Paul and the Law* (Louisville, KY: Westminster John Knox, 1990); N. T. Wright, *What Saint Paul Really Said: Was Paul of Tarsus the Real Founder of Christianity?* (Grand Rapids: Eerdmans, 1997); idem, *Paul: In Fresh Perspective* (Minneapolis: Fortress, 2009); and idem, *Paul and the Faithfulness of God* (Minneapolis: Fortress, 2013). It should also be noted that though these three authors are generally grouped together, they all have significant disagreements with each other. Consequently, the New Perspective should not be viewed as monolithic.

Our first consideration should be methodological. For any metanarrative to be proposed, one must establish who controls the metanarrative. Do all authors of Scripture have the metanarrative in mind and consciously write toward it? Is it imposed in the canonical process at the end? Is it God's intended metanarrative that is executed without the knowledge of the authors? We have pursued the methodology that gives greatest weight to text in context. In such a methodology, a metanarrative that is imposed at the end of the canonical process, or one that derives from the hindsight of early Christian writers, or one that is supervised by the hand of God outside of the intentions of the human authors, would all fail the criterion in which the authority of Scripture is tethered to the author's intention—text in context. The only metanarrative that could be sustained from a text-in-context approach is one that the authors of the Old Testament were aware of and were knowingly promoting (as is found, for example, in the metanarrative of the history of Israel presented throughout Joshua, Judges, Samuel, and Kings, or the metanarrative of the ancestors of Israel found in Genesis 12–50). Earlier in this book, we proposed a recurring theme of the presence of God, but that is not a metanarrative. It is a theme that various authors discuss, though not all of the Old Testament authors address it and not all of those who do address it in the same way.[2] No overarching metanarrative can be identified from a text-in-context approach. Likewise, as discussed in proposition sixteen, nothing in the idea of the "unity of Scripture" or of a single divine author of Scripture demands that the text be reducible to a single story.

---

[2]A metanarrative has a linear structure—sometimes called a narrative arc—in which each plot point builds on those previously established. Normally an inciting incident (in salvation history, the fall) instigates a series of tensions (the conflict) leading up to a climax (in salvation history, the crucifixion), which is followed by a wrapping up of loose ends leading to the conclusion. In contrast, recurring themes and motifs have a more centralized pattern; that is, all the instances of the motif or theme reference the same thing (sometimes with different emphases or to different ends) but do not reference each other. Two or more authors who are unaware of each other's work can refer to the same motifs or themes, but they cannot contribute intentionally to the same metanarrative.

Second, salvation history runs into problems in that, as we will demonstrate in the remainder of this chapter, salvation from sins is not something that was expected in the Old Testament and is therefore not even a major theme of the Old Testament, let alone its defining and central subject. If one were to try to draw connections between salvation from sins in the New Testament and deliverance from slavery or exile in the Old Testament, again difficult obstacles would have to be overcome since these crises are very different from the problem of sin.[3]

The theological benefit of this redemptive-historical interpretation is self-evident in its affirmation of the coherence of the biblical text across the canon, but at what hermeneutical cost? For authority to be viewed as something outside of our own creativity, it must be derived with hermeneutical controls in place. Those who adopt this redemptive-historical position often look to the New Testament to supply a unifying theme or purpose and show little concern for the intentions of the Old Testament authors. The observation that the New Testament authors occasionally propose a redemptive-historical metanarrative (which is arguably demonstrable) is invoked to give some authority to that interpretation. However, as discussed in proposition fifteen, we cannot assume that the New Testament provides us with hermeneutical guidelines; the New Testament authors' reading of the Old Testament is a product of their time. The observation that interpreters of the Second Temple period were inclined to read metanarratives into the Old Testament still falls short of demonstrating that the Old Testament should be read only through that filter or that the Torah can be understood to address salvation.

To understand what is important, we have to start by investigating how the Israelites of the Old Testament thought about the concept of

---

[3]For more extensive treatment see John H. Walton, *Old Testament Theology for Christians: From Ancient Context to Enduring Belief* (Downers Grove, IL: InterVarsity Press, 2017), 225-37.

salvation. Speaking bluntly, on the basis of the evidence from the Old Testament, we find that they had no hope of what we call salvation.[4]

- They did not know that "going to heaven" was a possibility.[5]

- They did not imagine that one could spend eternity in the presence of God.

- They did not fear eternal punishment.

- They did not believe that they needed their sins to be resolved in any way beyond that which was available to the community in the sacrificial system.

- They did not believe that they could be saved from their sins (in the way we understand was accomplished by the death of Christ) or that they needed to be.

- They did not think of the Messiah as functioning in the sacrificial system to provide a mechanism for salvation;[6] they saw him only as playing a role in the restored order.

It is self-evident, then, that if the Israelites held none of these concepts or expectations, they did not expect the Torah to accomplish them. Moreover, Yahweh did not intend to accomplish these things through the Torah. The Torah had nothing to do with these issues.[7] The Israelites did not evaluate the Torah in that light, and neither should we.

---

[4]For more extensive discussion see Walton, *Old Testament Theology for Christians*, 225-37.

[5]A variety of passages have been interpreted to suggest that Israelites did have a hope of heaven. We cannot get into those here, but readers can find a thorough study in Walton, *Old Testament Theology for Christians*, 225-65.

[6]Isaiah 53 portrays the servant, putatively a messianic figure, as bearing the sins of the people as a substitute, but that imagery is arguably not associated with the sacrificial system. See Walton, *Old Testament Theology for Christians*, 229-37.

[7]Note this very straightforward assertion by Walter Kaiser: "The law was never intended as an alternative method of obtaining salvation or righteousness—not even hypothetically." Walter J. Kaiser Jr., "The Law as God's Gracious Guidance for the Promotion of Holiness," in Wayne G. Strickland, ed., *Five Views on Law and Gospel* (Grand Rapids: Zondervan, 1996), 178.

Torah provided the means for them to be in relationship with Yahweh through the covenant; it did not reconcile them to God by permanently obliterating their sin. (Reconciliation to God is another concept that is absent from Old Testament theology, except in regard to restoration of favor following covenant infidelity.) Individuals could be faithful to the covenant, and that put them in good standing in the covenant community, a community that continued to exist in covenant relationship with Yahweh generation to generation, though individuals would come and go. Individuals who failed to observe the Torah could be cut off from the community so that they would not negatively affect the good standing of the community as God's people. If the community as a whole failed to keep the covenant, the covenant curses would come upon them and they could lose the covenant benefits (land and the privilege of Yahweh dwelling among them) and instead suffer exile.

God's plans and purposes did not do something *to* the Israelites (other than give them a status as his people); his plans and purposes worked *through* them. His plan was not to cleanse them of their sins, provide for their eternal life, reconcile them to God, impute righteousness to them, or take their sin on himself. Instead, what he did was establish his kingdom on earth and dwell among his people as king. In the process, as we can see in hindsight, he was establishing what kind of God he was, so that when Christ appeared claiming to be God, people would have a way to understand that what he meant was not the same thing that the Greeks and Romans would have believed was represented by the word *God*. The Israelites were not anticipating incarnation, but they were to understand that their concept of their God was supposed to be slightly different from the understanding of other gods that both they and their neighbors shared.

Israel did not have to be "saved" to enter Yahweh's kingdom— Yahweh was building his kingdom through the Israelites. He had chosen them for that purpose. That is what it means that he declared them holy. Even when they proved uncooperative, they remained part of his kingdom; he was still their sovereign and they were still his vassals, even if they were rebellious vassals. The Torah gave them wisdom for being cooperative participants—it did not give them an individual eternal destiny.

Divine Instruction Can Be Understood as a Metaphor of Health Rather Than a Metaphor of Law

People reading the Bible today often begin with the assumption that the Torah provides divine moral instruction, then they go about trying to figure out how it does that. We have already considered some of these approaches, for example, separating what is identified as moral law from the civil and ritual law (see proposition sixteen). Others locate the moral law even more strictly in the Decalogue alone. The base assumption is fueled by the equation that morality is achieved by law and that law is intended to produce morality. Given this two-way equation, the Torah, which they identify as law, is seen as being the source of morality, and since the source of Torah is God, the Torah has moral authority. As we have been discussing, this breaks down at almost every level. If the Torah is not legislation and cannot be reduced to morality, the fact that it has divine authority does not establish a divine source for either legislation or morality since neither is the Torah's intent.

When we ask about the relationship between the Torah and morality in ancient Israel, we are asking whether the Torah tells the

Israelite people what they ought to do. Morality is the philosophical study of ought. To claim that the Torah offers moral instruction is to say that its imperatives contain rules for what people ought (or ought not) to do: honor your parents, do not kill, wear fringes on your clothes, do not boil a kid in its mother's milk, and so on. Alternatively, if someone claims that the Torah reveals the moral character of God, they are saying that it illustrates a principle by which they can determine what they ought to do since the character of God is the source of ought. Examples of such principles (though not necessarily derived from the character of God) are "do unto others what you want them to do to you"; "do what you will if it harms none"; "do that which produces the greatest good for the greatest number"; and so on. Based on the line of thinking that we have developed in the previous chapters, the Torah provides neither moral instruction nor moral example. We will discuss the issues of derived principles further in proposition nineteen, but we have proposed that, as aspective reflections of wisdom, the Torah is not offering binding principles or rules. Consequently, there is no ought of any kind.

The intention of the Torah is to produce knowledge, not obedience; it was not given because Yahweh wanted Israel specifically to do anything. What it offers is not an imperative but a choice: "See, I set before you today life and prosperity, death and destruction. . . . Now choose life, so that you and your children may live" (Deut 30:14, 19). The Torah does not tell the people of Israel that they ought to choose life or that death and destruction will be a punishment for failing to choose life. Yahweh is establishing a reputation for himself through his interaction with Israel. He does not tell them that they ought to reflect him in a certain way; his reputation will be established one way or another, regardless of what Israel does (see proposition six). What he tells them lets them know beforehand what they can do in order to receive favor and blessings, if they should decide that they desire favor and blessings. This is the point that the prophets drive home as they indict the Israelites of covenant unfaithfulness. Yahweh wants them to be faithful vassals, and they need to do so if they expect to enjoy the blessings of the covenant relationship.

Instead of conceiving of a moral system as analogous to laws, obedience, and crimes, it might be more helpful to conceive of morality as analogous to the category of health. In today's Western cultural river, few things are considered as important as good health, which requires vitamins, diet, exercise, nutrition, and numerous smaller factors. Doctors and researchers are constantly trying to determine what will lead to good health so they can pass those results on to a public that prioritizes that value above most others. Frustration can result when different studies produce different results: Is wine good for your health or not? Is fish oil beneficial? Does vitamin C fight colds? Do the benefits of red meat outweigh the possible disadvantages? The list goes on and on. Even in today's climate of advanced research and understanding, people recognize the goal (good health) and pursue it aggressively, but it is still difficult to provide a list of specific guidelines for how that goal can be achieved. Furthermore, although some potential foods are universally recognized as dangerous (e.g., some poisonous mushrooms) and must always be avoided, others are dangerous to some (sugar for diabetics) but necessary for others (the same sugar for those with hypoglycemia). No universal set of instructions exists that anyone anywhere could be given in order to achieve this goal of health. Further, when we visit the doctor, the doctor does not legislate how we ought to eat. The doctor will not inflict us with heart disease as punishment for failing to exercise. What the doctor does is provide us with knowledge about what we can do if we decide that health is something we want. Further still, the advice the doctor gives one person may differ from the advice for another because these two people are in different contexts. Even though they are listening to the same doctor and trying to achieve the same ideal of health, the differing contexts may require them to go about attaining health in different ways.

It would complicate the matter significantly and prove utterly unreliable to try to look to the Bible in order to derive universally applicable principles for good health. The Bible's authors would have either no knowledge or little concern for the pillars of good health that we consider essential (diet, exercise, nutrition, vitamins).[1] God has offered no revelation concerning how to achieve good health, though we would not thereby conclude that the idea of good health is irrelevant or imaginary. Neither the dietary lists for ancient Israel nor the idea of achieving health through obedience to God would serve as transferable principles.

This example helps us to see that we are capable of pursuing a goal that is desirable by whatever means are currently considered productive, even though the details are constantly being adjusted. For example, we no longer employ bloodletting as was done in the Middle Ages. The key is to have clear sight of the goal and to be committed to doing whatever represents the current wisdom in order to achieve that goal. If we try to reduce the goal to a checklist of practices and behaviors, it is likely that we will lose sight of the larger goal.[2] Extracting a list of principles has the potential to undermine the importance of some of the more abstract ideas.

We might have good reason to maintain that God would be interested in our good health, even if we cannot defend that reason by pointing to a biblical prooftext in which God issues a universally binding commandment to be healthy. If we want to pursue the goal of good health, however, we could not do so by going to the Bible in general or the Torah in particular, and most people do not attempt to do so. We would do better to use all the wisdom, insight, and research available in our modern context to make the best judgments that we can. The issues that contribute to our understanding of good health

---

[1] Attempts to do so (such as the Ezek 4:9 diet) border on the ridiculous, especially since that diet is referred to by Ezekiel as the hardship of exile, not as a diet to be promoted.

[2] We would contend that this is precisely the point that Jesus is making in Matthew 5:21-48.

today are complicated and very different from biblical times. We understand the issues differently and are unarguably better informed. Good health remains as important to us as it was in the past, perhaps even more so, but the Bible will not address how we should approach good health today. We share a goal, but the exact conception of that goal is likely to vary somewhat, and the means to achieve that goal are very different, though some principles might be transferable.

In the same way, we might have good reason to maintain that God would be interested in ethical behavior, and we could defend this reason even without identifying a specific biblical command to be moral.[3] If we want to pursue the goal of being ethical people, however, we would maintain that the Torah is not going to provide sure guidance to that goal. Just as we share the common goal of good health but differ in the ways we achieve it and differ in the situations that we face, so do we as human beings share with the ancient world the common goal of individual and corporate human goodness (of some kind or another, achieved in part by ethical behavior). At the same time, we may describe our personal and social ideals in terms different from those they used (i.e., happiness, human flourishing, or the common good versus order, structure, and coherence with longstanding tradition). Likewise, we may differ in the ways we achieve these ideals and in the situations that we face. Just as we have to continually adjust how we understand health and what specific behaviors will promote it, so we have to continually adjust how we understand goodness (achieved in part by ethical behavior) and how we can achieve it in the issues that we face.

The contrast between the principles of law and health is emphasized in 1 Corinthians 6:12 and 10:23: "'I have the right to do anything,' you say—but not everything is beneficial." Paul claims that all things are lawful, that is, that there is no legislation that prohibits them. This

---

[3]Or there could be one; Matthew 5:16 is one expression of this that we could point to: "In the same way, let your light shine before others, that they may see your good deeds and glorify your Father in heaven."

statement does not provide an authoritative biblical declaration that the Torah is not legislation (or that it is legislation that has been abolished), but it is nonetheless consistent with our own observation that the Torah does not designate anything as unlawful. At the same time, however, Paul does not leave his readers floundering with no behavioral guidelines. In the absence of law, one permitted behavior can be preferred over another based on the extent to which the behavior is healthful. This observation does not include an imperative to be healthy or indicate that unhealthy behavior is an offense to be punished; unhealthy behavior is essentially its own consequence. The use of this metaphor in the New Testament does not, of course, constitute a divine imperative to understand moral instruction this way—providing interpretive metaphors to theologians is not the purpose of the text in context—but the metaphor is consistent with the way we have demonstrated that the Torah functioned in its own context. And the ability of the New Testament to use the same metaphor indicates that it is not inconsistent with New Testament ideas either.

We Cannot Gain
Moral Knowledge or Build a
System of Ethics Based on Reading
the Torah in Context and Deriving
Principles from It

Before we continue the topic of the relevance of Torah as Scripture, and particularly its relevance for ethics, we need finally to address the approach that is very common today—applying the Torah by deriving behavioral principles point by point. We will refer to this as the "derived principles" approach.[1] For many years I (John) taught this

---

[1]The most extensive treatment of this approach can be found in Roy E. Gane, *Old Testament Law for Christians: Original Context and Enduring Application* (Grand Rapids: Baker Academic, 2017). Though I disagree with the principles approach, Gane works out such an approach in an admirably thorough treatment. He also differentiates the principles approach from the similar but not identical paradigmatic approach favored by Christopher Wright (Gane, 185). Wright defines his approach: "In applying the Old Testament in this way, we are taking it as a model or paradigm which can legitimately be brought to bear on issues of our contemporary world, with all appropriate allowances for cultural and historical differences." Christopher J. H. Wright, *Walking in the Ways of the Lord: The Ethical Authority of the Old Testament* (Downers Grove, IL: InterVarsity Press, 1995), 33. Similar approaches are also promoted in Walter C. Kaiser Jr., *Toward Old Testament Ethics* (Grand Rapids: Zondervan, 1983).

method for deriving the message of the Torah for us today as I looked for a relevant and applicable principle for each legal saying. More recently, I have become persuaded that such a methodology cannot yield consistently reliable results, and so I have changed my approach. Before we discuss individual examples, we need to address the usual validation for the practice of deriving principles from the Torah's stipulations. Paul appears to use such a method, and people have taken that as justification for also employing it.

The practice of deriving principles of behavior from the Torah is similar to the likewise common approach of deriving principles of behavior from the Old Testament narratives. We can demonstrate the flaws of the methodology in connection with Torah by examining the methodology applied to the narrative literature. As with the Torah, we sometimes substantiate a derived-principles method by pointing out that the New Testament authors show an inclination to use Old Testament characters as role models for behavior (cf. especially Heb 11). Such methodology is typical of children's curricula and is foundational to many sermons and Bible study series. The problems with this method are multitude. One problem occurs when, in some cases, it is not clear at all whether a character's behavior is acceptable or not, in which case no principle can be derived by claiming that it is biblical.

For example, endless arguments take place concerning Rahab's protection of the Israelite spies by lying to the king's men as she sends them off on a wild goose chase while the spies are hidden on her roof. Is her lie commendable or deplorable? Is lying always wrong? The text does not resolve this in the course of the narrative and is not intended to engage or answer such questions. No principle about lying can be derived as the biblical teaching.

Another more frequent problem occurs when the behavior is incidental to the intent of the narrative—obvious by the fact that the narrator offers no comment about it. Is the narrative about Abram and Lot (Gen 13) trying to teach us about the importance of letting others choose first? Or for that matter, does the feeding of the five thousand (Mt 14:13-21) offer a lesson about sharing because of the boy who shared his lunch? I would contend that these are illegitimate approaches to identifying the authoritative message of the text.[2] They are dependent on the imagination of the reader, not on the intention of the author. With no controls, abuse is inevitable and amply attested in the history of interpretation.

In contrast, we should evaluate what the narrator is doing with the characters rather than focusing on what the characters are (incidentally) doing. When Rahab lies to the king's men, she is demonstrating her new commitment to Yahweh and to what he is about to do in the land. It demonstrates how Yahweh is protecting the Israelites and carrying out his conquest of the land. In Genesis 13, when Abram lets Lot choose first, the text is not providing guidance for how we should act toward others. Instead, the question of who chose first is important because it shows that Lot chose to leave the land of his own accord. The text draws out this message as the chapter ends with Yahweh telling Abram that now all the land is his. The narrative has a literary/theological explanation, not an ethical one. In the feeding of the five thousand, the boy appears in only one verse of one of the Gospel accounts. The point of the narrative is clearly that Jesus is God and that he is fulfilling his messianic role as he recapitulates aspects of Israel's history (cf., e.g., 2 Kings 4:42-44). We do not know whether God approved of Rahab's lie. We do not know whether Abram was being altruistic. We do not know whether the boy felt peer pressure to share his lunch.

Though the ethical approach to narrative literature is often endorsed even by respected scholars,[3] it cannot be applied consistently and is difficult to defend as the intention of the narrative genre in the

---

[2]This concept is developed both in introductory articles dealing with methodology and in the examples of Bible stories found in John H. Walton and Kim E. Walton, *The Bible Story Handbook: A Resource for Teaching 175 Stories from the Bible* (Wheaton, IL: Crossway, 2010).

[3]See for example, Gordon J. Wenham, *Story as Torah: Reading Old Testament Narrative Ethically* (Grand Rapids: Baker Academic, 2004).

biblical text. This approach has long been popular in part because, on occasion at least, the ethical behavior of the characters is noteworthy and commendable in every way, at least by the standards the interpreters in question are already inclined to employ based on the values and priorities of their own context. We could easily point to examples of characters behaving in ways we consider to be admirable that are also approved of by God (or by the document's narrator): the faith of Shadrach, Meshach, and Abednego (Dan 3:16-18), for example, or the moral fortitude of Joseph to withstand seduction (Gen 39:8-12). However, that a particular behavior is approved by God or the narrator in the context of the text does not consistently establish the behavior as exemplary. Sometimes God approves of behaviors that we consider reprehensible (the slaughter of women and children by Joshua, Josh 6:2-21), and sometimes behavior that we would consider admirable is condemned by God (the mercy of Ahab and of an unnamed prophet, 1 Kings 20:34-42). Likewise, when behavior we consider exemplary does appear, we cannot assume that such commendable behavior appears in the text for the purpose of urging the reader to similar moral excellence. These examples strike us as intrinsically admirable (mostly because of things we happen to value that derive from our cultural river), but since they do, we do not need the Bible to tell us to act that way. This behavior already coincides with what we believe. Identifying characters as true moral exemplars becomes much more difficult when we are uncertain whether the behavior is to be emulated.

For example, the very same Joseph who withstood the temptation of Potiphar's wife instituted an economic policy that would be considered morally bankrupt today:

- In a time of plenty, tax the people excessively to build up reserves (Gen 41:47-49).

- Then in a time of need, sell the reserves back to people (Gen 41:56-57).

- When they can no longer afford to buy from the reserve, take their land (Gen 47:13-23).

Yet the text informs us that God provided famine relief not only to Abram's family but to all the world through Joseph (Gen 41:57; 45:7). The commendation is not implicit or incidental; this event stood as a prime example of how all the people of the earth were blessed through Abram's family (Gen 12:3). However, nobody today argues that the Christian moral standards that God commands through the Bible as a way to bless the whole earth in fulfillment of the promise to Abraham should include the oppressive economic policies exemplified by the great paragon of virtue Joseph.

Here is the main point that we must understand: if we have to be selective about which passages we mine for moral guidance and which we reject, it is not Scripture that is guiding us but our own preconceived notions of what is right and wrong. As a corollary, then, whatever is producing our sense of right and wrong, which we are using to filter and evaluate Scripture, is not Scripture.[4] If Scripture is not in fact producing our sense of right and wrong, then the question of whether it theoretically could is mostly academic, and the claim that it does not (as we have argued in the case of the Torah) is reduced to a technical discussion among scholars. On the other hand, if we are not filtering which passages are moral and which are not, we either need to say that all of it is, or none of it is, or that it is possible to tell the difference within the text itself (i.e., its own content and context). In this final case, an appeal to content and context requires much greater substantiation than the simple observation that the document is Scripture and that we consider the character's behavior to be exemplary.

---

[4]This is true even if the filter in question is asserted to be another passage in Scripture. Being able to designate one passage in Scripture as an acceptable filter as opposed to any other passage in Scripture indicates that simply "being Scripture" is not the criterion that is being employed to determine suitability as a filter.

The Bible does not provide its revelation by means of characters in morality plays that are supposed to be normative for the reading audience. We know this because of the abundance of counterexamples. If that is not what the author of Scripture consistently intends through the genre of narrative, then reading the narrative in this way does not engage the authority of the text. The narratives of the Old Testament undeniably illustrate certain sorts of behavior—all narratives do. But that does not mean we should conclude that they intend to teach that behavior or to be a source of ethical teaching. While the New Testament authors do occasionally use the Old Testament characters as examples to illustrate ethical principles, we recall that the purpose of the New Testament documents is not to dictate interpretive methods to future theologians (see proposition fifteen).

Consequently, we are misguided if we think that we can use the derived-principles approach to narrative literature, and we are equally misguided if we transfer the same approach to the Torah, for the same reasons. We should not be using it in narrative literature to begin with, and the flaws are evident in both genres. Just as narratives were sometimes mined for behavioral guidance by New Testament writers, principles were also derived from some Torah stipulations in the New Testament. These do not give us license to do likewise.

Now that we have demonstrated that we cannot use the method of deriving principles from Old Testament just because New Testament authors have done so, we can turn our attention to the Torah itself to consider the methodology on its own merits (rather than legitimating it as a method that the New Testament authors used). The problem in using the New Testament method as a model suffered the problem that it could not be applied with consistently reliable results. Just as we found that there are characters in the Bible whose behavior is commendable in every way and therefore demonstrates attributes that we would hope would characterize our own lives, we will find stipulations in the Torah that can easily be seen to offer common-sense principles that we would do well to emulate. That we can find such examples does not mean that every stipulation can be treated that way successfully. Nor does it prove that the Torah is meant to be interpreted in that manner.

PROBLEMS WITH DERIVING PRINCIPLES FROM THE TORAH

The first problem that we encounter in trying to derive principles from the Torah is the difficulty in determining which passages contain moral principles. If the derived-principles approach were to be used consistently, we would have to apply it equally to all the stipulations of the Torah since they are all of equal quality in establishing order; we cannot try to sort the stipulations into categories without violating the original context (see proposition sixteen). If we apply the derived-principles approach only selectively, then we are the ones deciding what does and does not have value as God's Word. Inevitably we will choose only the passages that we can readily attach to principles that we already believe are true. In this scenario, we are using Torah not to establish a moral system but to undergird one that we have already decided is valuable and coherent. In this case, Torah is used as little more than illustration.

The second problem with this approach is in trying to establish derived principles with confidence. When we are working from the text in context, we have numerous obstacles that exist because of the contexts in which Torah is situated. We have discussed these at length. Particularly challenging for this approach is the fact that the Torah is situated in the ancient world. As an example, it would be difficult to use the cosmic geography of ancient Israel (evident throughout the biblical text) to derive principles by which we could understand cosmic geography today. Their cosmic geography is too deeply rooted in the perspectives current in the ancient world to provide useful principles for us.

We likewise encounter such examples in the ancient context of stipulations in the Torah. The ancient peoples are so far removed from

our world and our ways of thinking that any attempt we might make
to derive principles from them would reflect more of our preconcep-
tions about moral principles than about what the text is doing in
context. The text offers us no guidance about how to derive principles
from it, and therefore our attempts to do so have shallow, if any,
rooting in the text.

If we have no consistent methods for determining which texts
contain moral principles and are faced with insurmountable obstacles
in deriving principles with confidence, we must confront the uncomfortable reality that both of these determinations are ultimately based
on our culture and our inherent sensibilities, not established by the
text independently. Some examples can help us to realize the shortcomings of this approach.

One example of a stipulation from which some derive universal
principles is found in Deuteronomy 22:8: "When you build a new
house, make a parapet around your roof so that you may not bring the
guilt of bloodshed on your house if someone falls from the roof."
People who are inclined to derive principles from Torah stipulations
feel very good about this one. Interpreters recognize that in its original
context, this was not some sort of OSHA code—the emphasis is on
avoiding bloodguilt, not on the particulars of guardrails. Even though
in common architectural practice in Western society inhabitants of
the house would not normally have occasion to be on the roof, interpreters identify an underlying principle that a homeowner has the
responsibility to assure that safety measures are taken to protect the
life and health of family and friends. Consequently, the principle
drawn from this is generally related to any number of liability issues
(our nearest equivalent to "bloodguilt"). However, since the verse is
just an illustration, it does not offer clear boundaries for where liability
starts and stops. Therefore, though we could easily identify a principle,
the text offers little actual guidance for behavior and leaves the controversial specifics undefined. The "principle" therefore does not offer

resolution of difficult cases; it derives from common sense that we could have employed without the Bible's instruction. It does not even tell us generally that looking out for the well-being of guests is something that will always serve God's will; God's will can also be served by murdering a guest with a wooden stake (Judg 4:19-21).

As another example, Deuteronomy 25:4 states, "Do not muzzle an ox while it is treading out the grain." This is one of the showcase examples in which the apostle Paul extracts a principle from the Torah—specifically about paying God's workers for the ministry that they do (1 Cor 9:9-12; 1 Tim 5:18). As already addressed above, however, Paul's use cannot offer legitimation for us to do the same. He is using methods that were legitimate in his time, arguments described by many New Testament scholars as similar to those of the rabbis, but that does not necessarily make them methods that everyone should use. Because he is inspired, the recognition that his methods are deeply problematic (note that virtually no Christians today consider the rabbis to be a legitimate source of exegetical authority) is irrelevant to the integrity of his arguments. It does not mean, however, that, for the sake of the integrity of our own (uninspired) arguments, we should not use them. Again, like the passage about guardrails, people find it easy to infer the principle behind the verse and to apply it to a variety of arguably related situations. In some cases, the extension of the principle would be obvious, but we might easily see that we would need to impose limits lest the message be extrapolated beyond its legitimate range. In this case, for instance, why would an employee not use it as justification for taking supplies from the office? Perhaps employees at a college might invoke it to excuse taking dishware from the student cafeteria for use in their offices. As before, it is only our good common sense that resolves the gray areas for us—not the Bible.

In each of these examples, we have shown how a principle that could legitimately be derived from the Torah as good common sense fails to be productive for more complicated ethical determinations.

Now we progress to the next step—stipulations from which the principles derived would be contrary to common sense. One of the most obvious in this category is the well-known *lex talionis*: an eye for an eye, a tooth for a tooth, a life for a life (Ex 21:24; Lev 24:20; Deut 19:21). It is common to draw from this the idea that the punishment must be commensurate with the crime—but that is not what this says. We can talk about how in context this is meant to limit the punishment so that it does not become excessive (e.g., a whole head for an eye, a whole family for a life, and so on), but most today would find putting out someone's eye to be excessive.

Many would find the talion law resistant to principle derivation, and the more extreme examples of putting to death the rebellious son (Deut 21:18-21) or marrying a captive woman (Deut 21:10-14) are significantly more impenetrable. If even a few of the stipulations cannot be interpreted to produce clear-cut principles, the methodological approach is jeopardized. So we have found that we cannot imitate the New Testament authors, that even when principles can be drawn, they are common sense and do not resolve complicated issues, and that many stipulations (most?) resist principles. In addition to all these obstacles, most readers of the Torah struggle with the opacity of the legal sayings.

Just as some narratives are opaque about the motives and behavior of the characters (and thus resist extrapolation of ethical principles), many of the legal sayings in the Torah fail to provide clear understanding of the underlying reason for the stipulation. Consequently, we cannot apply the derived-principles approach consistently. For example, we might think we can infer reasons that a donkey and ox should not be yoked together (Deut 22:10),[5] but even if we can, extrapolations of those principles remain controversial. That is, the text does not settle the issues for which we seek guidance (e.g., marriage

---

[5]For example, unequal strength results in crooked furrows and tired animals.

of couples who are different in one way or another).[6] Similarly, we may think that we can unravel the reasoning behind the prohibition of wearing clothing that mixes wool and linen, but we are only guessing. It would be no surprise if there were more to it than we recognize. The degree of opacity is far higher in, for example, the prohibition about cooking a kid in its mother's milk. The unsettling fact is that many of the legal sayings in the Torah are based on ways of thinking in the ancient world that are foreign to us as they transcend modern reasoning and intuition. This fact argues against the idea that their scriptural authority is to be realized by deriving principles from them.

Torah Not Intended to Provide a Moral System

We should not expect the Torah to be able to provide a moral system because that is not its genre. By this point in the book this is now just a reminder of that which we have already addressed in detail elsewhere (propositions four through six). Our expectations of a text and our use of the text must be coherent with the intention of the text— and that is determined in major part by its genre. As an example, imagine trying to derive timeless moral truths from a chocolate-chip cookie recipe. While this might theoretically be possible—"the mixing of the wet and dry ingredients teaches us that we have to work together with those who are different from us in order to accomplish goals that would be impossible to achieve by ourselves"—if you do not use your cookie recipe for its intended purpose, you'll never enjoy a nice batch of warm cookies.[7] The Old Testament legal texts do exist for a purpose, but that purpose is not for the formation of moral principles. The purpose might potentially have some application to the formation of

---

[6]The concept of being unequally yoked is invoked in later Scripture in relation to marriage, but as we have discussed, that does not give us what we need to establish the method safely within the bounds of authority.

[7]Illustration reused from John H. Walton and J. Harvey Walton, *The Lost World of the Israelite Conquest: Covenant, Retribution, and the Fate of the Canaanites* (Downers Grove, IL: IVP Academic, 2017), 94.

moral principles, but not in the form of lifting direct quotations. Instead, we need to be trying to understand what God was doing through the Old Covenant in its context. This will help us determine what he is doing through the New Covenant and ultimately will aid us in understanding what we must do to participate today as God continues to work through the New Covenant. We are not going to succeed in this endeavor by choosing selected statements from the Torah and deriving principles from them of our own design to undergird a moral system that represents our own sense of appropriate morality.

DETERMINING LIMITS

As we have seen in all these cases, deriving principles is a subjective enterprise and suffers from lack of limitations. It is our responsibility as faithful interpreters to be tethered to the text. If we readers of the text can derive our own set of principles and apply them to whatever situations strike us as appropriate, we are no longer benefiting from the authority of the text. We become duplicitous (or at least fallacious) when we appeal to that authority by referencing the text. If we seek to retain the authority of the text, we must use methods that reflect our accountability to the text, particularly as it is represented in the author's communicative intention, which is set in the context of culture, language, and genre.

If we were theoretically to approach the stipulations of the Torah as providing principles, we would have to recognize that we are engaging in a two-step process. We would first have to determine what the underlying principle is, and then we would have to exercise discretion in discerning the situations to which it can legitimately be applied. We have already noted the handicap that we have in trying to discern the underlying principles, but that is not the only obstacle to overcome. When we try to carry an idea from one cultural river to another, many hazards line the way.

A few examples can help identify the challenges. The first example is the prohibition concerning charging interest (Ex 22:25). In some periods of history, Christians understood this to mean that they had to refrain from charging interest to other Christians, which in turn made banking unprofitable and therefore not an allowable profession for Christians living in Christian communities. In such a setting, the Jews living among them were left to conduct the business of banking. That most of us today no longer consider banking to fall under the category of usury makes it easy to see how difficult it is to derive workable principles from such statements in the Torah. How it applies to one situation or another would always be subject to differences of opinion.

In the next example, the ability of the interpreter to derive principles is hindered from the start by the challenge of arriving at an accurate translation. Exodus 21:22 describes the unlikely situation of a pregnant woman who has inadvertently become entangled in a fight between men. Because of the unfortunate turn of events, the woman's pregnancy comes to an abrupt end. The text does not make clear whether she has a miscarriage or delivers her baby prematurely. Furthermore, it is uncertain whether the injury referred to is injury to the woman or to the prematurely delivered baby. These uncertainties make it difficult to reconstruct what has happened with any confidence, which jeopardizes any attempt to derive a principle from the scenario.[8]

A third example concerns a prohibition that many choose (arbitrarily?) to ignore as irrelevant: the prohibition against having sexual relations with a menstruating woman (Lev 18:19). This stipulation is embedded within an extensive list of sexual offenses that

---

[8]Current use of this passage, however, goes yet another step beyond the extraction and application of a principle. Interpreters do not tend to argue over how this scenario can be transferred to other presumably similar scenarios. Instead, they try to draw principles about the status of the child—is the fetus considered a person under the law or not? The text has therefore been given a prominent role in modern discussions about abortion and even, by extension, fetal stem cell research. The difficulty of translation only adds to the problem of discerning what this passage does or does not say about the standing of the fetus.

most interpreters consider to be of the most serious sort (e.g., incest, bestiality). Dismissing it stands as an obvious case of special pleading since all the others are generally recognized as important moral absolutes. Here the problem of limits is the opposite of some of the other cases. Instead of failing to impose limits that would restrict illegitimate extensions, here the imposed limitations (of modern logic) relegate the stipulation to a place where it can be utterly neglected despite the fact that all the surrounding stipulations are taken seriously.[9]

In a final example, we want to contrast two categories of stipulations. Any reader of the Torah is aware that there are many passages that address how the Israelites should treat outsiders who live among them (the *gērîm*). It is common for interpreters who derive principles from Torah to reflect on Yahweh's obvious concern for outsiders. Even though this falls short of helping us formulate immigration policies, it is also used to determine how we should care for outsiders. The question, however, is not about whether God cares for outsiders or whether we should. In fact, other passages could be used to support a principle of exclusion of outsiders (Deut 23:3). The question is, what is the role of the Torah in giving God's authoritative word on the matter?

We can demonstrate the problem by turning to another example. Just as readers are aware of the stipulations concerning outsiders, most readers are aware of the stipulations concerning diet. Someone reading the stipulations literally could hardly avoid the conclusion that Yahweh cares about diet. If our methodology is going to be consistent (deriving principles from what God cares about), would we not have to conclude that if God cares about diet, we should too?[10] We cannot

---

[9]Following the same line of reasoning, Gane concludes that this prohibition should remain in place today. Gane, *Old Testament Law for Christians*, 358-61.

[10]Some would say that when the New Testament weighs in, we see that caring for outsiders continues to be of significance whereas diet does not. But this cannot be applied consistently as the criterion for distinguishing since the New Testament does not have the role

avoid subjectivity when we are picking and choosing according to some outside criterion. Inevitably, that outside criterion, rather than the biblical text, carries the authority.

These examples, and many others that could be identified, demonstrate the methodological flaw of applying the Torah through derived principles. The methodology is not and cannot be applied consistently. History testifies to this as early as the attempts of the Pharisees to engage in such a process—a procedure that Christians decry (the legalism of the Pharisees!) even as they employ similar methods in their own interpretations. The fundamental problem is that in this approach we end up putting ourselves in the position of authority with no clear way to determine limits concerning which principles can safely be extracted and how far they can be taken.

The preceding discussion and examples have demonstrated the problems with the methodology. Most importantly, however, the inherent problem in the derived-principles approach is that it fails to take account of the actual purpose of the Torah. Even if those methods did work according to their own internal logic, they would still be wrong. Throughout the book we have tried to demonstrate that the Torah is not provided for us to construct a contemporary system of legislation or morality. It did not serve in that role for Israel and certainly should not be given that role by us. It is not legislation, and it is contextually situated in three important ways that together prevent us from treating it as an authoritative repository for principles of behavior. Such treatment goes against the intended significance of the genre of the Torah.

We also have to recognize that the Bible (in both testaments) is more interested in order in the community of God's people than in

---

of evaluating each of the stipulations of the Torah (see proposition 15). The question of whether we can formulate a moral system from the teachings of Jesus and the Epistles— which is by no means clear in itself—is unrelated to the question of whether we can formulate a moral system from the Torah.

establishing personal ethics/morality, though that does not necessarily mean that our personal ethics are unimportant to God. Having laid the theoretical foundation in this chapter, we now need to turn our attention to how we can address the current issues of today by taking advantage of the Bible's revelation while trying to be aware of potential fallacies. This is the topic of the next proposition.

Torah Cannot Provide Prooftexts for Solving Issues Today

Although many Christians believe that the Law is obsolete, that we are no longer under the Law, and that the Law is impenetrable, and sometimes just silly, whenever a socioethical issue arises, they are quick to go to the Pentateuch to find the "biblical" position. It is probably not surprising that the position they find supported in the Bible just happens to be what they were inclined to think anyway. Too often, one feels that the biblical text has been used or even exploited in support of a personal or group agenda. Years ago Donald McCullough spoke about trivializing God and referred to this tendency as treating God as the "God of My Cause."[1] We decide what we want to believe and then dig around in the Bible to dredge up support so we can "take a stand on biblical authority." Too often the authority of the Bible is not well represented by extracting prooftexts, yet this is one of the major ways that Christians attempt to make the Torah relevant and to resolve controversial issues.

---

[1]Donald W. McCullough, *The Trivialization of God: The Dangerous Illusion of a Manageable Deity* (Colorado Springs, CO: NavPress, 1995).

In this chapter, we will briefly examine three of the fallacies that are common when trying to use the Torah as prooftexts to resolve issues. After presenting the fallacies and examples, the chapter will conclude by identifying why these fallacies in particular, and prooftexting in general, will not suffice as the means for applying the Torah to today or for resolving contemporary issues.

Imprecise Cultural Transfer

Tattoos have become more popular in recent years and increasingly mainstream, but it was not long ago that church people railed against tattoos as unbiblical. At that time, it was common for people to believe that only certain sorts of disreputable people were inclined to sport tattoos, so the church decided that Christians just did not do that sort of thing. They associated most tattoos with rebels or miscreants. In support of their opinion (inherently based on sociological factors), they would produce the evidence of Leviticus 19:28: "Do not cut your bodies for the dead or put tattoo marks on yourselves. I am the Lord."[2] Using the Torah in this way illegitimately assumes that tattoos in the ancient world (including the Bible) had the same associations that they have in contemporary society. This is an uninformed view and reflects the fallacy of reading something from the ancient cultural river as if it were addressing the same practice and understanding in our cultural river.

In the ancient Near East (ANE), the textual and iconographic evidence indicates that body marking (whether tattooing or piercing) was used as a mark of servitude.[3] In cases of forced servitude, this would have a negative connotation, perhaps comparable to the tattooed

---

[2]It should be noted that even the translation "tattoo marks" is uncertain since this word (qaʿaqaʿ) occurs only here in the biblical text. Without a broader usage, it is difficult to be certain whether we have captured the correct nuance of the word.

[3]Nili S. Fox, "Marked for Servitude: Mesopotamia and the Bible," in *A Common Cultural Heritage: Studies on Mesopotamia and the Biblical World in Honor of Barry L. Eichler*, ed. Grant Frame et al. (University Park, MD: CDL Press, 2011), 267-78.

numbers on the forearms of prisoners in Nazi concentration camps. More commonly, however, these marks were taken on voluntarily and represented an adopted identity (e.g., Is 44:5). Why then are they prohibited in Leviticus? Since in this context it is paired with the prohibition of lacerating oneself as a mourning practice, one possibility is that this marking of the skin was intended to protect one against the spirit of the dead.[4] Whether that explanation or any of the other possibilities that have been proposed is correct, it should be obvious that, regardless of our inability to confidently penetrate the ancient world's thinking, the prohibition relates to the norms of the ancient world regarding body marking. We have no reason to think that the practice in antiquity had the same purpose that it has today.

A second example can be found in the prohibition in Deuteronomy 22:5: "A woman must not wear men's clothing, nor a man wear women's clothing, for the LORD your God detests anyone who does this." In the mid-twentieth century, fundamentalist churches would use this passage to prohibit their female congregants from wearing pants of any sort. I (John) well recall visiting such a church in the 1970s and hearing the announcement that for the winter youth retreat (where sledding would be a main activity), the girls were permitted to wear slacks or jeans . . . under their skirts! Though this view regarding women wearing pants would be even rarer today, the passage is still often used as a prooftext to explicate the biblical view of cross-dressing, or transvestite practices, and then factored into a larger conversation about gender identity.

Again, however, we have to ask what this prohibition referred to in the ancient world. We cannot simply assume that it reflects the same social and moral values that are found in today's controversies. We have to begin by understanding the ancient cultural river and what this prohibition would mean there. This begins by asking about the

---

[4]John E. Hartley, *Leviticus*, Word Biblical Commentary 4 (Dallas: Word, 1992), 321.

significance of dress in the ancient cultural river and in what circumstances people might adopt the clothing of the opposite gender.[5] We
will recall that order is the highest value in the ancient world. Consequently, each person's behavior was expected to conform to the norms
of his or her identity, status, and role in society. Conformity was
valued, uniqueness or individualism was eschewed, and violation of
customary boundaries was repudiated. In this cultural context, gender
ambiguity was a violation of the first order.

Gendered dress is one means by which society defines and enforces
gender ideology. In and of itself, dress does not carry inherent meaning,
but its meaning is ascribed culturally. As a visible extension of the
body, its social message is understood by both the wearer and the
viewer. Thereby, dress, marked by clothes, ornaments, utensils, and
body modifications (hair, skin, etc.), functions as a text documenting
social and ethnic identity as well as gender roles and boundaries.[6]

We get a glimpse of these elements in play in the persona of the
Babylonian goddess Ishtar (who identifies closely with Sumerian
Inanna). As a goddess associated with both love and war, life and
death, she embodied polarities and paradox. She was a perpetual
virgin and a promiscuous prostitute as well as an adolescent yet se-
ductive woman of the world. She was often portrayed as androgynous,
personifying the disruption of order. One of the primary contexts in
which we find cross-dressing in the ancient world is in the context of
the Ishtar cult and its festivals.[7]

---

[5]Nili S. Fox, "Gender Transformation and Transgression: Contextualizing the Prohibition of
Cross-Dressing in Deut 22:5," in *Mishneh Todah: Studies in Deuteronomy and Its Cultural
Environment in Honor of Jeffrey H. Tigay*, ed. Nili S. Fox, David A. Gilad-Glatt, and Michael
J. Williams (Winona Lake, IN: Eisenbrauns, 2009), 49-71.

[6]Fox, "Gender Transformation and Transgression," 50. One only needs to recall the Disney
movie *Mulan*, in which a young woman passed herself off as a man, and all the societal
perspectives that action challenged.

[7]Rivkah Harris, "Inanna-Ishtar as Paradox and a Coincidence of Opposites," in *Gender and
Aging in Mesopotamia: The Gilgamesh Epic and Other Ancient Literature*, ed. Rivkah Harris
(Norman: University of Oklahoma Press, 2000), 158-71; L. M. Pryke, *Ishtar* (New York:
Routledge, 2017).

This is not to say that the Israelites were aware of the Ishtar cult (though they may have been) or were inclined to engage in its customs. It merely offers an example of one context in which cross-dressing was practiced in the ancient world. Based on this example and others that could be discussed,[8] we see that the practice of cross-dressing in the ancient world operated under different premises than it does in modern society. Most importantly, it is not demonstrably associated with homosexuality. Blurring of boundaries violates order, but that sense of order is inherent in the ideology of the society.

COINCIDENCE OF WORDING

Sometimes, while misunderstanding of culture may be involved when mining Scripture for prooftexts, the fallacy may lie in the words used in the translation and how their meanings have changed for us. A good example can be seen in the way Christians popularly interpret the third commandment. When a young person uses profanity, a parent may well admonish the child not to "take the name of the LORD . . . in vain" (Ex 20:7 KJV).[9] This prooftexting approach seems intuitive because we have come to associate taking the Lord's name in vain with profanity.

It is true that profanity in the modern world devalues God's name. Although profanity would likely be covered by the wording of the third commandment, that interpretation does not capture its focus. People in the ancient world, however, were less inclined to treat the name of a deity as powerless. They were more inclined to recognize its inherent power and attempt to wield it for their own benefit. This concern is the polar opposite of the way that the commandment is used today in prooftext.[10]

---

[8]Another proposal is based on the use of gender association in magical rituals. See Harry A. Hoffner, Jr. "Symbols for Masculinity and Femininity: Their Use in Ancient Near Eastern Sympathetic Magic Rituals," *JBL* 85, no. 3 (1966): 326-34.

[9]Of course, this is not the only application that is made from the third commandment. Prohibition of false oaths would be another.

[10]We will deal with the third commandment more extensively in the appendix when we treat the Decalogue in more detail.

INADEQUATE TRANSLATION

When the church desires to formulate policy on important social issues of the day, it is common for people to look to the Torah for guidance in understanding what they believe to be God's view of the matter. This is evident in the attempt by churches to decide how to respond to the growing trend of divorce and remarriage. The Torah has little to say about the issue, but the one passage that addresses it, Deuteronomy 24:1-4, is often given a central place in discussions:

> If a man marries a woman who becomes displeasing to him because he finds something indecent about her, and he writes her a certificate of divorce, gives it to her and sends her from his house, and if after she leaves his house she becomes the wife of another man, and her second husband dislikes her and writes her a certificate of divorce, gives it to her and sends her from his house, or if he dies, then her first husband, who divorced her, is not allowed to marry her again after she has been defiled. That would be detestable in the eyes of the LORD. Do not bring sin upon the land the LORD your God is giving you as an inheritance.

The key to this complex case is in the reasoning behind the ruling cited in Deuteronomy 24:4: "after she has been defiled." On this all translations are in virtual agreement, though it has been demonstrated to misrepresent the situation. The grammatical form of the verb "defiled" is the problem. All the translations render it as passive, "has been defiled," but the verb form is a passive reflexive and should be rendered by the admittedly complicated construction, "since she has been made to consider herself to be defiled."[11] We discover that it was the

---

[11]John H. Walton, "The Place of the *Hutqaṭṭēl* Within the D-stem Group and Its Implications in Deuteronomy 24:4," *Hebrew Studies* 32 (1991): 7-17. For a more accessible and nontechnical presentation see E. Carpenter, "Deuteronomy," in *The Zondervan Illustrated Bible Backgrounds Commentary*, ed. John H. Walton (Grand Rapids: Zondervan, 2009), 1:500, abridged in Craig S. Keener and John H. Walton, *NIV Cultural Backgrounds Study Bible* (Grand Rapids: Zondervan, 2016), 335. For commentary support, see Daniel I. Block,

initial divorce that caused her to consider herself defiled (not a divorce for moral turpitude, but for a physical condition) and was the act of an insensitive husband (demonstrated by the fact that a second husband was willing to marry her even though her condition had been made public). Finally, we note that the prohibition is not against the woman remarrying but specifically against the first husband marrying her again. She is not guilty of any violation; the first husband is prevented from preying on her vulnerability. Consequently, this case has nothing to offer in modern discussions of divorce and remarriage because it is constructed on the social realities of the ancient world, which are very unlike ours.

Both Deuteronomy 24:4 and the earlier example in Deuteronomy 22:5 include the comment that the proscribed behavior is detested by Yahweh (alternatively translated as an "abomination to the LORD"). Often it is this sort of statement alone that has been used as the basis for extending a prohibition universally. Such designations are often present in Leviticus and Deuteronomy and reflect the Hebrew word *tô'ēbâ*.[12] The term classifies an object or behavior as contrary to order. In some contexts, it may carry a visceral revulsion or a sense of disgust, but it does not necessarily do so. It is important to recognize that when something is contrary to order, even when it is contrary to order by Yahweh's perspective, that does not mean that the object or behavior so identified should be considered universally immoral, sinful, impure, or otherwise deficient or flawed. Something that was contrary to order in the view of the ancient world may not be contrary to order from our perspective and cannot necessarily be identified as inherently sinful behavior. Specifying that the order is Yahweh's, means that the order

---

Deuteronomy, NIV Application Commentary (Grand Rapids: Zondervan, 2012), 556-59.

[12]For extensive discussion of the word, see John H. Walton and J. Harvey Walton, *The Lost World of the Israelite Conquest: Covenant, Retribution, and the Fate of the Canaanites* (Downers Grove, IL: IVP Academic, 2017), 151-56; or John H. Walton, *Old Testament Theology for Christians: From Ancient Context to Enduring Belief* (Downers Grove, IL: InterVarsity Press, 2017), 175-79.

in question is Israel's covenant order, not intended for all of God's creation. We know this because the Torah is situated in the context of the covenant with Israel, and its purpose (inferred from its genre) is to define the nature of the covenant order.

These examples should not suggest to us that in these specific sorts of cases prooftexting is unacceptable but that in all others it is fine. In all these examples, and many others, the flaw lies in the inconsistent or uneven application of that methodology. For example, other passages in the same context and carrying the same weight and wording are ignored (e.g., the prohibition against weaving wool and linen together or the requirement to make tassels for the four corners of the cloak, Deut 22:11-12).

The inherent flaw in prooftexting goes beyond particular fallacies to the larger concept of misidentifying the Torah. The procedures by which we seek the relevance of the Torah must recognize what we have been observing about the Torah throughout this book. Decisions about the relevance and application of the Torah (as with any text of Scripture) must be made on the basis of the genre (in this case, wisdom insight rather than legislated commands), the context (written to Israel in the context of covenant and temple), the rhetorical strategy (how a section of literature functions within the larger work), the author's intention (what he intends the communication to accomplish— the expected response), and the backdrop of the cultural context (understood in relation to the ancient cultural river, not ours). Only by consistently maintaining these standards of interpretation and methodology can the authority of God's Word be appropriated to our modern contexts. Extracting prooftexts never gets us there.

The Ancient Israelites Would Not Have Understood the Torah as Providing Divine Moral Instruction

If the Torah cannot be divided so as to isolate a moral segment (see proposition sixteen), we must either conclude that its entire focus is moral in nature, which very few interpreters consider seriously, or that in the literary function of the Torah as a whole, morality is simply not its focus. We will maintain the latter and, as is our general procedure, will begin by getting a sense of the ancient Near Eastern (ANE) cultural river. We will begin with an examination of how ancient people thought about norms of behavior and whether those ideas have a divine foundation in the ANE. We will then be able to compare that to what we find in the Old Testament. This will help us to think about morality in an Old Testament context instead of letting the New Testament, Christian theology, or modern philosophical ideas drive the discussion.

THE ANCIENT NEAR EASTERN CULTURAL RIVER

Every culture has specific standards of acceptable behavior as well as some general conception of what people ought or ought not to do, no matter how much various cultures may disagree and regardless of how they have arrived at their understanding. To attempt to grasp the ways people thought in the ANE, we begin by assessing the ancient perception of what we call "morality" in light of kingship. This is not an intuitive association for moderns, but it represents well the ANE cultural river that was grounded in community identity. Morality in the ANE, to the extent that the idea existed, is communal in nature rather than individual. The king was the link between heaven and earth and established order in society. That order would result in content gods and people. Beate Pongratz-Leisten makes the observation that "any violation of the normative value system that occurs between individuals was considered to affect the entire collective and the divine world."[1] This corporate mentality is utterly foreign to those of us accustomed to a highly individualistic way of thinking. In the ANE, a well-ordered society, rather than a moral system of behavior, was the hallmark of civilized life. Despite having over a million cuneiform texts from which to work, we see little to suggest that morality as we think of it was a religious or even cultural virtue.[2] This is sufficient to warn us that we cannot simply assume that people in the ancient world thought about morality in the same ways that we do today.

---

[1] Beate Pongratz-Leisten, "Bad Kings in the Literary History of Mesopotamia and the Interface Between Law, Divination, and Religion," in *From Source to History: Studies on Ancient Near Eastern Worlds and Beyond*, ed. Salvatore Gaspa et al. (Münster: Ugarit-Verlag, 2014), 527-48 (quote from 527). This articulation is not unique to Pongratz-Leisten but is representative of the general sense among scholars specializing in the ANE. Other resources include classic seminal articles such as W. G. Lambert, "Morals in Ancient Mesopotamia," *JEOL* 15 (1957–1958): 184-96, and more recent treatments such as Karel van der Toorn, *Family Religion in Babylonia, Syria and Israel: Continuity and Change in the Forms of Religious Life* (Leiden: Brill, 1996); Giorgio Buccellati, "Ethics and Piety in the Ancient Near East," *CANE*, 3:1685-96; and Daniel C. Snell, "The Invention of the Individual," in *A Companion to the Ancient Near East*, ed. Daniel C. Snell (Oxford: Blackwell, 2005), 357-69. I have provided a more extensive though still summary discussion in John H. Walton, *Ancient Near Eastern Thought and the Old Testament: Introducing the Conceptual World of the Hebrew Bible*, 2nd ed. (Grand Rapids: Baker Academic, 2018), 115-27.

[2] Jean Bottéro, *Religion in Ancient Mesopotamia*, trans. Teresa Lavender Fagan (Chicago: University of Chicago Press, 2001), 169-70.

At the same time, we can observe that they took the need for proper behavior seriously. This is evident from a variety of texts, one of the most important being the *Shurpu* incantations:

> He us[ed] an untrue balance, (but) [did not us]e
>   [the true balance],
> he took money that was not due to him, (but) [did not ta]ke
>   mo[ney due to him],
> he disinherited the legitimated son (and) [did not est]ablish
>   (in his rights) the le[gitimate] son,
> he set up an untrue boundary, (but) did not set up
>   the [tr]ue bound[ary],
> he removed mark, frontier, and boundary.
> He entered his neighbor's house,
> had intercourse with his neighbor's wife,
> shed his neighbor's blood,
> put on [var.: took away] his neighbor's clothes,
> (and) did not clothe a young man when he was naked.
> He ousted a well-to-do young man from his family,
> scattered a gathered clan.
> His mouth is straight, (but) his heart is untrue,
> (when) his mouth (says) "yes," his heart (says) "no,"
> altogether he spoke untrue word.
> He who is . . . , shakes and trembles (of rage),
> destroys, expels, drives to flight,
> accuses and convicts, spreads gossip,
> wrongs, robs and incites to rob,
> sets his hand to evil.
> His mouth is . . . lying, his lips confused and violent,
> who knows improper things, has learned unseemly things,
> who has taken his stand with wickedness,
> transgressed the borderline of right,

committed things that are not proper,

set his hand to sorcery and witchcraft.

Because of the evil taboo he has eaten,

because of the many transgressions he committed,

because of the assembly he divided,

because of the tightly united company he dispersed,

because of all the contempt for the god and goddess,

because he promised in heart and by mouth but did not give,

omitted the name of his god in his incense offering,

made the purifications, (then) complained and withheld (it),

. . . , saved something (for the gods, but) ate it.

After he behaved arrogantly, he started to pray,

disarranged the altar that had been prepared,

made his god and his goddess angry with himself,

standing up in the assembly, said inadequate words.

He trampled in bloodshed,

he used to follow wherever blood was shed,

he a[te] what was taboo in his city,

he betrayed the affairs of his city,

he gave his city a bad reputation.[3]

The *Shurpu* incantation series was used as a remedy for misfortune that was considered the result of evil forces (human or demonic) at work. It was intended to provide an extensive list of possible offenses that might just happen to address an offense of which the gods actually considered the sufferer guilty (one could only guess). An offended god would be inclined to neglect a person, leaving that one vulnerable to evil forces. The ritual connected to these incantations was conducted by two specialized personnel: a priest and an incantation expert. The line items address activities that were viewed as potentially offensive to the gods. Both its incompleteness regarding moral categories and its

---

[3]Lines 42-97 of tablet II, translation by Pongratz-Leisten, "Bad Kings," 532-33.

inclusion of many behaviors that are not moral in nature indicate that morality is not its focus. The gods expected what we might call moral behavior only secondarily as part of a system of order or disorder (see proposition seven). Even a casual reader of this list will notice that, not unlike the Torah, it includes offenses against individuals, against the community, and against the gods. It is self-evident that they are not exclusively in the area that we would classify as ethical or moral.[4]

The important question, then, is not whether any of the listed behaviors can be construed as in the moral/ethical realm but whether the literature can be interpreted as intentionally addressing anything akin to what we call moral law. Moral law is generally considered a way to talk about rules people ought to obey (either in general[5] or by means of a specific list). Some believe that it derives from God, or perhaps from the character of God (divine law) while others believe it reflects a common sense of right behavior that is inherent in people or even more broadly in the operations of the world (natural law).[6] Some blend the two together.[7] These are the categories that result from ways of thinking that are anachronistic to the Torah. We cannot trust this later classification system to shed light on the ancient world.

The way of thinking that we have described in the ANE does not consider law to be divine.[8] The people of the ANE believed that the aspects of their society that comprised law (e.g., justice, wisdom) were

---

[4]Similar lists can be found in the Egyptian Book of the Dead, Spell 125, or in the negative confession of the Babylonian Akitu Festival.

[5]Avoid all harm, golden rule, and the like.

[6]J. Budziszewski defines "natural law" as "the foundational principles of right and wrong which are both right for all and at some level known to all." J. Budziszewski, *Natural Law for Lawyers* (Nashville: ACW Press, 2006), 21.

[7]Cf. C. Stephen Evans, *God and Moral Obligation* (Oxford: Oxford University Press, 2013). Christine Hayes, *What's Divine About Divine Law?: Early Perspectives* (Princeton: Princeton University Press, 2015), 88-89, defends the idea that the Stoics were the first to equate divine law to natural law.

[8]Here we are not referring to the literature found in the legal collections—we have already demonstrated that they are not legislative, and not law. We are referring to the more abstract category of law, however it is preserved in society.

woven into the fabric of the cosmos, but not by the gods. They are expressed by the Sumerian term ME, roughly translated "control attributes." Though these laws did not have their origins in the gods, they were thought to be administered by the gods through decrees.[9] In the ANE there was no special revelation (outside of the very limited answers to oracular questions in the divinatory practice of extispicy), and the gods did not legislate their will for society. The control attributes ranged across the boundaries of cosmos and society (as what we call natural law also does), and they could be perceived by gods, kings, and people (so, loosely corresponding to what we would call natural or general revelation). There is a coercive will of the king that is expressed in decrees, to be sure, but not in a formal body of legislation.

When we turn to Israel, however, Yahweh is positioned as the king, and like the kings in Mesopotamia he establishes order. Nevertheless, everyone in the ancient world understood that order was not maintained by following a rigid set of rules. Yahweh's combined role of God and King does not serve to equate his decrees (for order in the human world or loyalty of a vassal) with cosmic control attributes applicable to all people everywhere and apprehensible through general revelation as natural law. We should not conflate divine and royal functions simply because they are being performed by the same person.

In conclusion, we can now return to the claim made in the proposition. The designation "moral" would not be a fitting description since the Torah includes so much that cannot be associated with morality.[10] Literarily, then, the Torah must be considered to have a focus

---

[9]For extensive treatment of the ANE literature informing us about these, see John H. Walton, *Genesis 1 as Ancient Cosmology* (Winona Lake, IN: Eisenbrauns, 2011), 46-65, and the footnotes that lead to more technical treatments.

[10]Even Paul Copan, with whose overall view we have many disagreements, accepts this premise: "Mosaic legislation is not to be equated with the moral law. Laws are often a compromise between the ideal and the enforceable." Paul Copan, "Are Old Testament Laws Evil?," in *God Is Great, God Is Good: Why Believing in God Is Reasonable and Responsible*, ed. William Lane Craig and Chad Meister (Downers Grove, IL: InterVarsity Press, 2009), 134-54, quote on 149.

that is not moral in nature (though we undoubtedly could find material that overlaps with people's moral sensibilities). It includes divine instruction (as per the association with Wisdom previously established), and moral instruction would be appropriately involved, but no systematic or universal moral system is found there.

Israelites being faithful to Torah would mean maintaining a particular state of order in all aspects of their society. It would be characterized by what we call "moral behavior" suitable to their ancient world, their covenant relationship with God, and their responsibilities as hosts to the presence of God. But Torah only conveys that morality incidentally and partially. So, Torah is "divine"—it has a divine source. Torah is instruction—in the very nature of the word and in the Wisdom orientation of the material. But Torah cannot be considered moral because that is too restrictive a term to describe how it functions. Instead, the Torah is instruction, and the expected response is comprehension of the nature of the order it describes ("you will know") rather than a response of obedience to the specific rules it reportedly dictates ("you ought").

New Testament View of Torah as Divine Instruction

Based on the evidence we have presented concerning the Old Testament perspective, neither the Torah nor any segment of it should be considered moral law since (1) the Torah cannot be segmented if it is read in the context of either testament, (2) morality is not its focus, and (3) it is not legislative. It was not moral law for the Israelites and therefore cannot stand as moral law for us today (if we find the text's authority in its authors' intentions). Taking the Torah seriously in its Old Testament context eliminates the idea that we should read it as a moral treatise. As has been proposed in previous chapters (see propositions four and five), the Torah in its Old Testament context should be viewed as instruction for maintaining God's favor by reflecting his desired reputation through the order of the nation of

Israel, not legislation or rules for morality. However, we have also argued that the New Testament understands the Torah differently from the way the Old Testament does (see proposition fifteen). Therefore, it is theoretically possible that the Torah, as the Second Temple period understood it[11] (as opposed to the form that appears in the Old Testament), is being established by the New Testament as a basis for divine moral law going forward. This is worth some examination.

To begin the discussion, let's return to the story of Jesus and the rich young ruler. Jesus indicated that, in this case, for the young man to fulfill what Torah asked of him he should sell all that he had and give the proceeds to the poor. It has not been in the practice of the church to believe that Jesus was saying that all who want to take the Torah seriously should feel obliged to go and sell all that they have and give to the poor. That was an application to this young man's case. Such an idea is not explicitly stated in the Torah (either in the Hebrew Bible or in the Second Temple extrapolations from it), and though Jesus expressed it, it has not been picked up as a moral principle that all should follow. We therefore see that there is precedent for recognizing a relative aspect to the Torah and its application.

As we examine the remainder of Jesus' use of Torah, we find that he takes it seriously, that he draws application from it, and that he bases some of his teaching on it (notably the Sermon on the Mount, which literarily recapitulates Moses giving the Torah to Israel). Nevertheless, he does not attempt to build a moral system on it or derive a moral system from it. In the teaching of Jesus, Torah is to be fulfilled, not established as legislation. By that, Jesus means that he, as Israel's king (Messiah), fills the role of the faithful regent to the divine sovereign as Israel's previous kings did not. Because the regent is faithful and his people likewise follow him in faithful execution of order (now as the concept is understood in the Greco-Roman world, not according to

---

[11]Either as a concept in general or in those parts of it that the New Testament incorporates directly, i.e., commandments 5-9 in Luke 18:20.

the ANE anymore, as illustrated especially throughout the Epistles), God's favor is restored to the regent and his people, who are now represented by the church, the true remnant of Israel.

When Paul wants to encourage morality, he does not do so from the Torah. Instead, he builds a case from logic—both philosophical and theological (see Rom 2). Paul's approach to the question reflects the common way of thinking in the Greco-Roman world. The New Testament authors in general encourage Christians to be paragons of Greco-Roman order (explicitly in Titus 2:10). The early Christian apologists relied heavily on this idea as they argued that the Christians were exemplary citizens unjustly persecuted, and the book of Acts consistently represents Paul as a law-abiding Roman citizen in contrast to his unruly and pernicious accusers. But the specific behaviors that are advocated are all drawn from Greco-Roman cultural expectations, not from the details of the Torah. The objective of the New Testament instructions is the same as that of the Torah—preserve the ideal of order in one's own time—but it does indicate that even the New Testament authors did not see the Torah as the basis by which to define what ideal order in their time should consist of. Based on these observations, we would contend that the Torah in particular, and perhaps even the entire Bible in general, does not have the literary-theological purpose or function of revealing a moral system. As indicated above, the Old Testament does not use Torah that way, and we seek in vain for the New Testament to do so.

Proposition 22

A Divine Command Theory
of Ethics Does Not Require That
the Torah Is Moral Instruction

People who want to read the Torah as providing a moral system generally fall into two categories. The first want to take the Bible seriously and read the Torah as a list of moral rules because it does not occur to them that the Torah could be anything else. The second expect that the Bible must provide moral instruction of some kind and assume that the Torah is the place where it does so. The first group is concerned about what the Torah is and how to take it seriously; the second group is interested in the process by which moral truths are extracted from the Bible.[1] We have already argued that taking the Torah seriously in either testament does not entail reading it as moral instruction; that is not the function of the Torah, any more than it is instruction for an ideal diet or for ideal agricultural practice. We will now address the question of where we might find moral instruction if we cannot find it in the Torah.

It is understandable that people who take the Bible seriously want to draw from it guidance from God for living their lives as God would

---

[1]For an introduction to a variety of perspectives, see R. Keith Loftin, ed., *God and Morality: Four Views* (Downers Grove, IL: InterVarsity Press, 2012).

desire. It is no surprise then that people would include the Torah in God's directions and look to it as a guide for moral behavior. We have suggested that, in the context of the ancient Near East (ANE) and Israel's covenant, the Torah did not function that way for them, and it was not commended as the source of moral instruction by the New Testament either. But does it function that way for us?

Many Christians believe that if the Bible in general and the Torah in particular do not provide a moral system, they would not know where else to turn for moral guidance from God. They believe that any human moral system must derive from God because the "moral character" of God is the basis for our morality; that is, the reason why we ought to do certain things ultimately derives from the nature of God. If God has not communicated his moral commands and moral character, they fear that there could be no reliable moral foundation for life and society. In this book, I have been contending that the Torah does not present a moral system.[2] We must therefore examine whether we can alternatively discover God's moral commands without deriving them from the Torah.

The idea that a moral system must derive from the moral character of God is the converse corollary of the well-known moral argument for the existence of God. This argument states that if the concepts of right and wrong are to have any substantive meaning (that is, relate to something beyond the simple preferences of the person applying the label), then there must be a transcendent universal "ought" from which that meaning is derived. This universal ought is called the will of God or the moral character of God (from which his will is derived).[3]

---

[2]It is of passing interest that even divine command theory supporters do not suggest that all of morality or ethics can be traced to divine commands (of whatever sort they are). See C. Stephen Evans, *God and Moral Obligation* (Oxford: Oxford University Press, 2013), 88. This observation likewise argues against the idea that the Torah provides any sort of comprehensive moral system.

[3]"[A divine command theory of ethics] affirms that 'moral rightness and wrongness consist in agreement and disagreement, respectively, with the will or commands of a loving God.'" Paul Copan and Matthew Flannagan, *Did God Really Command Genocide? Coming to Terms*

Consequently, for any particular action or behavior to be properly called right or wrong, that action or behavior must be known to correspond to the will of God. Therefore, in order to be able to know what is right or wrong, God's will in these matters must have been made known to us somehow. This understanding of moral formation is called divine command theory by philosophers of ethics.[4] Many readers of the Torah and of the New Testament assume that the various imperatives contained therein are the basis by which God delivers his divine commands for the purpose of instructing us in how to behave according to his will. Patrick Miller, for example, indicates that the Decalogue belongs to the framework of divine command theory, though he hastens to add that that is just its starting point.[5]

The Decalogue, however, is no different from the rest of the Torah in this regard. The Decalogue is part of the Torah, but it does not have a different function from the rest of the Torah. Neither the Old nor the New Testament distinguishes it in such a way. Consequently, as with the rest of the Torah, we can recognize that the Decalogue may reflect moral sensibilities, some of which are universal or nearly so, but it is not intended to give voice to a moral system, nor can it stand as one.[6] It cannot be used to formulate a moral system, though we may recognize some moral principles in it that we value.

It is worth noting, however, that apologists and proponents of divine command theory do not always locate the knowledge of God's commands in the text of the Bible. Philosophers Paul Copan and

---

with the Justice of God (Grand Rapids: Baker Books, 2014), 148, citing Robert M. Adams, The Virtue of Faith and Other Essays in Philosophical Theology (New York: Oxford University Press, 1987), 145.

[4]Divine command theory that includes both special and general revelation is defended in Evans, God and Moral Obligation. He assumes that Scripture contains such divine commands without defending that idea based on discussions of genre or speech-act theory.

[5]Patrick D. Miller, The Ten Commandments (Louisville, KY: Westminster John Knox, 2009), 415-23. He also sees the significance of the Decalogue as an ethic of correlation, particularly reflecting a grounding in the imitatio Dei, 426-27.

[6]For more detailed discussion of the Decalogue, see the appendix of this book.

Matthew Flannagan, for example, present a case for a moral system based on divine commands without referencing the Bible at all:

> A divine command theory is not the claim that morality is based on knowledge of, or belief in, commands revealed in a sacred text such as the Bible, Torah, or Qur'an. While most divine command theorists accept that God has revealed his commands through a sacred text, this is due to other theological commitments they have, independent of belief in a divine command theory. A divine command theorist could argue that, in principle, the rightness or wrongness of an action is identical to and constituted by God's commands and prohibitions but that we know what is right and wrong through our conscience and not from any purported written revelation like the Bible.[7]

In *Mere Christianity* C. S. Lewis argues for a natural intuition of right and wrong without coming within "a hundred miles of the God of Christian theology": "All I have got to is a Something which is directing the universe, and which appears in me as a law urging me to do right and making me feel responsible and uncomfortable when I do wrong."[8] As we have already noted, Paul himself argues in Romans 2 that right and wrong can be known from nature. Thus it is clearly possible to derive a coherent and functioning moral system, even a moral system based on conformity to the will and commands of God, without specific reference to the text of Scripture. This in turn allows us the freedom to examine whether the text of Scripture might be concerned with something else, with no danger of compromising the integrity of a system of divinely inspired morality.

A derivative of divine command theory, which states that right and wrong are defined in general by conformity to the will of God, is a moral system called *imitatio Dei*. In this system right and wrong are

---

[7]Copan and Flannagan, *Did God Really Command Genocide?*, 153-54.
[8]C. S. Lewis, *Mere Christianity*, near the end of chap. 4.

defined not as following a list of divine demands but as doing what God does, or perhaps more accurately doing what God would do in your particular circumstance. The point is for readers to manifest the same moral character as God so that they will choose to do the same things that God would choose to do. This in turn requires a more detailed understanding of what God would or would not do than can be deduced abstractly, thus requiring God to reveal not a list of demands but a depiction of himself so that people will know what they are supposed to imitate. This concept, when drawn from the Old Testament, is usually based on Leviticus 19:2, which is taken as a divine injunction to pursue holiness, and that holiness is equated with morality. These ideas call for careful consideration.

At issue in this discussion is the questionable assumption that God's people are called to be holy and that they are thereby called to be moral as God is moral. This reflects flawed thinking on several counts. Since God's people are not called upon to be holy (instead they are declared to be holy), we cannot base a putative call to morality on the equation of holiness and morality. The English word *moral* does not match the semantic range of Hebrew *qdš*; a closer English semantic equivalent to *qdš* is *divine*.[9] We might note that the vast majority of holy things—such as objects (the temple articles), places (Mount Sinai, Jerusalem), geopolitical abstractions (the land, the nation), or time (the Sabbath)—have no moral agency. When a thing becomes holy, whether that thing is the abstract community of Israel (which is what is addressed in Lev 19, not each Israelite individually) or an object like the ark or the sanctuary, that thing is or does in some way identify something about what God is or does. As we discussed in detail in proposition seven, for the nation of Israel to be holy means that Yahweh will identify—that is, reveal—himself through his interaction with them. If Israel is faithful to the covenant, that interaction will be

---

[9]See previous detailed discussion in proposition seven.

characterized by favor and blessing; if not, the interaction will be characterized by curses and calamity. This is what the text means when Israel is offered the choice between "life and prosperity" and between "death and destruction" in Deuteronomy 30. But whichever choice they make, they are still holy; that is, God's identity is still being defined through his treatment of them.

Moving to the New Testament, we note that 1 Peter 1:15 is an exhortation to a particular kind of behavior, as opposed to a declaration of a conferred status: "But just as he who called you is holy, so be holy in all you do." But the word used here for "be" (*ginesthe*) is not the same word that the Septuagint uses in Leviticus 19:2 (*esesthe*).[10] Based partly on a paradigm shift in the cultural conception of the metaphysics of the divine, the Greek word *hagios* (holy) does not mean the same thing as the Hebrew word *qdš* (holy). Also, as discussed in proposition fifteen, in the interpretive tradition of the Second Temple period, *Torah* is understood differently by the New Testament audience than it would have been by the original Israelite audience to whom it was written. Peter is invoking a contemporary (first century) understanding of what holiness means (*hagios* means "dedicated to God")[11] and what Torah is for (divine legislation) to exhort the audience of his epistle to a particular kind of behavior. Perhaps the exhortation also

---

[10]The LXX form is future indicative of *eimi*, "to be"; the form in 1 Peter 1:15 is present imperative of *ginomai*, "to come into being." The use of *ginesthe* again in 1 Peter 1:16 (the quote from Leviticus) is a common variant, although *esesthe* is better attested. However, *esesthe* cannot be translated as an imperative. See John H. Walton and J. Harvey Walton, *The Lost World of the Israelite Conquest: Covenant, Retribution, and the Fate of the Canaanites* (Downers Grove, IL: IVP Academic, 2017), 108n9.

[11]In the LXX *hagios* translates *qdš*, but that decision represents an interpretive choice of the translators. The concept of divinity represented by the divine constellation cannot be accurately conveyed within the categories of Greek metaphysics; see Michael B. Hundley, "Here a God, There a God: An Examination of the Divine in Ancient Mesopotamia," *AoF* 40 (2013): 68-107; and Barbara N. Porter, "Blessings from a Crown, Offerings to a Drum: Were There Non-Anthropomorphic Deities in Ancient Mesopotamia?," in *What Is a God?: Anthropomorphic and Non-Anthropomorphic Aspects of Deity in Ancient Mesopotamia*, ed. Barbara N. Porter (Winona Lake, IN: Eisenbrauns, 2009) 153-94. *Qdš* means "divine"; a closer Greek semantic equivalent would be *theios* (e.g., Acts 17:29; 2 Pet 1:3-4).

applies to all Christians beyond the original audience of Peter's letter, but that is beyond the scope of this study. For our purposes, Peter's appropriation of a quote from Leviticus does not constitute a demand for all Christians to read Leviticus as a guide to the particulars of moral behavior. Peter is referencing the Septuagint for his own purposes, not telling his audience (ancient or modern) how Leviticus ought to be read or what the text of Leviticus meant in context.

As we extend these concepts beyond the scope of Israel, it is probably not unreasonable to maintain that God's people have been given an identity with God and that it is our responsibility to honor God as we reflect him in our lives. Moral behavior would unquestionably be part of that, but only a part. The basis of this claim, however,

ON OBJECTIVE MORALITY

The concept of objective morality can be defined in a couple of different ways. A moral system could be designated objective if it finds its source outside of humanity (e.g., divine command theory). Another possible definition allows that such a system could be considered "objective" if it attempted to derive its components objectively (i.e., from "pure reason") rather than subjectively.

In either case, if someone believes that there is objective morality, they have to determine where to get it. Given the approach that we have taken in this book, one could not derive objective morality from Torah because it does not provide a full moral system. If we have to pick and choose which components to use, it is not objective. Furthermore, a moral system cannot be derived from God's revelation of his character because not enough of God's character is revealed for us to derive a full morality. Even the glimpses of moral insight that the text does contain do not carry the authority of God because authority is tied to context and the context of the insights is not to define a moral

system. Finally, the problem with deriving morality from nature/conscience is that such an approach leaves too many gaps and ambiguities; the observers of nature and experiencers of conscience are themselves human, and so their insights cannot really claim to transcend humanity. In the end we have to pick and choose which human insights about nature or which human experiences of conscience will guide our moral conclusions, and which will not.

Morality may well find anchors in all these sources, but none is complete and our use of each is selective, so no objectivity. An objective moral system based on the Bible is simply impossible to produce. Whether an objective moral system based on something else can be produced is a question for philosophers, not exegetes. However, even if someone were to conclude that there is no objective morality (as defined above), that is not the same as saying there is no morality, that right and wrong have no meaning. Of course there is morality, but if it does not have an identifiable source outside of humanity from which it can be objectively

would not be a universal revelation of the character of God in the Torah but rather an idea derived from the New Testament's own context (i.e., the idiom "in Christ" as a declaration of identity) and the assumption of thematic recapitulation in the parallel portrayals of the church and Israel (see proposition twenty-three). Most importantly, however, this observation in itself does not help us to ascribe a particular shape to moral behavior, let alone the shape that is described in the Torah. Morality may well comprise some universal absolutes (i.e., do not steal), but it is also defined by norms that are culturally relative (i.e., do not run around naked in public). But our knowledge of the particular shape of the universal (or situationally relevant) constituents of moral behavior need not be assumed to come directly

derived, we have to come at the question from a different direction.

Regardless of where right and wrong come from, no one is free to make an individual morality. Morality is a function of communities, not individuals. Every community desires order, and morality entails establishing behavior, customs, and traditions as well as social norms and taboos that preserve order.

We do have moral obligations, and we have no reason to think they are not grounded in God. Moral obligation may depend on God ontologically whether or not someone believes in God and whether or not morality can be objectively determined. Some suggest that God can be considered a moral authority without believing that we can objectively determine the shape of morality.[a]

Given this ontological understanding, we could say that there is no uniquely Christian morality, any more than there is a uniquely Christian cosmic geography, and for the same reasons (addressed below and in proposition nineteen). Whether morality is objective or subjective, morality is a part of reality, just like

the structures and arrangement of the cosmos are part of reality. A Christian who happens to be a physicist can examine the structures of the cosmos and understand how they work, or perhaps even correct the consensus. Likewise, a Christian who happens to be an ethicist can examine morality and understand how it works, or perhaps correct the consensus. But in neither case will anything in the Bible or any work of the Spirit (except perhaps subliminally) help them to do so. Our particular morality is a product of our cognitive environment, just as our particular physical cosmology also is; it represents something we have to work within, not something we have to create. The task of the church is not to determine rightness and wrongness; the task of the church is to make disciples, which it can only do by both maintaining the integrity of its identity (regardless of what the culture thinks is right or wrong) and by being careful not to make itself unnecessarily offensive to the surrounding culture (that is, in light of what a particular culture thinks is right and wrong).

[a]Evans, *God and Moral Obligation*, 2, 21.

from the text of the Bible, though divine command theory admits the possibility that God's commands can be known from general revelation, and neither the Old Testament nor the New Testament teaches that it should come from the Torah.

Some will respond that by contending that the Torah is not establishing morality or legislation for us today, we are diminishing the Old Testament and negating its relevance. Nothing can be further from the truth. Trying to identify the precise function of the Torah makes it more significant to us, not less important and relevant. By denying it one role, we are in a position to give it a different role, one that we contend is more important. Indeed, when we read it for the kind of literature it is, we will inevitably recover a more significant role for it. We are certainly not saying that the Torah has no significance for Christians today—only that it does not have the sort of significance that many try to give it. To give it a significance that is not in line with the character of the literature is not a way to honor it as God's Word. We have to understand the Torah according to the revelation it provides, to which we now turn our attention.

Taking the Torah Seriously Means Understanding What It Was Written to Say, Not Converting It into Moral Law

As might be anticipated, most Christians approach the issue of Torah through a New Testament perspective.[1] Despite the variety of positions taken, the centrality of morality as the focus of the Law (*nomos*) in the Second Temple period is something that most studies agree on. It is not the purpose of this study to examine whether the New Testament as a whole is intended to provide moral instruction or the basis for constructing a moral system. Instead, we have been exploring the

---

[1]An array of positions from this vantage point has been presented in Wayne G. Strickland, ed., *Five Views on Law and Gospel* (Grand Rapids: Zondervan, 1996). Many books and articles deal with these questions, and trying to delve into all the philosophical discussions concerning moral theology would quickly drive us well beyond the scope of this book. The following sources are only a few of the wide variety that we have consulted: David Baggett and Jerry L. Walls, *God and Cosmos: Moral Truth and Human Meaning* (Oxford: Oxford University Press, 2016); J. Budziszewski, *Natural Law for Lawyers* (Nashville: ACW Press, 2006); Christine Hayes, *What's Divine About Divine Law?: Early Perspectives* (Princeton: Princeton University Press, 2015); James W. Thompson, *Moral Formation According to Paul: The Context and Coherence of Pauline Ethics* (Grand Rapids: Baker Academic, 2011); and James M. Todd III, *Sinai and the Saints: Reading Old Covenant Laws for the New Covenant Community* (Downers Grove, IL: IVP Academic, 2017).

question of whether the New Testament teaches that the Torah is sup-posed to be used as moral instruction, such that taking the New Tes-tament seriously might dictate how we are to use the Torah regardless of what it meant in its own context. Most interpreters assume that this is indeed what we are supposed to do, and these assumptions define how people think about the relevance of the Law for us today. However, we argued in proposition fifteen that Paul's teaching on the Torah does not include a declaration that it should be used for moral formation. Further, we argued that when Peter references Leviticus, he does not do so as part of an instruction on how Torah ought to be used. Finally, we argued that assumptions about how the Old Testament was sup-posed to be used by the interpreters in the Second Temple period (including the New Testament authors) are not normative for inter-preters today. Thus the question of moral instruction in the New Tes-tament is essentially a purely New Testament discussion, with no real consideration from the Old Testament in context at all.

We have discussed issues related to the use of biblical material in general for the formulation of a moral system through principles in proposition nineteen and concluded that, in all these positions, as-sumptions about morality and moral formation have dictated how the Torah should be read. None of them bases either the conclusion that the Torah ought to be read as moral instruction or even the particulars of what the instructions actually consist of on a contextual exami-nation of the Torah itself.

Thus the desire to take the teaching of the Bible seriously, whether the Old Testament or the New, does not entail an obligation to read the Torah, even the Decalogue, as moral instruction. Whether a com-plete and coherent formulation of an applied system of morality can be constructed from the Bible without appealing to the Torah as moral instruction is a different issue that can only be addressed within a discussion of how a biblical moral system ought to be formed and a contextual examination of whatever the resulting supporting texts happen to be. However, since reading the Torah seriously does not entail using it as the basis for a moral system, we must consider the possibility that those who try to use it as the basis for a moral system are, in fact, the ones who are not taking the text seriously.

Alternatively, some Christians see in the Torah a reflection of the "moral character of God" that itself should stand as our guide to behavior. The idea of God having "moral character" can stand heuristically even though theologians and philosophers will raise technical objections; that is not the subject of this study. However, since God's character is only revealed to us in scattered glimpses (not comprehensively, in the Torah or even in the biographies of Jesus), we cannot know the character of God fully. Given this lack of full disclosure, we are not sufficiently informed to define morality based on our understanding of his character.

Our sense of how we ought to conduct ourselves cannot come fully from the revealed character of God, though if anything is revealed of his character, it may be an important consideration for our conduct (e.g., 1 Cor 11:1). Our understanding of God's character also cannot come fully from abstract laws of nature, though Paul insists that nature is sufficient to give us insight into some of the qualities of God (Rom 1:20, though Paul mentions nothing of divine character there). Third, our sense of what we ought to do cannot be fully derived from social convention and traditional customs. Such an approach would find no moorings outside of our own fallen sensibilities. The widely recognized shortcomings of these three approaches have led to the fourth approach: developing our sense of what we ought to do from commands delivered through special revelation. However, if this approach is to be distinct from the other three, it must locate those commands entirely within the context in which they supposedly appear, both in identifying them as commands and in describing their content. We have demonstrated that, in the case of the Torah, this cannot be done. Both Torah and the New Testament writings can perhaps inform our

THE LOST WORLD OF THE TORAH—PART 5

moral sensibilities, but they do not stand as a comprehensive system or provide an authoritative source for determining all behavior. Their purpose is not to dictate God's demands for our conduct but to let us know what God is doing—what his plans and purposes are—so that we can choose whether we want to participate or suffer from not participating as its own consequence. Participation may perhaps entail some particular behavior, but that would have to be determined based on what those plans and purposes are, which is not the subject of this study. Israel chose to participate by accepting the covenant (Ex 24), but once they did so no further action was required of them for God to reveal himself through them; their actions determined only the consequences of those actions (blessings or curses). Whether under the New Covenant we choose to participate once and for all (as Israel did), and thereafter only suffer consequences based on that status, or our participation is dictated moment by moment by behavior is beyond the scope of this study.

In conclusion, we cannot reconstruct a moral system from the Torah or any part of it (e.g., the Decalogue or the Holiness Code, Lev 18–20) because that is not what it is designed to do. Christians and non-Christians are interested in morality for the same reasons; culture and society demand conformity to whatever set of values it has decided to prefer (though non-Christians will often be interested in morality without any concern for God's plans and purposes). Christians cannot use knowledge of God's purposes to create an ideal morality to impose on their own environment. They use that knowledge to know where (and how) to conform or deviate from what the society created, based on whether the particular actions are harmful ("everything is lawful, not everything is beneficial," 1 Cor 6:12; 10:23; harm can come either inherently, as when we eat too much and get fat, or as a consequence of a status given by God, as when Israel's holy status subjected them to the covenant curses) or they are useful for their participation in God's purpose (assuming behavior dictates participation).

Paul's treatment of Law is customized to the perspectives and issues of his day. He is not interacting with Torah as it was understood and used in the Old Testament. He is not giving a universalistic understanding of law that comments on the Torah in the Old Testament Covenant. He is debating the role of divine law and natural law as it should be understood within his contemporary context. Whether the Epistles themselves can provide any basis for moral instruction applicable outside of a Hellenistic context would have to be determined by a close examination of those texts in context and is a topic for separate discussion, but it has nothing to do with the Torah (as understood in either testament) and is beyond the scope of this study. For our purposes, we can claim that it is possible to have moral knowledge, even moral knowledge that has its source in God, without needing to get it from the Torah, or even from special revelation of any kind, including the New Testament (see proposition fifteen).

This does not mean that the Torah does not contain any principles that can be valuable to us, but its authoritative role is not to consistently provide those point by point. In this way, it is comparable to what has already been acknowledged concerning the narrative literature. Any narrative, whether Scripture or not, can potentially provide instructive role models (note the discussion of Joseph in proposition nineteen). We have to ask, however, whether the authoritative intention of the text is to provide such models. We have contended that it is not. Such models are at times instructive, but incidental. The same is true of the Torah. Inevitably, we will be able to identify wise insight in some of the principles of behavior that are inherent in the Torah's stipulations, but the same could be said of Hammurabi's collection. We have to ask, what makes it Scripture? For this, we need to understand the goal of the genre and its literature. What is the appropriate response to the Torah—for the Israelites or for us? If it is not provided to derive principles that can be applied to other aspects of life, what is it?

We have already laid the groundwork to give us direction in addressing this question. We have built a case to suggest that the Torah provides Israel wisdom for establishing order that upholds the reputation of Yahweh, their king and their God, and thereby secures his favor in the form of continuing presence and blessing. This is far different from the idea that it provides principles or rules for morality. As we have proposed, Yahweh's revelation to Israel was not to provide legislation, an ideal social system, or a moral system.

If the Torah is to be read as originating from God, it needs to be read in its proper context, which includes its genre. One of the reasons why we conclude that the Torah is not legislation is because it is not comprehensive enough to stand in that capacity. Likewise, the scope of its moral teaching is also not comprehensive enough to cover all that would be necessary to formulate a complete moral system. Because of this limited coverage, trying to construct a moral system from the teachings of the Torah (or even from the New Testament, which is not comprehensive either) is like trying to build a skyscraper out of seven two-by-fours and a pot of glue. It simply cannot be done. Any real analysis of the nature of the skyscraper would have to focus on the steel, concrete, and glass that the building is actually made of, not the wood and glue. It does not matter if the two-by-fours are exceptionally high quality (treated mahogany) or incorporated into the structure so that they can be pointed out to visitors; a claim that the building is made of—or even founded on—wood and glue is simply nonsensical, especially if you did not use any of the glue. Likewise, we might note that some of the moral advice in the Torah is good advice (i.e., parts of the Decalogue), and we might be able to point out how this advice has been incorporated into the moral system we happen to have. But if we want to have any real analysis of our moral system, we need to pay more attention to the things it is actually composed of, which is not the Torah, and mostly derives from our cultural river. Claiming that this moral system is derived from or based on the Torah is likewise nonsensical, especially since we do not even use most of the contents of the Torah in that system.

We should not expect the Torah to apply to us directly because the two covenants do different things. Some interpreters treat the Old Testament as passé, a failed system that God has replaced and is therefore no longer relevant to us. That is not the position that we are advocating. Yet it is a mistake in the opposite direction to think that God is doing the same thing in both testaments with the result that we merge them to extrapolate how he might communicate with us today. Such an approach makes one of the testaments redundant and distorts both of them by obliterating their respective cultural contexts and theological focuses.

We believe that the Torah also provides revelation for Christians today. As we have noted, however, since the Torah is situated in the ancient world, in the covenant with Israel, and in the context of sacred space, the revelation that we receive (we could call it the canonical revelation) takes on a different focus. The purpose of the Torah was to give Israel—and through them, the nations—an understanding of their God. If we want to understand the value of the Torah today, we might ask what our understanding of God would be if we did not have it. Imagine what Moses might have thought if confronted by Jesus and the New Testament writers in the second millennium BC. Without any further resources, he would have assumed that the God Jesus was claiming to be was more or less the same as the gods he knew from his culture—self-interested and exploitative, expecting Israel to provide for his needs but willing to offer benefits in exchange.[2] We can see this kind of thinking in reaction to Jesus by people who do

---

[2]It is worth noting that when God does appear to Moses, and also to Abram before him, both without the context of the Torah, he does not present them with demands but simply makes them an offer: land and nation to Abram, deliverance from Egypt to Moses. There is no reason to think that the religion of the Patriarchs would not have been essentially symbiotic; Abram builds altars for a reason, and Moses tells Pharaoh that he wants to take the people to make sacrifices to their God.

not have the Torah even in the Greco-Roman world (where the Great Symbiosis also defines divine-human relations in certain ways). The Gentiles of the Decapolis believed that Jesus was at least a prophet of some kind, and their reaction was to beg him to go away (Mt 8:34; Mk 5:17; Lk 8:37). Roman gods, like ancient Near Eastern (ANE) gods, could grant blessings and favors, but they were petty and demanding, and their attention was as likely as not to result in calamity when the humans under scrutiny failed to live up to expectations. Consider how we tend to think of the government today; we enjoy the infra-structure and security that government provides, but we do not want the police looking over our shoulders. Similarly, when the people of Lystra think that Paul and Barnabas are Hermes and Zeus, their im-mediate reaction is to rush to pamper them (Acts 14:13). This is the reasonable and natural reaction to the presence of gods; fall over yourselves to try to keep them happy so at the very least they will refrain from smiting you.

Without the establishment of a particular divine-human relationship in the Torah—one based on loyalty to a suzerain rather than codepen-dence—the natural reaction to the moral instruction of the New Tes-tament is to psychologize the Great Symbiosis. This means we would imagine that God requires specific actions on our part to meet his emo-tional and psychological needs—that we are expected to make God happy by satisfying his craving for worship and moral punctiliousness—and that failure to do so will bring horrendous consequences. Indeed, a great many Christians today, having neglected the Torah or failed to understand it, believe exactly this, usually justified by a misinterpre-tation of Hosea 6:6. At the same time, however, the value of the Torah is not primarily to convey the theological fact that the God of Israel has no needs. Many worldviews already believe that God or the gods have no needs, but the Torah has value for them as well. The primary value for the Torah outside of the original context of covenant Israel is the role it plays in helping us make sense of the New Testament.

The Torah was not written to provide the Israelites trivia about God (e.g., the fact that he has no needs), and the New Testament was not written to provide trivia about God either. Making sense of the New Testament does not entail extracting theological facts. The New Testament contains very little in the way of theological facts such as we might find in a dogmatic treatise or a textbook. Its description of what God is like—specifically, what God is doing in and through the New Covenant—is presented in a manner that is more illustrative than didactic and is based on parallels to the history of Israel. The details used to establish the parallelism are not important, but it is crucially important for us to understand the fact of the parallel itself. The details present in the New Testament are (necessarily) drawn from what the Second Temple authors and audiences believed about the history of Israel; this is the only way communication is possible. However, there is a reason why the Christian Scripture contains the original Hebrew Scriptures and not any of the Second Temple translations or expositions of it, such as Targum, Midrash, or Septuagint, or any of the supplementary documents (e.g., Enoch or Jubilees) that provided alternative or expanded interpretations. All these sources (to varying degrees) are highly speculative and represent significant distortions of the original material (even accounting for varying document traditions apart from the Masoretic text). Because these sources do not faithfully represent the Scriptures and are not Scripture themselves, there is no basis for assuming that what they teach about God is accurate, any more than the Roman poets or Greek philosophers would be (though all of these served as inspiration for later theologians). Not all the Old Testament references in the New Testament establish parallels, but when a study of the New Testament text in context determines that it is intending to say "this recapitulates something that was done in/by/to/through Israel," we have to look at the original to understand what the recapitulation is supposed to mean, even if that is different from what the New Testament author would have thought.

This is what it means for a Christian theologian to treat both testaments as Scripture; we do not consider the Hebrew Bible to be merely a background supplement to the New Testament, and we do not consider the Christian Scriptures to consist of the New Testament and the Septuagint (as opposed to the Hebrew text). But that in turn means that if we want to understand New Testament recapitulations, we have to first understand what the original was, and we have to understand it in its capacity as Scripture and therefore in its own context. Thus, the intention of the Torah is the same for us that it was for ancient Israel; we are to understand what it is saying and what God is doing through it. Israel was supposed to understand so they could know how to retain God's favor; we today are supposed to understand so that we know how to make sense of the New Testament, the church, and our present lives and circumstances.

For example, most scholars agree, based on a variety of indicators, that the Sermon on the Mount in Matthew 5 is intended to recapitulate Moses giving the Torah to Israel. However, the content of the sermon is notably different from the content of the Torah. Jesus has little to say about such things as goring oxen, tassels on clothing, or instructions for wave offerings. The literary recapitulation combined with the divergent content leads many interpreters to argue that Jesus is overwriting the Torah in its entirety (supported by the series of "you have heard . . . but I tell you" statements, e.g., Mt 5:27-28), or at least redacting it such that only the "moral" category of stipulations remains relevant, even if their content is not repeated in the sermon itself (usually supported by a misinterpretation of Mt 6:6-8). This is not how canonical theology is supposed to be done. Neither of these approaches entails treating the entirety of the Torah as Scripture in its own right with a message to convey and incorporating that message into our theological conclusions.

The Sermon on the Mount consists of a sequence of moral commands delivered with the authority of God. However, that does not mean that Matthew (or Jesus) is teaching that the Torah was always a list of moral commands, or that only the moral commands remain relevant. We recall that in the Second Temple period the Torah was, in fact, considered to be a list of moral commands, as evidenced by the use of the word *nomos* in the Septuagint (see proposition fifteen). This means that a recapitulation of the giving of Torah, in order to be meaningful, would have to consist of moral commands; otherwise the connection would be lost. For example, if someone today wanted to recapitulate the start of the Reformation, they would have to take a giant hammer to a church and nail a statement of protest to the door because that is how we imagine that the Reformation began. It would not have the proper effect if they tacked an advertisement for a seminar on controversial topics up on the school bulletin board, even though that would more closely replicate what Martin Luther actually did.[3] The observation that the statements in the sermon were moral commands for their primary audience (the crowd listening to Jesus) may not actually serve any purpose beyond establishing the literary recapitulation. After all, the ritual instructions contained in the Torah really were instructions for their primary audience (the priests), but the literary use of the material by the compilers of the Pentateuch, which in turn grants their status as Scripture, has changed their genre such that they no longer carry an imperative of mandatory worship procedure for the audience of the book of Leviticus. (The literary intention of the Sermon on the Mount for the audience of Matthew's Gospel would require a detailed study of Matthew and is beyond the scope of this study.)

Because of the shift in the cognitive environment between the testaments, we would not expect New Testament recapitulations to replicate their Old Testament precursors in either form or content. Instead, in order to treat the recapitulation as theologically meaningful,

---

[3]Iain Provan, *The Reformation and the Right Reading of Scripture* (Waco, TX: Baylor University Press, 2017), 4.

we should expect a replication of function. The Sermon on the Mount is not a treaty and does not duplicate the instructions of the Torah. However, because it recapitulates the Torah, we should expect the literary purpose of the sermon in the Gospel of Matthew to be similar to the literary purpose of the Torah in the documents of the Pentateuch. In other words, we should expect the sermon to contain an aspective description of the kind of order that should define the kingdom of God under the New Covenant—which, because the New Covenant works differently from the covenant with Israel, will probably be different, thus explaining the need for new revelation. How exactly the sermon defines the order of the New Covenant would require an examination of the principles of the individual statements. A tentative guess might be the principle of the inversion of common sense, which is consistent throughout the sermon and is also a recurring theme throughout the New Testament (the first is the last, the least is the greatest, joy comes through suffering, and so on). The point is that doing canonical theology in this way respects both the context and setting of the New Testament material (as a literary allusion or recapitulation) as well as the context of the setting of the original on which it is dependent (God's revelation of himself to Israel) and thus respects both of them as Scripture as opposed to simply overwriting or censoring one with the other.

The Israelite community was chosen to participate in Yahweh's plans and purposes in many ways. Among the most important of these roles was to be a medium of revelation and to serve as hosts to the presence of Yahweh. In these roles they also served as a light to the nations. Being a light to the nations did not call on them to go to the nations to evangelize them or draw them into the covenant relationship. Instead, the nations would see what Yahweh had done in Israel and give honor to his name. The New Covenant has a different purpose. God is no longer using his people to establish a reputation for himself. That was done through Israel and does not need to be done again, which is why the

Old Testament has been preserved as Scripture. But God has other plans and other purposes now. Just as he was carrying out his plans and purposes through Israel, he is now carrying them out through the church.[4]

The Torah is not infinitely pliable. It cannot be productively carried over into any other cognitive environment—not the Greco-Roman world, not the world of medieval France, not the Byzantine world, not the world of nineteenth-century Tibet, and not our postmodern twenty-first century. Yet, at the same time, it cannot simply be set aside as no longer relevant. If we give up the Old Testament, whether by judging it as irrelevant or by making it into something that it is not and was never intended to be, we have given up a significant portion of God's revelation to us. And we must remember that this Old Testament revelation was the only Scripture that Jesus and the New Testament authors knew. We would be rejecting the divine testimony that narrates the way God has worked in the past to unfold his plans and purposes for the world. Through his story we come to know him better and to recognize how important it is that we participate in ways appropriate to our covenant.

---

[4]It is possible that he also continues to carry them out through Israel. Paul seems to think so in Romans 9–11.

Summary of Conclusions

We began with the methodology that has characterized the Lost World series, working from the recognition that the Old Testament is an ancient document. Though its authority is derived from God, it is channeled through the author's communicative intention based on his language and cultural context. This fact compelled us to investigate how collections of legal sayings functioned in the ancient world. Legal sayings were accumulated using the genre of list making, which functioned on the basis of an aspective approach to wisdom. We consequently noted that the focus of this genre in the ancient world was not to provide legislation but to provide wisdom for bringing about order in society. Order in turn enhances the reputation of the administrator of the social order (the king in most of the ancient world; Yahweh as suzerain king over Israel). The objective of the Torah is to teach the Israelites about the kind of order that they will need to uphold if they want to receive the blessings of God's favor and presence. This should not be confused with the commonly assumed idea that the Torah provides Israel with a divine law and is unrelated to anything that is accomplished by the New Covenant.

On the basis of this analysis, we turned attention to the legal corpus of Israel in the Old Testament. We concluded that its genre was similar to what we found in the ancient Near East (providing legal wisdom), but also served as the stipulations to the covenant. These stipulations outlined for Israel how they could serve as the people of God, particularly in the role of vassals to their suzerain. We noted that the order the stipulations provided for included ritual and had the major focus of holiness (incorporation into divine identity, an element not found in the ANE literature).

As we explored these issues, we noted that the Torah was therefore situated in three important ways. First, it is situated in the ancient world and therefore reflects ancient values and ideas. Second, it is situated in the covenant between Yahweh and Israel and in that way is unlike what is found in the ANE legal wisdom texts. Since the Torah is embedded in a covenant, it is not directly applicable to those outside that covenant. At the same time, even though the legal texts in the ANE are not part of covenants and there is no precedent in the ANE for a god making a covenant with a people group, we did find a similarity between Torah and treaties of the ANE. Although the Torah comprises legal sayings that overlap with the legal texts of the ancient world, we noted that they also serve as stipulations in a treaty format. As such, the Torah needs to be read similarly to the treaty stipulations and therefore stand as Israel's response as vassals to their suzerain. Third, Torah is situated in a context of sacred space in that it is instructing Israel in how they can retain the blessing of Yahweh's presence among them and the favor this presence represents.

Once we arrived at conclusions about what the Torah was in its context, we began to explore what the Torah is not. In this analysis, we concluded that the Torah should not be divided into categories of moral, civil, and ceremonial law. These divisions can only be artificial and fail to help us understand the impact of the Torah as a whole. They assume that the Torah is legislation and that as legislation it intends to lay down laws for those various aspects of life. The long tradition of suggesting these divisions primarily served the purpose of allowing interpreters to separate out the moral law, which could in turn become the basis for determining a moral system based on the Torah—something that it was never intended to do. We then continued to propose that not only did the Torah not provide the basis for a system of morality; it likewise did not provide an ideal social structure. This allowed us to offer a way to resolve a longstanding problem: why the inclusion of slavery or patriarchy in the Torah should not concern us. The Torah spoke into the Israelites' culture as it was rather than trying to transform their culture to some ideal. In contrast, we attempted to demonstrate why transforming culture is not the purpose of Torah and why this understanding should not be attempted.

Even today we are aware of the need for God's people to be transformed (a concept expressed in Rom 12:1-2), and a case could be made that this in fact is the purpose of the New Covenant, variously called regeneration, glorification, or theosis. However, transforming people is not a means to transforming culture. Jesus let Caesar keep what was his; he did not take what was Caesar's for God. We do not know the end to which transformation is a means, just as Israel never knew that the reputation that Yahweh established through them would eventually serve as the basis by which future generations would understand further revelation. For the vast majority of God's people, transformation does not actually occur until after their death.

Beginning with proposition twenty, we undertook a more concerted effort to understand how the Torah should be used and what it was designed to do. We discussed the common approach of deriving principles from the Torah for application today. We rejected that approach as overspecifying and lacking the necessary controls. Such an approach could not be applied consistently enough to achieve reliable results. Instead, the practice bristles with subjectivity and, to the extent that it does so, is not tethered to the authority of the text. Likewise we cannot mine prooftexts from the Torah to establish what our behavior or position should be. That gave us the basis for returning to the conclusion that the Torah was not intended to serve as legislation or as a means of salvation.

Finally now, we can offer a way forward with regard to how we should proceed as we try to resolve important issues for today in the light of biblical authority. No book can resolve all the problems, but we hope that we have offered some insights that can help us forge a way forward in difficult times.

Just as Israel in the Old Testament was identified as the covenant people of God through whom he would carry out his plans and purposes, so in the New Testament the church is co-identified with God as the Body of Christ to carry out his plans and purposes. In this way, though, the church does not reproduce or replace Israel; it recapitulates Israel. Israel was defined by an ethnic marker and the sign of circumcision; the church is defined as being "in Christ" (e.g., 2 Cor 5:17) and the sign is baptism "of water and the Spirit" (Jn 3:5). This recapitulation is well established in the New Testament's own context, even if it occasionally molds the Old Testament to its own purposes in order to do so. In both cases, God's co-identification is with a community (corporate Israel / church universal) composed of individuals who receive the sign to mark their commitment to the co-identification. Both participate in the kingdom of God, but at different levels and in different ways.

The Torah provides wisdom to the Israelites to help them understand what their co-identification should look like as Yahweh carries out his plans and purposes through them in their time and culture and enables them to be appropriate hosts to Yahweh's presence. The church does not serve the same function so the Torah will not enable the church to live out its identity. To say it another way, the Torah was not given as God's revelation to help the church be the church; it was given to help Israel be Israel. How then can we discern how the Torah can remain as God's revelation for us today? If we have learned what Torah was and how it functioned, we will be able to use that understanding of God's plans and purposes to gain insight into how these are being carried out today through the New Covenant. Because God chose to reveal the New Covenant in terms of the work he did through Israel, if we want to understand the New Covenant, we must understand what that work through Israel was.

The New Covenant does not replace the Torah because the latter was somehow considered deficient or a failed program; neither should it be viewed as progress. The New Covenant is simply another way through which God carries out his various plans and purposes. What we can learn from the Torah is important, but we are not participants in that program.

When we read the Torah, we are encountering the wisdom that God offered to Israel so that they could establish the order that he expected of his vassals. However, God is working differently through the church than he did with Israel. The terms of participation have changed because Torah was culturally and contextually situated. Israel was co-identified with God in connection to a vassal treaty; we are not.[1] The wisdom that we gain from the Torah is not a point-by-point wisdom that is built on deciphering how each line of Torah offers a principle to which all of God's people at all times should adhere. It is a cumulative wisdom based on the whole (see the example of health in proposition eighteen). This conclusion is the natural result of the aspective nature of the Torah. All the pieces are working together to achieve a big picture of a community identity. Some of the pieces may have more independent value than others, but in the end what we need is found in the composite profile, not in the individual bits.[2]

---

[1]Christ is depicted as our king, but whether being characterized as citizens under a (Roman) ruler happens to mean the same thing as being characterized as vassals under an ANE suzerain is beyond the scope of this study. For Roman Imperial imagery used of Christ (in Revelation specifically) see, for example, David Aune, *Apocalypticism, Prophecy, and Magic in Early Christianity: Collected Essays* (Grand Rapids: Baker Academic, 2008), 99-119.

[2]A similar approach is adopted in Christopher J. H. Wright, *Walking in the Ways of the Lord: The Ethical Authority of the Old Testament* (Downers Grove, IL: InterVarsity Press, 1995), 31, though he still wants to develop principles.

The value of the Torah for us does not consist in requiring us to do anything. The value is to see the reputation that Yahweh has established for himself, read through the lens of the ANE context. From the Torah, we can know that the God we worship is not petty, arbitrary, co-dependent, indifferent, or (conversely) cruel, tyrannical, or monstrous. The Torah and the covenant establish these qualities (reputation) in the context of the ANE cultural environment. This is useful to know because many modern people often do not know this. Unfortunately, misreading the Torah usually gives us the opposite impressions because we do not understand the context.

When we think of our relationship to Torah, we should recognize that, technically speaking, the counterpart to status is status; "in Christ" (our new covenant status) fits the template of *qdš* (status of holiness). There is no treaty formulation (or recapitulated contract) circumscribing the New Covenant status because the New Covenant does not work that way (although the Greek word *pisteuō*, usually translated "believe," may have connotations of swearing allegiance to a ruler).[3] The closest recapitulation of the Torah in the New Testament is, arguably, the Sermon on the Mount, but the emphasis there is on the act of giving the law, not on a revised content of the law. The Sermon on the Mount is not a list of obligations we have to fill in order to earn good marks on our efforts to be "in Christ." As a recapitulation of the giving of the covenant, it reaffirms what the message of the covenant was. As discussed in proposition twenty-three, God is taking responsibility for order in the human world. It is what Christ has done that brings order to the world, not what Christians do (or fail to do). Human efforts do not bring order to the human world. In fact, most of the statements in the Sermon on the Mount (and those concerning the order of the kingdom in general) are inversions of common sense.

---

[3]Matthew W. Bates, *Salvation by Allegiance Alone: Rethinking Faith, Works, and the Gospel of Jesus the King* (Grand Rapids: Baker Academic, 2017); cf. R. Bultmann, πιστευω, *TDNT*, 6:177.

Christ will accomplish his purpose regardless of what his people do or do not do. Moral performance is valuable because it is the means to avoid the natural consequences of vice ("everything is lawful but not everything is beneficial," 1 Cor 10:23).

As a final thought, when we participate in the Eucharist (Communion or Mass), we do not do so in order to gain an understanding of the nature of the Trinity. But among many possible functions, it does help us to focus on Christ. This also means that we realize that our gathering together is not about the oratorical or exegetical skills of the preacher or the musical abilities of the worship team or organist, or about how we respond emotionally to the music or the sermon.[4] The church took centuries to arrive at wording to express the nature of Christ, but the Eucharist does not depend on that or on our understanding of it. God's work through Christ will be done regardless of what we do or do not do.

Our commitment as individuals and as the body of Christ to be above reproach, self-controlled, submissive to transformation, and committed to being salt and light will all continue to drive us to think and work together toward solutions that will bring honor to the name of our God in all the complicated issues of our modern world. The mandate we have is to be the people of God bringing honor to his name, "so that in every way [we] will make the teaching about God our Savior attractive" (Titus 2:10). We must be attractive because the Christian community can only sustain itself through recruitment. If we make ourselves reprehensible in the eyes of our culture, we will be unable to make disciples. Note that in 1 Corinthians 5:1 the deviant is accused not of violating God's law but of behavior "of a kind that even pagans do not tolerate." This should not encourage us to pander to our culture in every respect. If we become indiscernible from non-Christians, the community will vanish and there will be nothing to recruit to. But it

---

[4]Reflections shared by Josh Walton.

also does not mean that we rigidly conform to the cultural values of the ANE (expressed in the Torah) or of Hellenized Judea (expressed in the Gospels and Epistles). The decision between "do not conform to the pattern of this world" (Rom 12:1-2) and "become all things to all people so that by all possible means [we] might save some" (1 Cor 9:22) does not default in either direction. It means that we exercise wisdom in knowing where to conform to the culture of our day. This wisdom must be exercised by those who can understand the culture well enough to understand the cost of either decision, and it is these people whom we should appoint to lead the community. But making those decisions is not the same thing as following a rigid set of rules, especially not a rigid set of rules that was written to a different culture. Perhaps this book can provide one small step in helping us to think about how we can do that most effectively.

Appendix

The Decalogue

We have already referred to the Decalogue in the discussion about the Torah and morality, noting that many who believe that the Torah establishes a moral system see the Decalogue as the core of that morality (propositions thirteen and twenty-two). The position adopted in this book argued against that interpretation. In this appendix, we will offer our overall understanding of the Decalogue as well as an interpretation of each of the ten items.[1]

Regardless of the connection to a moral system, the list known as the Ten Commandments is often understood as the summary and most important part of the Torah. The word *commandments* is itself misleading because everywhere the set is referred to in the Old Testament, it is called the "ten words" in Hebrew (five times: Ex 20:1; 34:28; Deut 4:13; 5:1; 10:4).[2] Exodus and Deuteronomy draw attention

---

[1]John has addressed these previously in *Old Testament Theology for Christians*, and some of this material is adapted from the discussion there. Some sections have also been incorporated from John H. Walton, "Interpreting the Bible as an Ancient Near Eastern Document," in *Israel: Ancient Kingdom or Late Invention?*, ed. Daniel I. Block (Nashville: B&H Academic, 2008), 298-327.

[2]There are even questions about how they should be divided. Daniel I. Block, "Reading the Decalogue Right to Left: The Ten Principles of Covenant Relationship in the Hebrew Bible," in *How I Love Your Torah, O LORD! Studies in the Book of Deuteronomy* (Eugene, OR: Cascade, 2011), 21-55; and Block, Excursus A: "How Shall We Number the Ten Commandments? The Deuteronomy Version (5:1-21)," in *How I Love Your Torah*, 56-60.

to this list, though the iteration in Exodus 34, also called the Ten
Words (in Hebrew), differs from the others and is difficult to divide
convincingly into ten sayings.[3] Regardless of which list we use, how
we number them, or how we translate what they are, it is important
for us to recognize that they cannot stand as the summary of the Law
and be singled out as more important than the rest. If for no other
reason, when Jesus is asked to identify the most important parts of the
Law, he gives the two great commandments rather than citing the ten
(Mt 22:37-40).[4]

The Decalogue, then, like the rest of the Torah, is focused on instructing Israel as to the nature of the societal order that would reflect
the reputation God desires for himself. The ten "words" provide information about the shape of the covenant community, both in terms of
how the community interacts with Yahweh and how the Israelites interact with one another. This focus on the covenant community is nowhere clearer than in the motivation cited for honoring parents: "so
that you may live long in the land the LORD your God is giving you"
(Ex 20:12). As stipulations to Israel's covenant with Yahweh, the words
are not intended to establish morality; they characterize the ways that
Israel, Yahweh's covenant people, can retain God's favor and thereby
receive life in the land. They describe the sort of society that Yahweh
wishes to establish for the reflection of his identity in the context of the
cultural river of the ancient Near East (ANE) as he administers favor,
blessing, and presence as opposed to curses, abandonment, and exile.

Finally, like the rest of the Torah, the Decalogue should also be
understood in comparison to its ANE background. Such an investigation has some startling results. We learn that a few of the sayings
stand in stark contrast to typical ancient practice while many of
them coincide fully with what we can find in the ANE. Furthermore,
similarities are not limited to the ANE. Moshe Weinfeld draws our

---

[3]This is an intriguing issue, which we will unfortunately not be able to probe here.
[4]Notice that in Luke 18:19-20 he includes only five.

attention to a remarkable inscription from the city of Philadelphia in Lydia (Asia Minor) dating to the first century BC in a shrine of the goddess Agdistis. The builder describes a list of commands he was given by Zeus in a dream:

> Not to destroy a fetus or cause an abortion
> Not to commit a robbery
> Not to murder
> Not to steal anything
> To be loyal to the sanctuary
> No man will lie with a strange woman other than his wife . . .
>   nor with any boy or maiden.[5]

The inscription continues by prohibiting any who are guilty of such crimes from entering the shrine "for here sit enthroned mighty gods who keep an eye on all these transgressions and will not tolerate sinners. . . . The gods will look with favor on those who obey, and will grant them blessings, but will hate those who transgress, and will inflict on them great punishments."[6]

When we find contrast to the ancient world, we will need to be aware of the ancient world's practices that the Israelites are spurning in order for the contrast to be meaningful. When we find similarity, we will see that the order found in the covenant was not so different from the recognized ways of preserving order in the ancient world. This should be no surprise. As we begin to analyze each saying, we will also notice that in some cases, cultural changes among the Bible-reading audiences over the centuries have pushed interpretation far from the original contextual understanding.[7]

---

[5]Moshe Weinfeld, "The Uniqueness of the Decalogue and Its Place in Jewish Tradition," in *The Ten Commandments in History and Tradition*, ed. Ben-Zion Segal (Jerusalem: Magnes, 1990), 30-31.
[6]Weinfeld, "Uniqueness of the Decalogue," 31.
[7]For a more extensive discussion of the comparative issues and analysis of numbers 1-4, see Walton, "Interpreting the Bible as an Ancient Near Eastern Document," 298-327. For a

SAYINGS 1-4

#1 *Other gods*. A survey of the history of the interpretation of this commandment prior to the availability of materials from the ANE shows certain clear trends. The Heidelberg Catechism, the Westminster Confession, and the interpretation of the Reformers all go in the direction of interpreting the prohibition in terms of priorities. In the Westminster Confession, the extrapolation suggests that the point of the text is that in all thoughts, actions, and attitudes, God will be the highest priority. Nothing in our lives should detract from the glory of God. Earlier church fathers had even given the commandment a christological twist.[8] Other interpreters focused on a philosophical interpretation that sought to establish absolute monotheism that explicitly ruled out the existence of other gods.[9]

The availability of the ANE literature brought an increased recognition that the commandment dictated only monolatry or henotheism rather than what we now call monotheism—relating as it did to the question of whom the people worshiped rather than to whether other gods existed.[10] Earlier interpreters had made this same point, but the ANE material tended to push interpretation more firmly in this direction. This interpretation continued to frame the issue as prioritization even though it is more restricted to the issue of worship practices.

---

discussion of the presence of items 5-9 in the ANE, see Karel van der Toorn, *Sin and Sanction in Israel and Mesopotamia: A Comparative Study* (Assen, Netherlands: Van Gorcum, 1985), 13-20. All ten are treated in some detail with citations in *Zondervan Illustrated Bible Backgrounds Commentary*, ed. John H. Walton, vol. 1 (Grand Rapids: Zondervan, 2009), in the comments by B. Wells on Exodus 20 and those of E. Carpenter on Deuteronomy 5; and in David L. Baker, *The Decalogue: Living as the People of God* (Downers Grove, IL: IVP Academic, 2017).

[8]Gregory of Nyssa. See Joseph T. Lienhard, *Exodus, Leviticus, Numbers, Deuteronomy*, ACCS (Downers Grove, IL: InterVarsity Press, 2001), 102.

[9]As early as Philo (*De decalogo*, XIV.65, vol. 7).

[10]Most commentators take this view. For some of the more detailed treatments see Walter J. Harrelson, *The Ten Commandments and Human Rights* (Philadelphia: Fortress, 1980), 54-61; and Moshe Weinfeld, *Deuteronomy 1–11*, AB (Garden City, NY: Doubleday, 1991), 284-89.

The focus on priorities found support as far back as the Septuagint, which translated the Hebrew עַל־פְּנֵי ('al pǝnê, "before me") by the Greek preposition plēn ("except"). But if Hebrew meant to say "except," there are several ways to do it (e.g., 'ak or raq). Likewise, if Hebrew meant to express priority, it would have used wording such as that found in Deuteronomy 4:35 or Isaiah 45:21.[11] Twentieth-century theologians recognized the problem. Gerhard von Rad, for example, suggested that the Hebrew ought to be translated "in defiance of me" since that at least had the support of synchronic usage.[12]

A more defensible interpretation was suggested by Werner Schmidt in light of even deeper probing of the practices and beliefs that were current in the ANE. He proposes that when the first commandment prohibits other gods in the presence of Yahweh, it is ruling out the concept that he operates within a pantheon or a divine assembly or with a consort.[13] J. Bottéro describes this system as similar to a king at the head of the state with his family and functionaries around him operating in a structured hierarchy.[14]

This background suggests the interpretation that the Israelites were not to imagine any other gods in the presence of Yahweh: "You shall have no other gods in my presence."[15] This is supported by the fact that when the prepositional combination that occurs in the Hebrew text takes a

---

[11]Walter C. Kaiser Jr., *Toward Old Testament Ethics* (Grand Rapids: Zondervan, 1983), 85.

[12]Gerhard von Rad, *Old Testament Theology*, trans. D. M. G. Stalker (New York: Harper & Row, 1962), 1:204. Genesis 16:12, Job 1:11, and Psalm 21:13 (Eng. 21:12) show this meaning.

[13]Werner Schmidt, *The Faith of the Old Testament: A History*, trans. John Sturdy (Philadelphia: Westminster, 1983), 71.

[14]Jean Bottéro, "Intelligence and the Technical Function of Power: Enki/Ea," in *Mesopotamia: Writing, Reasoning and the Gods*, trans. Zainab Bahrani and Marc Van De Mieroop (Chicago: University of Chicago Press, 1992), 233.

[15]Weinfeld, *Deuteronomy 1–11*, 276-77. Daniel Polish, "No Other Gods," in *The Ten Commandments for Jews, Christians, and Others*, ed. Roger E. Van Harn (Grand Rapids: Eerdmans, 2007), 24; cf. Anthony Phillips, *Ancient Israel's Criminal Law: A New Approach to the Decalogue* (New York: Schocken, 1970), 38-39. Miller wants to hold onto all the possibilities in the meaning of 'al pǝnê. Patrick D. Miller, *The Ten Commandments* (Louisville, KY: Westminster John Knox, 2009), 20.

personal object, the meaning is consistently spatial: עַל־פְּנֵי (ʿal pənê) with
personal object of preposition. The following examples express location:

- Genesis 11:28: Haran died ʿal pənê his father Terah
- Genesis 23:3: Abraham arose from ʿal pənê his dead wife and spoke
- Genesis 32:22 (Eng. 32:21): And the present passed ʿal pənê him
- Genesis 50:1: And Joseph fell ʿal pənê his father and he wept for him
- Exodus 33:19 (34:6): I will cause all my goodness to pass ʿal pənê you
- Leviticus 10:3: I will be honored ʿal pənê all the people
- Numbers 3:4: [Nadab and Abihu] made an offering of unauthorized fire ʿal pənê him
- 1 Kings 9:7: I will cast [Israel] from ʿal pənê the land
- 2 Kings 13:14: Jehoash went down and wept ʿal pənê him
- Job 4:15: A spirit passed ʿal pənê me
- Job 21:31: who denounces his conduct ʿal pənê him
- Psalm 9:20: let the nations be judged ʿal pənê you
- Ezekiel 32:10: when I brandish my sword ʿal pənê them

With an understanding of the practices of the ANE, this spatial
sense gains much greater credibility. The gods in the ANE operated
in a pantheon, and decisions were made in the divine assembly. In
addition, the principal deities typically had consorts. The lifestyle
and operations system for deity, then, constituted a community experience. The destinies of the gods were decreed in assembly as
were the destinies of kings, cities, temples, and people. The business
of the gods was carried out in the presence of other gods. This
system is well summarized as a hierarchy of authoritative deities
and active deities.[16]

---

[16]Lowell K. Handy, *Among the Host of Heaven: The Syro-Palestinian Pantheon as Bureaucracy*
(Winona Lake, IN: Eisenbrauns, 1994), 97.

On the other hand, Yahweh is occasionally depicted as having a
divine council (most notably in 1 Kings 22:19-22 and Job 1–2), and the
text makes no attempt to disabuse its readers of that conception.[17]
Consequently, the "presence" of Yahweh, where the other gods are not
to be, most likely refers to his terrestrial presence (in the temple and
ruling over his territory), not his royal audience chamber in the divine
realm. In Ezekiel 8, Yahweh objects to the practice of placing images
and altars of other deities in his temple, a practice of the Baal cult in
which King Manasseh also participates in 2 Kings 21:1-7. Furthermore,
in accordance with suzerain treaties, no other god (read: ruler) was to
be recognized in Yahweh's territory. The significance of this is that the
pantheon/divine assembly concept carried with it the idea of distribution of power among many divine beings. The first commandment
becomes a simple statement that Yahweh's power—at least within the
boundaries of Israel—is absolute. He is not one of many who share in
the distribution of divine authority. It is understandable that the Israelites would struggle with this concept. First of all, it removes Yahweh
from the community of the gods. In the ancient world people found
their identity in their place in their community. They assumed the
gods did the same. To separate Yahweh from such a community
identity would have been a confusing concept. Autonomy and independence were not valued in ancient society, and to ascribe these
qualities to their God would have seemed impious.

Furthermore, Israelites would wonder whether just one God having
jurisdiction and authority in every area made any sense. Even kings,
who ruled from a seat of solitary authority, distributed that authority
down through the bureaucracy. Consider life on a college campus.
Would it make any sense for the president to be personally involved

---

[17]Even Psalm 82, which is commonly thought to depict Yahweh sentencing other gods to
death and thus stripping their divine status, is not a commentary on the nature of the divine council. The "gods" who "die like mere mortals" in Psalm 82:6-7 are not the same as
the members of the council in Psalm 82:1.

in every decision? Instead of going to the resident assistant in the dormitory to resolve roommate problems, or to the registrar for class problems, or to the teacher for homework problems, imagine that you were supposed to take all your problems directly to the president. We would wonder why he would care about our little issues or whether she would have time or resources to manage everything herself. We would assume that operating without a bureaucratic management structure would result in chaos. Yet this is effectively what Israel was being told to do.[18]

Israel was to be distinct from the nations around them. That is the very point of the prohibition. Although it does not say explicitly that no other gods exist, it does remove them from the presence of Yahweh. If Yahweh does not share power, authority, or jurisdiction with them, they are not gods in any meaningful sense of the word.[19] The first of the Ten Words insists not that the other gods are nonexistent but that they are powerless; it disenfranchises them. It does not simply say that they should not be worshiped; it leaves them with no status worthy of worship.

The issue here is not metaphysics. Rather, it concerns the God who is making the covenant with Israel. He is their suzerain; they are his vassals. No other gods are involved in this relationship—the covenant is not being made with a council of gods. In treaties in the ANE (and remember that the covenant has adapted a treaty format), many gods are called as witnesses and are involved as sponsors of the agreement. Here it is only Yahweh.[20] He is giving them their covenant status, and they are going to identify with him—no other. Yahweh's absolute

---

[18]Illustration provided by Ashley Edewaard.

[19]This idea may have even further significance if we attach to it the idea that in the ANE something was not considered to exist if it had not been assigned a name, a place, and a function. If this concept maintains, other gods, given no place or function, would not be thought to exist.

[20]Heaven and earth are called to witness the covenant (Deut 4:26; 30:19) and again to testify to Israel's infidelity (Is 1:2), but they do not share the responsibility of enforcing the treaty alongside Yahweh.

exercise of power throughout the territory of Israel can be observed by other nations (1 Kings 20:23-29), and other peoples occasionally recognize Yahweh's power as superior to their own gods even outside of the territory of Israel (2 Kings 5:17-18; Dan 4:34-37), but other nations do not usually even try to worship any gods within the territory of Israel, Yahweh or otherwise. (Foreigners within Israel are still required to worship Yahweh in the same manner as the Israelites, as the Assyrian settlers discover in 2 Kings 17:25-28.) There is no prohibition against nations who are not under the covenant worshiping gods other than Yahweh in places other than the territory that Yahweh rules as the suzerain of Israel.

#2 *Images*. Four factors have had significant influence on modern popular interpretation of the prohibition of the use of images: (1) early rabbinic interpretation, (2) controversies concerning icons in the Orthodox tradition, (3) statues of the saints in Roman Catholic tradition, and (4) questions concerning Christian art in general. In derived-principles approaches, the concept of idols has been reduced to the concept of anything that is valued higher than God (e.g., in effect making one's family, position, or possessions gods). It is well known that in classical Judaism, the commandment led to the prohibition of any artistic representation of a living creature.[21] When we research the writings of the church fathers and interpreters into the nineteenth century, we find a dominant philosophical/theological idea that God is transcendent or "other" and therefore cannot be contained within an image.[22]

---

[21]We must exercise caution lest we overextend this interpretation in Judaism since it only has limited expression. For a defense of the plastic arts in Judaism, see Polish, "No Other Gods," 25-27.

[22]Philo, Calvin, Heidelberg Catechism. This interpretation carries over into the modern period and is reflected in the writings of a large number of commentators who are well aware of the ANE materials. For examples see Harrelson, *Ten Commandments and Human Rights*, 61-72; and Weinfeld, *Deuteronomy 1–11*, 289-300. Kaiser covers this territory in its broadest form: "Every form of neglect, substitution, or contempt for public and private worship of God is rejected." Kaiser, *Toward Old Testament Ethics*, 86-87.

Gerhard von Rad counters the focus on transcendence found in the history of interpretation with observations from the broad range of comparative religions: "The pagan religions knew as well as Israel did that deity is invisible, that it transcends all human ability to comprehend it, and that it cannot be captured by or comprised in a material object."[23]

Although our knowledge of the worldview underlying the use of images (which I will refer to as image ideology) is still limited and there are significant differences between Mesopotamian and Egyptian thought, some sense of the general aspects of the ideology can inform our understanding of this commandment.[24] The ANE beliefs can be explored through three aspects: the manufacture of the image, the use of the image, and the perception of the image.

---

[23]Von Rad, *Old Testament Theology*, 1:214. Transcendence in the biblical sense is not easy to locate in Mesopotamian thinking. For some discussion see Thorkild Jacobsen, "The Graven Image," in *Ancient Israelite Religion: Essays in Honor of Frank Moore Cross*, ed. Patrick D. Miller, Paul D. Hanson, and S. Dean McBride (Philadelphia: Fortress, 1987), 15-32 (esp. 22). For the idea that the gods are beyond human understanding, see *Ludlul bēl nēmeqi*, in W. G. Lambert, *Babylonian Wisdom Literature* (Oxford: Oxford University Press, 1960), 41, lines 33-38. On the point of being captured by a material object, see H. W. F. Saggs, *The Encounter with the Divine in Mesopotamia and Israel* (London: Athlone, 1978), 15-16. Further support can be found in the fact that the deity cannot be destroyed by destroying the image.

[24]This ideology has been developed in many sources, the following being among the most significant: Angelika Berlejung, "Washing the Mouth: The Consecration of Divine Images in Mesopotamia," in *The Image and the Book*, ed. Karel van der Toorn (Leuven: Peeters, 1997), 45-72; Edward M. Curtis, "Images in Mesopotamia and the Bible: A Comparative Study," in *The Bible in the Light of Cuneiform Literature, Scripture in Context III*, ed. William W. Hallo, Bruce William Jones, and Gerald L. Mattingly (Lewiston, NY: Mellen, 1990), 31-56 (also in his 1984 dissertation); Michael B. Dick, *Born in Heaven, Made on Earth* (Winona Lake, IN: Eisenbrauns, 1999); William W. Hallo, "Cult Statue and Divine Image: A Preliminary Study," in *Scripture in Context II: More Essays on the Comparative Method*, ed. William W. Hallo, James C. Moyer, and Leo G. Perdue (Winona Lake, IN: Eisenbrauns, 1983), 1-18; Victor Hurowitz, "Picturing Imageless Deities: Iconography in the Ancient Near East," *BAR* 23, no. 3 (1997): 46-48, 51; Tryggve Mettinger, *No Graven Image?: Israelite Aniconism in Its Ancient Near Eastern Context* (Stockholm: Almqvist & Wiksell, 1995); J. J. M. Roberts, "Divine Freedom and Cultic Manipulation in Israel and Mesopotamia," in *Unity and Diversity: Essays in the History, Literature, and Religion of the Ancient Near East*, ed. Hans Goedicke and J. J. M. Roberts (Baltimore: Johns Hopkins University Press, 1975), 181-90; and Jack M. Sasson, "On the Use of Images in Israel and the Ancient Near East: A Response to Karel van der Toorn," in *Sacred Time, Sacred Place: Archaeology and the Religion of Israel*, ed. Barry M. Gittlen (Winona Lake, IN: Eisenbrauns, 2002), 63-70.

Manufacture of the image. Since the existence of the idol needed to be approved by the god, only the gods could initiate the manufacturing process.[25] At the end of the process, rituals were performed to transfer the deity from the spiritual world to the physical world, referred to by Walker and Dick as "actualizing the presence of the god in the temple."[26] Consequently, the undertaking is viewed not in human terms but as a miraculous process through which the deity works,[27] not unlike our concepts regarding the inspiration of Scripture.

The most significant ritual is the mouth-opening ritual. This enables the image to eat bread, drink water, and smell incense,[28] that is, to receive worship on behalf of the deity. It purifies the image from the human contamination involved in the manufacturing process and thereby enables the statue to function as deity.[29] At the end of the ritual the incantation priest whispers in the ear of the image, "Ea has determined as your lot divinity and rule, walk around: You can move about, bless a blessing, make the gesture of blessing with your right hand! You are free! You are released!"[30] Another whispered prayer says, "You are now counted with the gods, your brothers. From today may your destiny be counted as divinity, and with the gods, your brothers you are counted."[31]

Berlejung concludes, "The whispered prayer of the priest suggests that the transfer of the image's perceptive and vital functions, and its

---

[25]C. B. F. Walker and Michael Brennan Dick, *The Induction of the Cult Image in Ancient Mesopotamia: The Mesopotamian Mīs Pî Ritual*, SAALT 1 (Helsinki: Neo-Assyrian Text Corpus Project, 2001), 8.

[26]Walker and Dick, *Induction*, 4 (quoting Peggy Jean Boden's dissertation on the "Mesopotamian Washing of the Mouth (*Mīs Pî*) Ritual" [PhD thesis, Johns Hopkins University, 1999]).

[27]Berlejung, "Washing the Mouth," 62. See Prayer to Asshur and Marduk, "Esarhaddon's Renewal of the Gods," in Walker and Dick, *Induction*, 25.

[28]Walker and Dick, *Induction*, 14; see Incantation Tablet 3, ll. 70-71.

[29]Walker and Dick, *Induction*, 14. For Egyptian rituals see Siegfried Morenz, *Egyptian Religion* (Ithaca, NY: Cornell University Press, 1973), 155-56.

[30]Jacobsen, "Graven Image," 27.

[31]Berlejung, "Washing the Mouth," 63.

integration into the divine community have now been completed."[32] Every aspect of the manufacture of the image was working toward this end result. At the end of the mouth-washing ceremony an incantation is pronounced as the deity enters the holy of holies, indicating that hereafter the god will remain in his house, where he will receive his food each day.[33]

Use of the image. All public worship revolved around the image. It marked the deity's presence and was the center of any ceremony involving the divine.[34] It was awakened in the morning, washed, clothed, offered two sumptuous meals each day (while music was played in its presence), and put to bed at night.[35] Thus worship took place by caring for the needs of the god through his image. We have discussed this ideology previously as part of the Great Symbiosis. This care was intended to ensure the continued presence of the deity in the image.

The image was also considered to mediate revelation from the deity. In Egypt of the early first millennium, for instance, court cases that were being tried were set before Amun. The various outcomes of the trial were placed oracularly before the image, which, manipulated by the priests, issued verdicts.[36] In Mesopotamia, extispicy divination (involving the examination of the entrails of a sacrificed animal) took place before the god in order to receive oracular instructions.

Perception concerning the image. From the preceding discussion we can conclude that the material image was animated by the divine essence. Therefore, it did not simply represent the deity; it manifested

---

[32]Berlejung, "Washing the Mouth," 63.

[33]Berlejung, "Washing the Mouth," 67.

[34]Walker and Dick, *Induction*, 5.

[35]A. Leo Oppenheim, *Ancient Mesopotamia: Portrait of a Dead Civilization*, rev. ed. completed by Erica Reiner (Chicago: University of Chicago Press, 1977), 188-90. For Egypt see Morenz, *Egyptian Religion*, 88.

[36]William W. Hallo and William Kelly Simpson, *The Ancient Near East: A History* (Fort Worth: Harcourt Brace, 1998), 285.

its presence.[37] We should not conclude, however, that the image was therefore the deity. The deity was the reality that was embodied in the image.[38] This same concept is observable in Egyptian literature when in the *Memphite Theology* Ptah forms the bodies of the gods.[39] In Egyptian thinking, the images were animated by the *ba* of the deity, which united with the image, thus permitting it to manifest the presence of the deity and reveal the deity—a phenomenon referred to as "habitation." In this way the image was not a physical picture of the deity but a characterization of the divine nature.[40] In terms we have previously used, the image is an important part of the god's divine constellation. It forms and shares an integral aspect of divine identity, representing the kind of relationship that later theologians would describe using the term *homoousion*.[41]

We may conclude then that the image functioned in the cult as a mediator of the divine presence. It is the means by which humans gained access to the presence of deity. As such it represents the mystical unity of transcendence and immanence, a theophany transubstantiated.[42] Jacobsen therefore sees the functioning image as an act of the deity's favor: "The image represented a favor granted by the god. . . . It was a sign of a benign and friendly attitude on the part of the community in which it stood."[43] Berlejung provides a useful summary

---

[37]Walker and Dick, *Induction*, 4 (quoting from p. 13 of I. J. Winter, "'Idols of the King': Royal Images as Recipients of Ritual Action in Ancient Mesopotamia," *Journal of Ritual Studies* 6, no. 1 [1992]: 13-42).

[38]Walker and Dick, *Induction*, 6; and Jacobsen, "Graven Image," 22. Walker and Dick suggest the relationship between statue and deity is somewhat like the relationship between body and soul as in Aristotelian dualism.

[39]Translation available in Miriam Lichtheim, *Ancient Egyptian Literature* (Berkeley: University of California Press, 1975), 1:55, ll. 60-61.

[40]Erik Hornung, *Conceptions of God in Ancient Egypt: The One and the Many*, trans. John Baines (Ithaca, NY: Cornell University Press, 1982), 128-35; and Morenz, *Egyptian Religion*, 150-52.

[41]Reference to a divine image is actually used to describe Christ in Colossians 1:15.

[42]Jacobsen, "Graven Image," 22-23; and Berlejung, "Washing the Mouth," 61.

[43]Jacobsen, "Graven Image," 22.

of our study: "A cultic statue was never solely a religious picture, but was always an image imbued with a god, and, as such, it possessed the character of both earthly reality and divine presence."[44]

How would we then interpret the second commandment in light of all this information? As we have seen, from deity to people, the image mediates presence and revelation.[45] From people to deity, the image mediates worship. Werner Schmidt draws the conclusion, "The important thing is that [the image] embodies the deity and so reveals him. It is not the appearance of the image that is basic, but its power."[46] In the same vein, von Rad defines an image as a "mediator of revelation claiming cultic adoration."[47]

In Israel, the temple housed the presence of Yahweh but did not mediate it. The ark mediated the presence of deity in a limited fashion but not in the same way that an image did. The ark was part of the throne (footstool); it did not contain the divine essence. Furthermore, it did not mediate revelation or worship. As part of the throne, it stood for Yahweh's kingship and was the place where offerings were brought, but as tribute, not as sustenance. The priests served a mediatorial role, but their role was to present the offerings on behalf of the people more than to receive the offerings on behalf of the deity.

We can now interpret the second commandment in light of the ANE data on the second commandment. No image is to be used as the mediator of revelation or presence from deity to people, or as the mediator of worship from the people to deity. The prohibition particularly excludes the sort of worship that is understood as meeting the needs of the deity through the image—what we have been referring to as the Great Symbiosis. This differs from the traditional

---

[44]Berlejung, "Washing the Mouth," 46.
[45]Cf. von Rad's observation that the image is a "medium of the spirit," which is "first and foremost the bearer of a revelation." Von Rad, *Old Testament Theology*, 1:214.
[46]Schmidt, *Faith of the Old Testament*, 82.
[47]Von Rad, *Old Testament Theology*, 1:219.

interpretations of the commandment in that, rather than insisting that God is transcendent or not to be replaced by material things, it specifically targets mediation.[48]

Having images of other deities would of course be a violation of the covenant arrangement between Yahweh and Israel. In this case, however, even images of Yahweh are prohibited. Aniconism is observable in various ways in other times and places in the ANE,[49] but it is nowhere as programmatic as it is in Israel.[50] Divine identities in the ancient world were extended into their images. Having different images of the deity fragmented the deity's identity into localized aspects: the aspect of Ishtar in Nineveh is distinct from the aspect of Ishtar in Arbela (enough so that they can even fight each other). In contrast, there is to be only one "aspect" of Yahweh who holds one covenant over all Israel. There are to be no local aspects of Yahweh who serve only a portion of the community; there can be no Yahweh of Samaria standing apart from Yahweh of Jerusalem, which is what Jeroboam is trying to establish with his calf altars. This statement is not about sculpture or art,[51] nor about icons or statues of the saints.[52] Through the image, divine revelation and care of the gods were mediated. That is not how Yahweh's covenant relationship with Israel was supposed to work.

---

[48]This was precisely an issue that early Israel struggled with as early as Mount Sinai. There Moses had been the human mediator of God's presence and revelation. When he appeared to have left them, they substituted the gold calf as a replacement mediator of God's presence.

[49]See Brian R. Doak, *Phoenician Aniconism in Its Mediterranean and Ancient Near Eastern Contexts* (Atlanta: SBL Press, 2015).

[50]Othmar Keel and Cristoph Uehlinger, *Gods, Goddesses, and Images of God in Ancient Israel*, trans. Thomas H. Trapp (Minneapolis: Augsburg Fortress, 1998), trace aniconism through the iconography known from the Levant.

[51]Acknowledged by Jewish commentators as well. See Moshe Greenberg, "The Decalogue Tradition Critically Examined," in Segal, *Ten Commandments in History and Tradition*, 100. He also offers some concise remarks about the way that the image and the deity overlap and yet are distinct.

[52]John Barton, "'The Work of Human Hands' (Psalm 115:4): Idolatry in the Old Testament," in *The Ten Commandments: The Reciprocity of Faithfulness*, ed. William P. Brown (Louisville, KY: Westminster John Knox, 2004), 194-203; note the last two pages.

#3 Name. The traditional interpretation of the third commandment links it to false oaths.[53] Some have considered this direction unacceptable if it is not clearly differentiated from the ninth commandment (false witness). A few interpreters have favored the view that the commandment prohibits blasphemy or profanity, a common popular-level interpretation today. Augustine took it this way but with a more specifically christological bent, indicating that denying the deity of Christ was a violation of the third commandment.[54] Anthony Phillips refutes both of these interpretive directions, arguing that such a command would be unnecessary given the jeopardy inherent in invoking the divine name. He concludes instead that the commandment was "designed to prevent the use of the divine name for magical purposes."[55]

Phillips's conclusions were based on analysis of the ANE materials that demonstrate the use of the divine name in magic. Magical use was documented primarily on the horizontal level, in which the divine name was invoked to protect against magical spells or to exorcise demonic forces. Some add to that a vertical level in which the divine name could potentially be used to summon, command, or bind the deity. Schmidt examines the ANE data and concludes along with Phillips that "the third commandment is intended to exclude conjuration or magic."[56] Stamm and Andrew go so far as to claim that "it is unanimously agreed that this commandment protects the name of Yahweh from that unlawful use which could take place in the oath, the curse, and in sorcery."[57] Access to the ANE materials has thus shifted

---

[53]From Philo to Calvin, in both the Heidelberg Catechism and the Westminster Confession, and in a wide array of commentaries. The occurrence of false oaths and the seriousness of the crime are well attested in ANE literature. For examples drawn from Babylon, Assyria, and Egypt, see Herbert B. Huffmon, "The Fundamental Code Illustrated: The Third Commandment," in Brown, *Ten Commandments*, 205-12, examples on 209-11.

[54]"Discourse of St. Augustine on the Ten Strings of the Harp" (Sermon 9), in *Works of St. Augustine*, ed. John E. Rotelle (New Rochelle, NY: New City Press, 1995), 3.1:261.

[55]Anthony Phillips, *Ancient Israel's Criminal Law: A New Approach to the Decalogue* (New York: Schocken, 1970), 53-54.

[56]Schmidt, *Faith of the Old Testament*, 75.

[57]Johann Jakob Stamm with Maurice Edward Andrew, *The Ten Commandments in Recent*

interpretation of the commandment in the direction of incantations, or what is often called magic.

A careful definition of magic can help us to articulate the pertinent issues in ANE thought and its relationship to this commandment.[58] Jean-Michel de Tarragon applies this self-interest to the function of domination.

> In antiquity, the recourse to magic is charted within the continuum of religious practice; there is no rigid boundary between the two. We tend to speak of magic when a religious ideology attempts to control, if not force, the divinity, or at least the world of nature. In magic, it is that domination which fascinates and causes fear. It could work especially by invoking the name of a god.[59]

We can see that the line between religion and magic was virtually non-existent in the ANE or even in the Greco-Roman world.[60] Under the influence of the medieval church and, eventually, the Enlightenment, stricter lines were drawn to separate the two. The understanding of names operating in the matrix of power was not evident to interpreters who were unaware of the ANE cultures.

These definitions have the advantage of focusing our attention not on a sociological situation per se (e.g., false oaths or occultism) but on the variety of contexts in which a name has efficacy. For this reason,

---

Research, rev. ed., SBT 2.2 (London: SCM Press, 1967), 89. See additional information and survey in Herbert Huffmon, "The Fundamental Code Illustrated: The Third Commandment," in *Pomegranates and Golden Bells*, ed. David P. Wright, David Noel Freedman, and Avi Hurvitz (Winona Lake, IN: Eisenbrauns, 1995), 363-71.

[58]Wim van Binsbergen, and Frans Wiggermann, "Magic in History: A Theoretical Perspective, and Its Application to Ancient Mesopotamia," in *Mesopotamian Magic: Textual, Historical, and Interpretative Perspectives*, ed. Tzvi Abusch and Karel van der Toorn (Groningen: Styx, 1999), 1-34.

[59]Jean-Michel de Tarragon, "Witchcraft, Magic, and Divination in Canaan and Ancient Israel," in *CANE*, 2075.

[60]John G. Gager, *Curse Tablets and Binding Spells from the Ancient World* (New York: Oxford University Press, 1999).

we do not need to solve the question about whether oaths, blasphemy, or magic at one level or another was in view. We simply have to understand the issues that informed the ancient understanding of how names, particularly divine names, worked. A. S. van der Woude attaches the significance of the name to the power of the deity.

> The meaning, the effect, and the "power" of a name lie not in the ominous character of the name per se but in the significance, the effect, and the "power" of the bearer of this name. . . . If one knows the name of a person or a god, one can summon, "invoke," him/her. In this sense knowledge of the name signifies a degree of power over the person known. If this person is very powerful, then the person's name also has corresponding effect and can be used for good or evil purposes. This situation also results in the use of the name of significant persons, but esp. of Yahweh's name, in magic.[61]

The name is equivalent to the identity of the deity, and the divine identity can be commandeered for illicit use. We are familiar with identity theft today, when a symbol such as a credit card number or social security number can be used to abuse or exploit the economic power or authority of an individual. Commandment three works on the same premise and prohibits divine identity theft (used for empty, vain purposes).

In light of this information, the third commandment, when read as ANE literature, concerns how Yahweh's power/authority was not to be perceived among the Israelites: people were to respect it by refraining from attempts to control or misuse it. It was not to be thought of as an efficacious symbol that could be used to pursue one's own self-interests.

Someone's name is not just what he or she is called; name is connected to identity. Everyone in the ancient world thought this way, and

---

[61]Adam S. van der Woude, "שֵׁם šem, name," in *TLOT*, 1351.

this concept serves as one of the fundamental components of magic. This is true of the gods' names as well as those of humans. A name is powerful.[62] Today when we think about honoring God's name, we often derive a principle along the lines that the casual use of the name of God fails to recognize its importance. That would certainly be one way to disrespect God's name.[63] However, a more significant violation in the ancient world would occur if someone recognized the power of the name and took steps to tap into that power for his or her own purposes. This abuse would include, for example, false prophecy.[64] Note that the Lord's Prayer begins by recognizing the sanctity of God's name. The prohibition does not concern pronouncing God's name; it involves invoking it for inappropriate purposes.

#4 *Sabbath*. Interpretations of the Decalogue prior to the surfacing of ANE literature were very vague about the fourth commandment. The command to observe the Sabbath was generally seen as prescribing a human rest that joined with the divine, thus sharing in his rest from work on the seventh day. Alternatives are even less specific about what the Sabbath is intended to accomplish beyond simply commemorating God's acts in history.[65] A minority position interprets the Sabbath as an expression of God's humanitarian concern for the well-being of his creatures.[66]

For several decades it was popular to posit ANE precursors to Sabbath observance.[67] But it is now widely acknowledged that no

---

[62]Stamm and Andrew, *Ten Commandments in Recent Research*, 89; Michael Coogan, *The Ten Commandments: A Short History of an Ancient Text* (New Haven, CT: Yale University Press, 2014), 66; and Harrelson, *Ten Commandments and Human Rights*, 73-76.

[63]See Walton, *Zondervan Illustrated Bible Backgrounds Commentary*, 1:232, 452. Expanded by Greenberg, "Decalogue Tradition Critically Examined," 102.

[64]Miller, *Ten Commandments*, 105-8.

[65]See for example Cornelis Houtman, *Exodus*, trans. Johan Rebel and Sierd Woudstra (Kampen: Kok, 2002), 3:40-48.

[66]For example, Eugene H. Merrill, *Deuteronomy*, NAC (Nashville: Broadman, 1994), 149-51.

[67]See a helpful summary in Stamm and Andrew, *Ten Commandments in Recent Research*, 90-95.

such observance has yet been found. ANE texts can be cited for the significance of seven days but not on a cyclical basis for theological observance. Likewise, most cultures had festival days that featured the absence of work but not in anything like a seven-day cycle. In the Torah, the Sabbath was interpreted as a recognition of Yahweh as the one who rules and brings order (order in the cosmos through creation, Ex 20, and order for Israel through deliverance from Egypt, Deut 5). Comparable at some level, festivals such as the Babylonian *Akitu* or the *Zukru* festival at Emar celebrated the reign of the patron god and his appointed king, but the *Akitu* was only an annual, or sometimes semiannual, celebration while the main *Zukru* was a seven-day festival held in the autumn every seven years. These likewise focused on order in the cosmos and in the country. This is an important point on which we can build our analysis.

The key to understanding the sabbath rest for people is found in the sabbath rest for Yahweh on the seventh day of creation as the formulation in Exodus tells us. The concept of divine rest can, in turn, be elucidated by the ANE literature, which demonstrates that deity's rest is achieved in a temple, generally as a result of chaos having been dispelled. The rest, while it represents disengagement from any process of establishing order (whether through conflict with other deities or not), is more importantly an expression of engagement as the deity takes his place at the helm to maintain an ordered, secure, and stable cosmos. This can be observed in the ANE literature.

First, we can observe that divine rest in the ANE is achieved after order-bringing acts of creation.[68] For example, in the Egyptian *Memphite Theology*:

> So has Ptah come to rest after his making everything and every divine speech as well, having given birth to the gods, having

---

[68]Bernard F. Batto, "The Sleeping God: An Ancient Near Eastern Motif of Divine Sovereignty," *Biblica* 68, no. 2 (1987): 153-77 (esp. 156).

made their towns, having founded their nomes [territories],
having set the gods in their cult places, having made sure their
bread offerings, having founded their shrines, having modeled
their bodies to what contents them.[69]

Second, we note that the divine rest is achieved in the temple.[70] This
concept of rest can also be illustrated by evaluating the names of
temples. Those built at Ur by Warad-Sin and Rim-Sin are called 'ki-tuš
ni-dub-bu-da-ni' (his dwelling place which will provide rest).[71] Finally,
the divine rest is characterized by ongoing control and stability.[72]

Niels-Erik Andreasen concludes, "We can say then that the gods
seek rest, and that their rest implies stability for the world order. The
gods rest because they want to see the world ordered."[73] He sees a
reflection of this same concept in Psalm 132:13-14:

> For the LORD has chosen Zion,
>   he has desired it for his dwelling:
> "This is my resting place for ever and ever;
>   here I will sit enthroned, for I have desired it."

---

[69]*COS*, 1.15, cols. 60-61 (trans. James Allen). Examples could be multiplied almost endlessly
since this concept is ubiquitous in the ANE literature.

[70]The material in support of this is conveniently gathered together by Victor Hurowitz, *I
Have Built You an Exalted House: Temple Building in the Bible in the Light of Mesopotamian
and Northwest Semitic Writings* (Sheffield, UK: JSOT Press, 1992), 330-31. Other key articles
are Moshe Weinfeld, "Sabbath, Temple and the Enthronement of the Lord—The Problem
of the Sitz im Leben of Genesis 1:1–2:3," in *Mélanges bibliques et orientaux en l'honneur de
M. Henrie Cazelles*, ed. A. Caquot and M. Delcor (Neukirchen-Vluyn: Neukirchener Ver-
lag, 1981), 501-12; Samuel E. Loewenstamm, "Biblical Studies in the Light of Akkadian
Texts," in *From Babylon to Canaan* (Jerusalem: Magnes, 1992), 256-64; Peter Machinist,
"Rest and Violence in the Poem of Erra," *JAOS* 103 (1983): 221-26; Batto, "Sleeping God,"
153-77; and John Lundquist, "What Is a Temple?: A Preliminary Typology," in *The Quest
for the Kingdom of God: Studies in Honor of George E. Mendenhall*, ed. H. B. Huffmon, F.
A. Spina, and A. R. W. Green (Winona Lake, IN: Eisenbrauns, 1983), 205-19.

[71]Hurowitz, *I Have Built You an Exalted House*, 330.

[72]This in contrast to simply sleeping peacefully, which is another concept in the ANE. For
rest as rule see Enuma Elish, *COS*, 1.111, 5:122-24 (trans. Benjamin Foster).

[73]Niels-Erik A. Andreasen, *The Old Testament Sabbath: A Tradition-Historical Investigation*,
SBLDS 7 (Missoula, MT: Society of Biblical Literature, 1972), 182.

The psalm concludes by enumerating all that God will provide from his throne as he assures the stability of the king and the people (Ps 132:15-18). Order in the cosmos is sustained not by God's being inactive but precisely by his continued activity.[74]

People are commanded to participate in the rest of God on the Sabbath, not to imitate his rest but in recognition of his work of bringing and maintaining order. His control is represented in his rest and is recognized by people yielding for the day their own attempts to provide for themselves. This is difficult but essential, as noted by Margaret Shuster,

> We are afraid to trust in a world that seems arbitrary and erratic at best; we ignore the fact that all we do assumes trust in the existence and regularities of a creation not under our control. If there is no sovereign God who holds and sustains us and the world, we are in far worse trouble than we generally care to think about. A vital lesson in humility comes from acting on the recognition that everything depends on Someone other and more faithful than we. If God is sovereign, we are not.[75]

This corresponds with the parallel observation throughout (especially) Genesis-Exodus that human efforts are not especially good at establishing and maintaining order or understanding the covenant as God working to establish and maintain order on humanity's behalf. This idea represents one of the most significant divergences of Israelite thinking from its broader context (where humans are usually delegated to sustain their own order on behalf of the gods) so it is not surprising that the festival encapsulating this idea has no direct parallel.

Investigation of the ANE background of these commandments has given us a revised view of our understanding of how Israelites were

---

[74]Andreasen, *Old Testament Sabbath*, 183.
[75]Margaret Shuster, "Response to 'The Sabbath Day,'" in Van Harn, *Ten Commandments for Jews, Christians and Others*, 83.

supposed to think about Yahweh's rule as their suzerain. It would no longer be sufficient for us to simply say they could not make statues or that they were not allowed to work on the Sabbath. Such statements are too reductionistic. These paragraphs of Torah reveal the essence of how Yahweh operates in the cosmos and among people, and how his power and authority are to be recognized—all in contrast to the common conceptions of deity in the ancient world though similar in some ways to the common conception of how kings are to be treated in the ancient world. Yahweh is, of course, both God and king.

This study turns modern readers away from placing too much emphasis on derived principles, philosophical abstractions, or theological systems. Instead these commandments strategically locate a particular perception of deity within a worldview and convey aspects of divine authority. We are now ready to turn our attention to the sayings that pertain to interactions among the Israelites.

SAYINGS 5-10

#5 Parents. Respect for parents was the norm in the ancient world, especially given the community identity that was characteristic of those cultures. Respect for parents would be reflected in how growing children responded to their parents. Among the Israelites, it would pertain specifically to honoring parents by receiving instruction in the covenant so that the covenant benefit (life in the land) might continue. One drew identity from family and clan, and values were preserved in that context. It would never have occurred to someone in ancient Israel to ask, would you still honor your parents if they tried to persuade you to abandon your faith or to engage in criminal activities?[76] Such unacceptable behaviors would not serve to preserve order in the covenant community's identity with Yahweh. The issue at stake here is the integrity of the community's identity and the individual's identity

---

[76]See discussion among the rabbis in Byron Sherwin, "Honoring Parents," in Van Harn, *Ten Commandments for Jews, Christians and Others*, 90-94.

within the community. It was the assumed parental obligation to raise children as covenant keepers (Deut 6:7).

But we too easily reduce the idea of honoring parents to young children obeying parents (undoubtedly with Eph 6:1-3 in mind). As important as this is, many modern interpreters have made a persuasive case that the fifth word is addressed primarily to adult children and focuses on their responsibility to their elderly parents.[77] This concern is evident not only in the Torah but in the ANE as well. As early as Sumerian texts at the end of the third millennium BC, Lipit-Ištar indicated in his prologue that he made the father support his children and made the child stand by his father.[78]

Following this line of thinking, the saying would pertain most importantly to the treatment of elderly parents who could no longer participate in the work of the community and therefore could be seen as a burden to their sons and daughters who maintained the household. In short, adult children have a duty to their parents, regardless of the circumstances.

> In instances in which a parent is extremely ill, senile, abusive, or morally corrupt, a person may not naturally be drawn to honor his or her parents. It may well be rational . . . to reciprocate parental generosity with filial duty. But neither are all parents generous, nor are all children either grateful or rational.[79]

In this way of thinking, it does not matter whether the parent has been true to the parental calling regarding the covenant. The stability of the

---

[77]Charlie Trimm, "Honor Your Parents: A Command for Adults," *JETS* 60, no. 2 (2017): 247-63, offers numerous examples of how important it was to honor parents in the ANE cultures; Miller, *Ten Commandments*, 181-93, also gives extensive treatment to this aspect. See Anathea Portier-Young, "Response to 'Honoring Parent,'" in Van Harn, *Ten Commandments for Jews, Christians and Others*, 100. She spends several pages delineating the various ways in which such honor will be lived out; see also Coogan, *Ten Commandments*, 76-79; and Harrelson, *Ten Commandments and Human Rights*, 93-105.

[78]*COS*, 2.154: 411 (trans. Martha Roth). Further examples of concern about adult children repudiating the care of their parents are cited in Baker, *Decalogue*, 86-88.

[79]Sherwin, "Honoring Parents," 90.

covenant community is dependent on families providing for the elderly in this way. In a context where this was the only social system provided for elder care, it was an essential aspect of order.

#6-9 *Murder, adultery, theft, and false witness*. These all prohibit behaviors that are disruptive to the community and destroy order within it. They are staples in any ancient literature that deals with order and justice in society, any society, so of course also a covenant community that has been co-identified with Yahweh. A few specific observations can help clear up some common misunderstandings of these sayings.

Many people have read the sixth saying and concluded that it prohibited all killing. Such an interpretation misunderstands the Hebrew vocabulary. The Hebrew word used here is *rāṣaḥ*, and it is properly translated as "murder."[80] It therefore does not pertain to any other sort of killing, such as capital punishment, war, suicide, or killing of animals for food. All those are fully acceptable in Israel, even at times required, and therefore do not stand as contradictory to this saying or to the preservation of order in the covenant community of Israel. Even when Jesus extrapolates from the saying in the Sermon on the Mount in the Second Temple cognitive environment, he extends the meaning from murder to the prior attitude of hate (Mt 5:21). He does not expand the principle to apply it to other ways in which killing takes place.

To understand the saying about adultery, we need to recognize a more restricted definition that existed in the ancient world. Throughout the ANE, adultery described sexual relations between a man and a *married* woman (cf. Lev 20:10). Sexual liaisons with an unmarried woman may have been considered promiscuous and unacceptable for a number of reasons (some related to clan relationships and the value of a woman for an arranged marriage rather than as purely a matter of sexual ethics) but are not classified as adultery. Adultery disrupted

---

[80]Stamm and Andrew, *Ten Commandments in Recent Research*, 98-99. Ample discussion, including careful nuancing, found in John K. Roth, "What Have You Done?," in Van Harn, *Ten Commandments for Jews, Christians and Others*, 113-26.

order in the community on a number of levels, but one of the most
important was that it resulted in questions about paternity and
therefore the essential identity of the child.[81] As in all these sayings in
this section, the broader ANE also found this behavior disruptive and
unacceptable; this one they labeled "The Great Sin."

Theft and bearing false witness were also behaviors that were commonly viewed as disruptive to order in society in the ancient world,
for transparent reasons. As a light to the nations, Israel was also expected to maintain the modicum of order that anyone in the ancient
world would expect for a well ordered society. Consequently, Yahweh
would be able to represent himself favorably by blessing them. These
behaviors would not reflect the wisdom, justice, and order that characterized Yahweh as demonstrated through his dealings with Israel.

#10 Coveting. Discussion of coveting is not found in the legal collections of the ANE, but it is addressed in Wisdom literature.[82] In
some ways this is a difference without a distinction since both Law and
Wisdom deal with order in society. Alexander Rofé has presented
evidence that the root *ḥmd* (covet) refers not only to the desire for
something but also "implies the adoption of measures to satisfy the
desire."[83] It thus entails both desiring and seizing (notice the

---

[81]Elliott N. Dorff, "Response to 'Sexuality and Marriage,'" in Van Harn, *Ten Commandments for Jews, Christians and Others*, 149-50.

[82]The best example is in the Ugaritic "Instructions of *Šūpê-amēli*" from the middle of the second millennium. Line 27 simply reads: "Don't covet another man's wife." Yoram Cohen, *Wisdom from the Late Bronze Age*, WAW 34 (Atlanta: Society of Biblical Literature, 2013), 86-87. Half a millennium earlier a treaty between Assyrians and some business partners in an area in Anatolia includes in the listing of expected business practices that the parties should not covet houses, slaves, fields, or orchards. Veysel Donbaz, "An Old Assyrian Treaty from Kültepe," *JCS* 57 (2005): 63-68; see also discussion in B. Wells, "Exodus," in Walton, *Zondervan Illustrated Bible Backgrounds Commentary*, 1:236. Egyptian wisdom (Ptah-hotep) likewise identified coveting as a vice to be avoided. For discussion and cita-tions of a number of sources, see E. Carpenter, "Deuteronomy," in Walton, *Zondervan Il-lustrated Bible Backgrounds Commentary*, 1:454.

[83]Alexander Rofé, "The Tenth Commandment in the Light of Four Deuteronomic Laws," in Segal, *Ten Commandments in History and Tradition*, 48. He finds the same to be true for the cognate root in Phoenician, as indicated in the Karatepe Inscription, which is sup-ported further in Stamm and Andrew, *Ten Commandments in Recent Research*, 102-3.

connection made explicit in Deut 7:25; Mic 2:2). This would suggest that the tenth saying is not restricted to a prohibition of thoughts and feelings; those thoughts and feelings are coupled with strategies to gain possession of that which is desired. The argument against this is that if the verb itself implied desiring as well as seizing, the second verb would not have to be specified.[84]

CONCLUSION

If we think of the Torah and the Decalogue as founding documents for Israel's covenant with Yahweh, they convey what Yahweh has a right to expect of his vassals. As a set, the Decalogue (regardless of which list one uses) serves as a short list (not a summary list) circumscribing covenant order by visiting some of the basic essentials. Yahweh is their king, and his authority must be respected in every way. As king, he establishes justice and right relationships in Israel. Thus, the Decalogue functions the same way that the rest of the Torah does. We might call it a mini-Torah. As one of the collections of legal sayings in the Pentateuch, the Decalogue stands as a list of illustrations that serve to circumscribe in part the realm of legal wisdom.

Coogan goes so far as to translate it "scheme against" rather than "covet." Coogan, *Ten Commandments*, 90-93.

[84]See Mark F. Rooker, *The Ten Commandments: Ethics for the Twenty-First Century* (Nashville: B&H, 2010), 164-67, who also proposes that the occurrences of the *qal* passive participle (Job 20:20; Ps 39:11 [12]; Is 44:9) suggest that the prohibition is directed toward the attitude, not just acting on it. The fact that the other sayings in this section pertain to actions would not rule out this one dealing with thoughts and attitudes; cf. Rooker's follow-up discussion on 172-74.

Further Reading

Select General Reading

Berman, Joshua A. *Inconsistency in the Torah: Ancient Literary Convention and the Limits of Source Criticism.* Oxford: Oxford University Press, 2017.

Daube, David, edited and compiled by Calum Carmichael. *Law and Wisdom in the Bible: David Daube's Gifford Lectures*, vol. 2. West Conshohocken, PA: Templeton Press, 2010.

Doorly, William J. *The Laws of Yahweh: A Handbook of Biblical Law.* Mahwah, NJ: Paulist Press, 2002.

Gane, Roy E. *Old Testament Law for Christians: Original Context and Enduring Application.* Grand Rapids: Baker Academic, 2017.

Morrow, William S. *An Introduction to Biblical Law.* Grand Rapids: Eerdmans, 2017.

Patrick, Dale. *Old Testament Law.* Atlanta: John Knox, 1985.

Schreiner, Thomas R. *40 Questions About Christians and Biblical Law.* Grand Rapids: Kregel, 2010.

Sprinkle, Joe M. *Biblical Law and Its Relevance: A Christian Understanding and Ethical Application for Today of the Mosaic Regulations.* Lanham, MD: University Press of America, 2006.

Strickland, Wayne G., ed. *Five Views on Law and Gospel.* Grand Rapids: Zondervan, 1996.

Todd, James M., III. *Sinai and the Saints: Reading Old Covenant Laws for the New Covenant Community.* Downers Grove, IL: IVP Academic, 2017.

Walton, John H. *Old Testament Theology for Christians: From Ancient Context to Enduring Belief*. Downers Grove, IL: InterVarsity Press, 2017.

Walton, John H., and D. Brent Sandy, *The Lost World of Scripture: Ancient Literary Culture and Biblical Authority*. Downers Grove, IL: IVP Academic, 2013.

Walton, John H., and J. Harvey Walton. *The Lost World of the Israelite Conquest: Covenant, Retribution, and the Fate of the Canaanites*. Downers Grove, IL: IVP Academic, 2017.

SELECT READING ON ANCIENT NEAR EASTERN LAW

Albertz, Rainer, and Rüdiger Schmitt. *Family and Household Religion in Ancient Israel and the Levant*. Winona Lake, IN: Eisenbrauns, 2012.

Beckman, Gary M. *Hittite Diplomatic Texts*. Edited by Harry A. Hoffner Jr. Rev. ed. WAW 7. Atlanta: Society of Biblical Literature, 1999.

Hayes, Christine. *What's Divine About Divine Law?: Early Perspectives*. Princeton, NJ: Princeton University Press, 2015.

Jackson, Bernard S. *Wisdom-Laws: A Study of the Mishpatim of Exodus 21:1–22:16*. Oxford: Oxford University Press, 2006.

Jackson, Samuel. *A Comparison of Ancient Near Eastern Law Collections Prior to the First Millennium BC*. Piscataway, NJ: Gorgias, 2008.

Kitchen, Kenneth A., and Paul J. N. Lawrence. *Treaty, Law and Covenant in the Ancient Near East*. 3 vols. Wiesbaden: Harrassowitz, 2012.

Knight, Douglas A. *Law, Power, and Justice in Ancient Israel*. Louisville, KY: Westminster John Knox, 2011.

LeFebvre, Michael. *Collections, Codes, and Torah: The Re-characterization of Israel's Written Law*. New York: T&T Clark, 2006.

Malul, Meir. *The Comparative Method in Ancient Near Eastern and Biblical Legal Studies*. AOAT 227. Kevelaer: Butzon & Bercker, 1990.

Roth, Martha T. *Law Collections from Mesopotamia and Asia Minor*. Atlanta: Society of Biblical Literature, 1995.

Strawn, Brent, ed. *The Oxford Encyclopedia of the Bible and Law*. 2 vols. Oxford: Oxford University Press, 2015.

Toorn, Karel van der. *Sin and Sanction in Israel and Mesopotamia: A Comparative Study*. Assen, Netherlands: Van Gorcum, 1985.

Van de Mieroop, Marc. *Philosophy Before the Greeks: The Pursuit of Truth in Ancient Babylonia*. Princeton, NJ: Princeton University Press, 2016.

Walton, John H. *Ancient Near Eastern Thought and the Old Testament: Introducing the Conceptual World of the Hebrew Bible*. 2nd ed. Grand Rapids: Baker Academic, 2018.

Westbrook, Raymond. *A History of Ancient Near Eastern Law*. 2 vols. Leiden: Brill, 2003.

Westbrook, Raymond, and Bruce Wells. *Everyday Law in Biblical Israel: An Introduction*. Louisville, KY: Westminster John Knox, 2009.

SELECT READING ON MORALITY AND ETHICS

Baggett, David, and Jerry L. Walls. *God and Cosmos: Moral Truth and Human Meaning*. Oxford: Oxford University Press, 2016.

Craig, William Lane, and Chad Meister. *God Is Great, God Is Good: Why Believing in God Is Reasonable and Responsible*. Downers Grove, IL: InterVarsity Press, 2009.

Evans, C. Stephen. *God and Moral Obligation*. Oxford: Oxford University Press, 2013.

Kaiser, Walter C., Jr. *Toward Old Testament Ethics*. Grand Rapids: Zondervan, 1983.

Kaye, Bruce, and Gordon Wenham, eds. *Law, Morality, and the Bible: A Symposium*. Downers Grove, IL: InterVarsity Press, 1978.

Loftin, R. Keith, ed. *God and Morality: Four Views*. Downers Grove, IL: InterVarsity Press, 2012.

Thompson, James W. *Moral Formation According to Paul: The Context and Coherence of Pauline Ethics*. Grand Rapids: Baker Academic, 2011.

Wilkens, Steve, ed. *Christian Ethics: Four Views*. Downers Grove, IL: IVP Academic, 2017.

Wright, Christopher J. H. *Old Testament Ethics for the People of God*. Downers Grove, IL: IVP Academic, 2004.

_____. *Walking in the Ways of the Lord: The Ethical Authority of the Old Testament*. Downers Grove, IL: InterVarsity Press, 1995.

SELECT READING ON THE DECALOGUE

Baker, David L. *The Decalogue: Living as the People of God*. Downers Grove, IL: IVP Academic, 2017.

Brown, William P., ed., *The Ten Commandments: The Reciprocity of Faithfulness*. Louisville, KY: Westminster John Knox, 2004.

Coogan, Michael. *The Ten Commandments: A Short History of an Ancient Text*. New Haven, CT: Yale University Press, 2014.

Harrelson, Walter J. *The Ten Commandments and Human Rights*. Philadelphia: Fortress Press, 1980.

Miller, Patrick D. *The Ten Commandments*. Louisville, KY: Westminster John Knox, 2009.

Phillips, Anthony. *Ancient Israel's Criminal Law: A New Approach to the Decalogue*. New York: Schocken, 1970.

Rooker, Mark F. *The Ten Commandments: Ethics for the Twenty-First Century*. Nashville: B&H, 2010.

Segal, Ben-Zion, ed. *The Ten Commandments in History and Tradition*. Jerusalem: Magnes, 1990.

Stamm, Johann Jakob, with Maurice Edward Andrew. *The Ten Commandments in Recent Research*. Rev. ed. SBT 2.2. London: SCM Press, 1967.

Van Harn, Roger E., ed. *The Ten Commandments for Jews, Christians and Others*. Grand Rapids, MI: Eerdmans, 2007.

Subject Index

Scripture Index

The Lost World Series

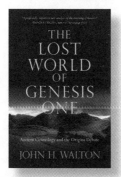

The Lost World of Genesis One
978-0-8308-3704-5

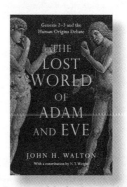

The Lost World of Adam and Eve
978-0-8308-2461-8

**The Lost World of the
Israelite Conquest**
978-0-8308-5184-3

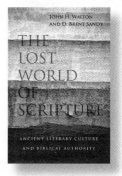

The Lost World of Scripture
978-0-8308-4032-8

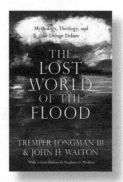

The Lost World of the Flood
978-0-8308-5200-0

Also by John H. Walton

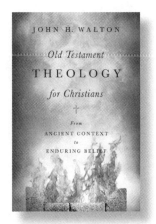

**Old Testament Theology
for Christians**
978-0-8308-5192-8

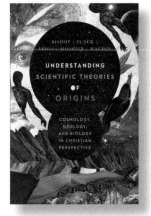

**Understanding Scientific
Theories of Origins**
978-0-8308-5291-8

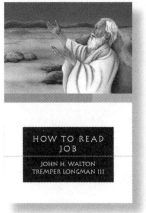

How to Read Job
978-0-8308-5184-3

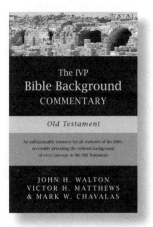

**The IVP Bible Background
Commentary: Old Testament**
978-0-8308-1419-0

Finding the Textbook You Need

The IVP Academic Textbook Selector
is an online tool for instantly finding the IVP books
suitable for over 250 courses across 24 disciplines.

---

ivpacademic.com